Political
Corruption
and
Public Policy
in America

Political Corruption and Public Policy in America

MICHAEL JOHNSTON
University of Pittsburgh

Brooks/Cole Publishing Company
Monterey, California

The Brooks/Cole Series on Public Policy

Charles O. Jones, University of Virginia
General Editor

Brooks/Cole Publishing Company
A Division of Wadsworth, Inc.

© 1982 by Wadsworth, Inc., Belmont, California 94002.
All rights reserved.
No part of this book may be reproduced, stored in a retrieval system,
or transcribed, in any form or by any means—
electronic, mechanical, photocopying, recording, or otherwise—
without the prior written permission of the publisher,
Brooks/Cole Publishing Company, Monterey, California 93940,
a Division of Wadsworth, Inc.

Printed in the United States of America

10 9 8 7 6 5 4 3 2 1

Library of Congress Cataloging in Publication Data

Johnston, Michael, (date)
   Political corruption and public policy in
America.

   (The Brooks/Cole series on public policy)
   Bibliography: p.
   Includes index.
   1. Corruption (in politics)—United States.

I. Title. II. Series: Brooks/Cole series on
public policy.
JK2249.J63   320.973   81-10026
ISBN 0-8185-0459-5   AACR2

Subject Editor: *Henry Staat*
Manuscript Editor: *Evan Lee*
Production Editor: *John Bergez*
Production Assistant: *Louise Rixey*
Design: *Vicki Van Deventer*
Cover Illustration: *Ron Grauer*
Typesetting: *Graphic Typesetting Service, Los Angeles*

```
Y O S L S
F T A W D
B I E H A
T A I A B
V P M G F
```

Foreword

Public opinion data reveal a distressing decline in the American people's confidence in their government. As James L. Sundquist observes, "The performance of the government has fallen far short of what the people have expected and have a right to expect."[1] It is generally agreed that among the causes of disillusionment is the public perception of malfeasance and corruption in government: Watergate, Abscam, and Koreagate at the national level; police scandals, kickbacks, and fraud at state and local levels. American politics is, and always has been, characterized by a bit of looseness in the exercise of governmental authority.

What is "corruption"? What are the roots and causes of corruption? How much corruption can a political system sustain? What are the costs of a corruption-free political system? Michael Johnston has treated these and other significant questions in this fascinating study. He has succeeded in offering a dispassionate analysis of a topic that typically arouses strong emotions. In the process, he contributes to our understanding of the workings of the American political system at all levels.

One expects a book on political corruption to be interesting, and Michael Johnston does not disappoint. The central issue is well conceived, the material is sensibly organized, and the examples are well chosen. A superb writing style encourages the reader to press on, always with rewards for the effort. Along the way Johnston provides the analytical perspectives required to comprehend why corruption exists and why it is unlikely ever to go away.

---

[1] James L. Sundquist, "The Crisis of Competence in Government," in Joseph Pechman (Ed.), *Setting National Priorities: Agenda for the 1980s* (Washington, D.C.: The Brookings Institution, 1980), p. 534.

In his last chapter Johnston wisely advises us to maintain realistic expectations regarding the honesty, efficiency, and levels of services we can expect from government. He does not propose that we ignore corrupt practices. He does suggest that we maintain our political trust and a sense of forbearance. This is an intelligent book about an important set of issues. I have no doubt that students will join me in thanking Michael Johnston for writing it.

Charles O. Jones
University of Virginia

Preface

When Richard M. Nixon resigned the presidency of the United States in August of 1974, I was on vacation in Ireland, staying at a small farmhouse in County Clare. In the months following the 1972 break-in at the Democratic headquarters in the Watergate office complex, I had become a confirmed Watergate addict, reading and watching everything I could about the unfolding drama. At 2 A.M. on August 9, I walked across the road to the Clare Inn, which had the nearest television set, and watched President Nixon deliver the speech I had been anticipating for some time. The resignation speech was the climax of America's worst political scandal. It also demonstrated all over again that political corruption arouses strong emotions. As Nixon spoke that night, heated arguments broke out over the conduct of the president and his men, even though most of those watching (and arguing) were Irish or English citizens who had followed the scandal from a great distance.

It is natural that corruption should make us angry. Here, after all, are people who spend our money, who are entrusted with great power, and who are supposed to serve the public; but some of them lie, cheat, and steal. At the very least, we are angry to see our taxes misappropriated; sometimes we feel bitter and foolish for ever having trusted our leaders and institutions.

Yet I am convinced that before we condemn corruption, we must understand it. Further, I believe that a thorough understanding of corruption will show us that many instances of official misconduct are really insignificant, and that some cases are even widely beneficial. To be sure, many cases of corruption do have substantial costs. And the worst costs are intangible: corruption undermines political tolerance and trust, and it is a "regressive" form of influence, serving the "haves" at the expense of the "have-nots." Corruption can thus reinforce or deepen social injustices and inequalities. After we realize these things about corruption, we may still get angry about it. But our anger can then be based on a more complete understanding of how corruption develops and persists; it can be focused upon the most damaging cases, rather than dissipated through diffuse outrage; and it can point the way to more effective countermeasures and strategies of adaptation.

These ideas will be developed in the chapters to come. In Chapter 1, I take up the surprisingly difficult task of defining just what corruption is. I then spell out three general perspectives on understanding corruption: *personalistic* approaches, which deal with the kinds of people who hold positions of public trust; an *institutional* view, which finds the causes of corruption in flaws or unrecognized biases in laws and institutions; and a *systemic* perspective, which suggests that corruption grows out of basic relationships between government and society.

Chapter 2 further develops the systemic view. I suggest that corruption is a form of influence. Like other kinds of influence, people use corruption because they stand to benefit from it; and, again like other forms of influence, corruption depends on the successful mobilization of political resources. One particular resource—money—is central to corruption-as-influence; Chapter 2 compares its uses and properties to those of other political resources.

Chapters 3, 4, and 5 are case studies of machine politics, police corruption, and Watergate, respectively. Machine politics is perhaps the first image that comes to mind when most people hear the word "corruption." Police corruption provides a particularly useful perspective on the relationship between government and society; the police, after all, operate at the point where law and society meet. And Watergate is a "tough case" for analysis, involving such diverse elements as campaign finances and Richard Nixon's personality. I argue that although institutional factors can be significant, these manifestations of corruption are best explained in systemic terms.

Chapter 6 is another case study—this time, of the difficulties of reform. Campaign finance practices were seen by many as a central problem in the Watergate mess; much effort and several pieces of legislation have since been devoted to reforming the way we finance election campaigns. Examination of basic problems of reform will show not only that reform of campaign financing is a most difficult task, but also that many kinds of "reforms" can produce results quite the opposite of those desired.

Chapter 7 takes up the broad social and political consequences of corruption, both costs and benefits. Sometimes corruption *can* have beneficial results; more often, it is insignificant. The biggest cost of corruption is not the dollars lost or the services not delivered, although these costs can be considerable. The major cost is that corruption is a highly undemocratic form of influence that fosters mass disenchantment with government and the law.

Chapter 7 concludes with observations on dealing with corruption. I offer a few reforms and policy proposals, but I also comment on the necessity of developing a realistic perspective on corruption in a democratic society. I do not contend that there is nothing we can or should do about corruption. I do argue that our efforts should be based on a recognition of corruption's role as a form of influence in the wider political system.

I owe a great deal to many people who helped bring this book into being. Series Editor Charles O. Jones provided encouragement and advice throughout the process. Patrick Fitzgerald offered an invaluable editorial perspective. The editorial efforts of Henry Staat, John Bergez, and Evan Lee of Brooks/Cole proved that it really is possible to translate semiliterate scrawlings into a finished book. Madelyn Leopold provided helpful critiques of various drafts. Todd Lueders and William Hicks of Brooks/Cole fielded questions from me, arranged for reviews of several chapters, and helped keep the project on track.

Many people were kind enough to read all or parts of the manuscript and offer helpful criticisms. They include Guy Beneventano, Robert Cindrich, Robert Lane, Alexander Lindsay, Jerome McKinney, Michael Margolis, Bruce Marshall, and Bert Rockman. Dean Robert Huckshorn of Florida Atlantic University provided a helpful review. My students at the University of Pittsburgh contributed greatly to the ideas and analysis of this book and also read drafts of the manuscript as a part of their coursework. Deborah Solomon did many hours of excellent bibliographic work. All these people have made this a better book.

Mary Hamler, Candy Wimer, Mary Ann Salapa, and Jane Marshall typed draft chapters of this book. That task involved deciphering my handwriting, which is only slightly more legible than hieroglyphics. How they did it, no one knows. Cece Candalor typed the revised manuscript, and did so with patience and good cheer; Patty Candalor was an excellent proofreader. I would also like to thank the office of Robert Cindrich, U.S. Attorney for Western Pennsylvania, for making available data on corruption prosecutions nationwide; the University of Pittsburgh, for computer time and facilities that I used to study patronage allocations; and Willie Stargell, for the 1979 baseball season.

Finally, there is my family. My wife, Betsy, is an excellent critic of writing and ideas, and she has contributed a great deal to all of my work. Our three children—Jonathan, Michael, and Patrick—helped out frequently by dragging me away from my desk for softball, story reading, and other activities much more sane and enjoyable than writing a book. To them, and to all, sincere thanks.

Michael Johnston

Contents

1 Corruption: Problems and Definitions   1

What is Corruption?   3
Types of Corruption   11
Explaining Corruption: Three Perspectives   12
The Data Problem   16
Summary   17

2 Corruption in Political Systems   18

What Is a Political System?   18
Corruption and Characteristics of Political Systems   24
Money as a Political Resource   33
Summary   34

3 The Political Machine   36

Machines and Corruption   37
The "Ideal Machine": An Organizational Analysis   38
The Political Base of the Machine   41
The Origins of the Machine: Three Theories   44
Machines in Action   56
The Death (?) of the Machine   66
Summary   68

4 Police Corruption 72

Police in the City 73
Police Corruption: Types and Techniques 74
Personalistic Views on Police Corruption 79
The Institutional Approach 84
Systemic Perspectives on Police Corruption 93
Consequences of Police Corruption 97
Police Corruption: What to Do about It? 101
Summary 105

5 Watergate 108

Analyzing Watergate 109
Cutting Watergate Down to Size 111
The Personalistic Perspective: Observations on the Presidential Psyche 112
The Institutional Perspective 117
The Systemic Perspective 124
Beyond Watergate: Consequences and Reforms 133
Summary 137

6 The Dilemmas of Reform 140

General Approaches to Reform 141
Why Is Reform So Difficult? 149
Dilemmas of Reform: From Theory to Practice 153
Summary 168

7 Corruption and Democracy 172

Costs and Benefits of Corruption 172
Assessing the Damage 175
Learning to Live with the Beast 183
Conclusions 186

Selected Bibliography 189

Index 193

Political Corruption and Public Policy in America

Corruption: Problems and Definitions

Not long ago, Pennsylvania Governor Milton Shapp decided that his state needed a new slogan. A statewide contest was held in which residents proposed slogans to take the place of "Keystone State" in promotional advertisements and on license plates. Shapp, while personally honest, was presiding over an administration beset by charges of corruption; indictments and convictions of state officials had become common front-page news. The eventual winning slogan ("Pennsylvania Naturally!") was chosen to celebrate the state's natural beauties, but many contestants and pundits concentrated on corruption instead: two of the more popular slogan ideas were "Nolo Contendere" and "Take the Money and Run."

This was a trivial event in the grand scheme of American politics, yet it reflects the fact that corruption and allegations of official misconduct have become major political concerns in recent years. Public response has ranged from apathy, to demands for reform, to cynicism, as in the Pennsylvania case. Mass disenchantment with government—fueled, to be sure, by such other problems as dissatisfaction with policy and rising taxes—has only been made worse by a widespread feeling that corruption pervades all levels of government. Tax money is wasted or misappropriated, many people feel, and, when it comes to having a say in how things are run, "the little guy" doesn't stand a chance.

Pennsylvanians did not invent corruption, to be sure; nor are bribery, extortion, favoritism, and patronage politics recent phenomena. In the year 1163 or 1164, King Louis VII of France wrote to his friend, the Bishop of Paris, and requested that the Bishop find a job in the construction of Notre Dame Cathedral for one of the King's young protégés:

> It is a frequent practice, and a wise policy, for those who through God's grace have risen to high station, to be well-disposed toward those who have helped them succeed, so that in the fullness of their own success they may return kindness for kindness.
>
> We are both aware that our clerk and yours . . . devotedly hoped and is now devotedly happy for your present eminence, and has in fact done all he could to help you succeed as you have. We take the occasion to repeat our request, and beg you to keep him in mind . . . so that if some worthy post were to become available, you might think of him.[1]

The language is from the 12th century, but the logic is the same as that used by a ward leader in sponsoring a loyal supporter for a city job. Then, as now, the tactic worked: the young protégé was appointed Dean of the Cathedral as soon as the post became vacant.

Corruption is frequently noted as a cause of the fall of Rome, and it played a clear role in sparking the Reformation. Shortly after the birth of the American Republic, two U.S. Senators, two Congressmen, an Associate Justice of the U.S. Supreme Court, two other high-ranking judges, and several prominent figures in New England state politics were implicated in the Yazoo land scandal, involving the sale of land that later became most of Mississippi and Alabama.[2] From then on, through the Credit Mobilier stock and bribery scandal, the Grant administration, Boss Tweed and the heyday of big-city machines, Teapot Dome, Harry Truman's troubles with the IRS, Watergate, Tongsun Park, and AB-SCAM, people have used illicit political influence in America. Almost every state and city could add its own stories of corruption to this incomplete list.

Today, a colorful vocabulary reflects corruption's worldwide presence. In parts of Asia and the Middle East, a little *baksheesh* can speed things along, while in Latin America *la mordida* ("the bite") is a frequent part of dealings with public officials. Italians are familiar with *la bustarella* ("the little envelope"), and in West Africa "dash" can work wonders. "Speed Money"—a term used in parts of India—perhaps captures the essence of corruption best of all.[3]

The most popular remedy for corruption, of course, is "Throw the scoundrels out!" Many candidates have ridden to victory on just such a pledge, and many have failed to clean things up for very long. Some have even become scoundrels in their own right. Yet the appeal of the "clean sweep" remedy remains strong. Other strategies for reform center on laws and formal structures. To fight corruption, Americans have provided for limited and fragmented power in our governmental agencies, weakened or abolished political parties (particularly at the local level), and sought to regulate the sources and use of money in electoral politics. Yet even "reformed" governments have experienced corruption, as in the case of Chicago, whose reform charter provides for a weak mayor and some nonpartisan positions. Still another strategy deals with the kinds of people we entrust with public power. Properly training public servants in the functional and ethical responsibilities of public life, we are told, will at least inhibit much of the corruption that plagues us. Yet today's state and local officials are probably the best-educated we have ever had, and still we find corruption. I hardly need add that nearly all the culprits of Watergate were college-educated, and most were lawyers.

I will contend in this book that corruption grows out of much more fundamental forces and tensions in the political system than individual misbehavior, structural deficiencies, or insufficient ethical training. Were we to clear individual miscreants out of government, subject our laws and institutions to the most painstaking structural reforms, and give our public officials the best training we could devise, corruption and the forces that sustain it would still play some part in our politics. This is so because government is an important source of goods, services, money, decisions, and authority in society—benefits that are vigorously pursued by many groups and individuals. The demand for government's rewards frequently exceeds the supply, and routine decision-making processes are lengthy, costly, and uncertain in their outcome. For these reasons, legally sanctioned decision-making processes constitute a "bottleneck" between what people want and what they get. The temptation to get around the bottleneck—to speed things up and make favorable decisions more probable—is built into this relationship between government and society. To get around the bottleneck, one must use political influence—and corruption, which by definition cuts across established and legitimate processes, is a most effective form of influence.

WHAT IS CORRUPTION?

Consider the following cases:

- In 1961, President John F. Kennedy nominated his brother Robert to be U.S. Attorney General. The nomination was approved, despite the fact that Robert Kennedy's experience as a prosecutor was viewed by some as quite limited. Was this a case of nepotism? Was it corruption?
- A large Eastern university opens a new $40 million classroom and office building, built largely with state funds. Part of the decor of the building is a very large and colorful mural executed in ceramic tile by a prominent artist. The mural, it is announced, is a gift to the university from the contracting firm that constructed the building. Is this a "kickback" on the part of the contractor? Is it a case of extortion by the university in return for a lucrative construction contract? Or is it merely a harmless demonstration of good will?
- An ambitious young woman realizes that tremendous amounts of money change hands as certain things are bought and sold and that buyers and sellers often have a hard time getting in touch with each other. So, by developing a network of personal contacts, she begins to seek out those who wish to buy and those willing to sell. For her troubles, she takes a flat 6% of every sale. Is this corruption?
- In 1969 and 1970, the Nixon administration launched a massive, covert bombing campaign in Laos and Cambodia. No declaration of war had been made against these nations; nor had they attacked the United States. In fact, flight

plans and bombing records were falsified throughout in order to hide the secret bombing from press and public. When the secret bombing was at last revealed in the pages of the *New York Times,* the government claimed that both the bombing and the efforts at maintaining secrecy were justified by legitimate needs of national security. Who, if anyone, acted in a corrupt manner in this case?
- A man takes his car to a service station for its annual inspection, as required by state law. It turns out that the car cannot meet safety standards; in fact, it will take $200 worth of repairs to bring it into compliance with the law. But the service-station owner is a friend, and, when the man offers him a crisp $20 bill, he agrees to certify the car as having passed inspection. Is this a case of corruption?

For all the public attention, scholarship, and litigation that has been focused on corruption in the last decade, corruption itself remains difficult to define. All the actions just cited could be viewed as corrupt from one perspective or another; most could also be defended as *not* being corrupt. It is clear that corruption involves conduct that violates some set of "reasonable standards," but what are those standards? To establish a case of corruption, must we show that a law was broken, or that money or gifts were received? What if seemingly corrupt acts benefit the public in some way, as in the case of a city boss who steals votes to stay in office but uses his powers to build schools, hospitals, and an airport? Can we construct a definition of corruption broad enough to capture its informality and its many manifestations, yet precise enough to help us analyze cases as diverse as machine politics, police corruption, and Watergate?

Not all behavior that breaks rules is corruption. Corruption involves abuse of a *public* role or trust for the sake of some *private* benefit. Martin Luther King, Jr., and his followers broke laws and cultural conventions, but few would call their deeds corrupt. Although King was a public figure, he was not responsible for a public trust; nor did he and his supporters break rules specifically to win private benefits such as money or business contracts. They sought to influence the actions of those who did hold public power, but they did not offer personal benefits, such as bribes, to those officials. Or consider the case of President Abraham Lincoln's decision to suspend habeas corpus rights during the Civil War. Lincoln definitely did hold public power, and perhaps his action transgressed reasonable standards of conduct. But we would still not judge this to be corruption, for Lincoln did not take his actions in pursuit of private benefit.

What, then, constitutes "abuse," and what are reasonable standards of conduct? James C. Scott points to three standards that could be used in answering these questions: the public interest, public opinion, and legal norms.[4] Hence, actions breaching one or more of these standards, performed for private benefit by a person holding a public trust, could be regarded as corruption. But which set of standards offers the best definition of corruption? Each has its advantages and drawbacks.

Public interest

A public-interest definition of corruption has an automatic appeal, for corruption is commonly regarded as harming the public interest, although, as we will see later, that is not always true. The problem is that the public interest offers no usable standard of judging conduct, for on all but the most general issues there is no such thing as *the* public interest. The public interest is at best merely a kaleidoscopic pattern of shifting and conflicting private interests, each pursued by varying numbers of people with differing amounts of skill and resources. Any significant political issue involves not just two or three but rather dozens of private interests; indeed, if it did not it would hardly be much of an issue. Consider, as an admittedly extreme case, the "issue" of motherhood. Few would depict motherhood as being against "the public interest"; yet even a superficial look reveals that zero-population-growth advocates and baby-food manufacturers will take differing positions on the motherhood issue. Mothers who wish to work and those who wish to stay at home are currently at odds over the Equal Rights Amendment. Many mothers (and fathers) want the federal government to take an active role in providing day-care services, while others see such a move as "creeping socialism" and a threat to the sanctity of the family. Many women have taken their employers to court over the treatment and benefits accorded pregnant women.

Each of these interests is advanced by members of the public, yet none could plausibly be called the "public interest." And if there is no clear public interest on the motherhood issue, can there be one on more familiar issues such as deciding how to change the tax laws or where to build an urban highway? We may well conclude, after the fact, that a corrupt act hurt (or helped) certain segments of the public and thus reach some sort of assessment of the costs and benefits of that particular act. But the public interest is not a sufficiently clear standard for defining corruption.

There are other problems with a public-interest definition of corruption. It suggests that the ends of political action may justify the means, a notion most advocates of democratic government find objectionable. Indeed, ex-President Nixon used just such an argument in contending that a President could order any actions he wished, including murder, in the name of "national security." A public-interest concept of corruption would allow any wrongdoers the defense that their actions were not corrupt because they were intended to serve the public interest. Several Watergate defendants used this defense, arguing that a public interest in quelling political disorder justified their illegal actions. The application of a public-interest definition after the fact can even lead to absurdities: if, as we are sometimes told, a political machine really did provide Mayor Daley with enough power to make Chicago "a city that works," does that mean the machine was not corrupt? A corollary of this last point is that a public-interest definition is of no help to us in looking for cases in which corruption may have had beneficial results for large segments of the public.

Perhaps the most serious objection to a public-interest definition is that if one argues that politics is, or ought to be, an enterprise serving the public interest, then corruption becomes an anomaly, an "exception" in the realm of well-ordered politics. This sort of notion prevents us from seeing corruption's systemic causes, diverting our attention instead toward individual "bad men" or presumed flaws of structures. This view of corruption as an exception makes it hard to account for its persistence: if corruption has been seriously harming the public for so long, why (at least in those systems where the public has a say in government) does the public so often fail to fight corruption, and why does it frequently lose when it does?

Public opinion

Can we use public opinion as our standard for judging whether or not a given action is corrupt? Consider the following case. In the late 1930s, some observers began to question the propriety of James Roosevelt's business dealings. James, one of President Franklin D. Roosevelt's sons, held the position of Secretary to the President and was also active in the insurance business. Questions were raised concerning whether or not James was improperly using his ties to the chief executive in order to drum up insurance business for his firm. Criticism became more intense when Eleanor Roosevelt joined the firm's Board of Directors.

Twice during the summer of 1938 the Gallup organization polled a national sample of citizens on the Roosevelt affair. Table 1-1[5] presents the results. What is the public-opinion verdict on James Roosevelt's actions? Clearly, there is no verdict at all. Three-fifths of the population, based on these poll data, had not even followed the allegations, and a number of those who had held no opinion. Even if we were to base our definition only on the replies of those who did hold opinions, we would still find no stable definition of corruption. In July 1938, those who felt James Roosevelt's conduct was improper outnumbered those who did not by 20% to 13%, but three weeks later, the verdict was reversed, 17% to 19%. Unless we are willing to conclude that Roosevelt's actions were corrupt in July but acceptable in August, it seems clear that we must judge this and other cases of alleged corruption by other, more stable and precise, standards.

TABLE 1-1. Gallup Poll results on James Roosevelt's business dealings, 1938

ITEM: "Have you followed the discussion about James Roosevelt (the President's son) and his insurance business? If Yes: Do you think James Roosevelt has made improper use of his relation to the President to get insurance business?"

	Made improper use	*Did not*	*No opinion*	*Haven't followed*
July 27, 1938	20%	13%	5%	62%
August 16, 1938	17%	19%	6%	58%

From "The Polls: Corruption in Government," by H. Erskine. In *Public Opinion Quarterly*, 1973–74, 37(4), 632. Copyright 1973 by The Trustees of Columbia University. Reprinted by permission.

Like the public-interest definition of corruption, public opinion as a standard for judging official conduct has its attractions. It is, after all, a democratic way to reach a definition. But defining corruption as that which the public regards as corrupt has some serious drawbacks. First comes the problem of deciding who "the public" is. Is it everyone, or just adults, or just registered voters? Is it only those who are knowledgeable about issues and events, or only those with a direct interest in a given area of politics and decision-making? Or do we regard "the public" as those who respond to surveys? There are, after all, *many* "publics," and they rarely agree on anything of importance.

Then there is the difficulty of achieving a stable consensus. Most of us would agree that for the President to sell the office of Secretary of State to the highest bidder, and then to pocket the money himself, would be a corrupt act. But what of more plausible actions? Throughout Watergate, for example, there were sizable shifts in opinion and widespread disagreement over whether certain Presidential actions were corrupt. On the issue of whether these deeds merited Nixon's removal, disagreement was even deeper. To have used a public-opinion definition of corruption during these months would have yielded shifting and unclear readings of Watergate.

Public opinion changes over time, and it yields ambiguous results, as in the James Roosevelt case. On some issues there may not even *be* a public opinion worth mentioning. How many New Yorkers really have an opinion on the honesty or corruptness of probating procedures in their city's Surrogate Court system? Appointments as receivers in large estate cases are an important and lucrative form of patronage for politically connected lawyers,[6] a practice on which public opinion renders no clear judgment. And anyone can claim the endorsement of public opinion for his actions; Richard Nixon, even in his final weeks in office, justified many actions by claiming vast public support for "the Presidency."

Public opinion also varies significantly from place to place. A Ghanaian might think nothing of giving a gift to a judge presiding over a case in which he was involved, whereas Americans would roundly condemn the practice. Significant variations occur within the United States as well. The 1962 Minnesota gubernatorial election may well have been decided by the revelation that concrete for a short section of a new highway was poured when the temperature was two or three degrees below the limit specified by construction standards. Newspapers charged that this "rush job" was done so that the incumbent governor could stage a ribbon-cutting just before the election. Much uproar resulted, and the incumbent was defeated in the closest election in Minnesota history. Minnesota has what Daniel Elazar has termed a "moralistic" political culture,[7] as exemplified by the mass concern over this seemingly trivial incident. It is difficult to imagine the more "individualistic" (Elazar's term again) residents of Pennsylvania, New York, or New Jersey getting very upset over such an incident; few of them would likely regard it as corrupt.

Even if a stable consensus on the corruptness of an action were to appear after the fact, it could not be the basis of a definition of corruption. To take a

1981 public-opinion reading on Watergate, for example, and project it back to 1973-74 not only would misrepresent the public opinion of the time but would impose an artificial structure and strategic analysis upon the whole controversy. Watergate was never a clear-cut case of a President transgressing "the people's" standards of conduct; significant portions of "the people" supported Nixon at various points during the conflict, and some still do. Reaching a working political consensus on whether Nixon's actions were wrong, and what—if anything—to do about them, involved a complex process of mobilizing public opinion, just as does any important controversy in American politics. This process is of much interest in its own right and had much to do with the ultimate outcome of Watergate. Imposing a *post hoc* public-opinion definition of corruption might keep us from looking into these interesting questions.

Finally, a public-opinion definition raises questions about corruption's persistence much like those left unanswered by the public-interest definition. If corruption is reliably and widely recognized for what it is by large segments of the public, and if that "public" opposes it, why is it so hard to eradicate?

Legal norms

Throughout this book I will employ a definition of corruption based on formal/legal norms. By this definition, corruption is *abuse of a public role for private benefit in such a way as to break the law* (or formal administrative regulations, which I will call "laws" for brevity's sake). This approach has some distinct problems, but they are outweighed by its merits. Laws or written regulations are much more precise and consistent for judging conduct than public opinion or the notion of the public interest. In spirit and content, formal/legal standards may well reflect dominant strains of public opinion, and they are at least occasionally formulated to serve some conception of the public interest. The courts constantly interpret and refine legal standards, and law-enforcement agencies apply them to official behavior, so that formal/legal concepts of corruption are constantly being tested against actual cases. Perhaps most important, the formal/legal definition gets right to the heart of the matter: it is in large part formal/legal standards that make up the bottleneck between what people want from government and what they get, and it is the bottleneck that encourages people to seek corrupt influence. A legal definition best captures this fundamental tension between the law and the behavior it seeks to regulate and hence best directs our attention to systemic causes of corruption.

Accordingly, I will employ J. S. Nye's definition of corruption: "behavior which deviates from the formal duties of a public role (elective or appointive) because of private-regarding (personal, close family, private clique) wealth or status gains: or [which] violates rules against the exercise of certain types of private-regarding influence."[8]

"Formal duties" here denotes obligations or prohibitions placed on the holder of a public role by the law or other formal regulations. "Public roles" are held not only by government employees but also (under certain circumstances) by members of political parties, interest groups, and even individual voters, as in the case of a person who sells a vote for a bottle of gin. The key is whether or not a person is taking direct part in decisions or processes that affect the use of public power or the disposition of public goods. Thus, a bank vice-president who embezzles is guilty of a crime but not of corruption. But if the same vice-president solicits illegal campaign contributions from other bankers and delivers them to a favored candidate, he or she has taken part in a process of corruption. "Private-regarding," as Scott notes, need not mean only benefits accruing to the role-holder alone; breaking the law to channel benefits to one's tribe, region, family, or neighborhood could also be seen as "private-regarding" behavior. "Behavior," of course, can mean deliberate failure to act as well as outright law-breaking deeds.[9]

There are problems with the formal/legal definition of corruption. The law can be vague or contradictory. It may at times be at great variance with public opinion or with common notions of the public interest. Moreover, the law is a political product, not holy writ, and many of those in a position to take part in corruption are also in a position to write or rewrite the law, perhaps legitimating their own conduct. This last point, however, may actually be an advantage of the legal definition, because it portrays the law and corruption as two forms of political influence. One is legitimate, the other not, and the two must by definition contend; but both represent strategies people use to advance their interests, and both are pursued within the general social, economic, and cultural context of the political system. Hence, while laws differ from place to place—meaning that behavior defined as corrupt in Albany might be perfectly legitimate in Accra—this diversity can be viewed less as a flaw in definition than as an invitation to study the interesting cultural and historical question of why legal norms have evolved as they have.

A similar point can be made about comparison of one time to another. Laws do change, of course; political behavior that may have been fully legal in Boss Tweed's day may be corrupt by legal standards today. Scott refers to such actions, legitimate during one era but later defined as corrupt, as "proto-corruption."[10] We will not encounter this problem very often in the chapters to come, but the political process by which proto-corruption becomes legally defined as corrupt can be of much interest in its own right. The alignment of various interests on one side or another of the legislation fight serves as a useful indicator of who benefits, and who loses, as a result of the practices in question.

On the whole, then, the formal/legal approach to defining corruption, despite its faults, is the best of those we have considered, and it is the one we will employ in the chapters to come.

The "tough cases" reconsidered

As we have seen, it is not always easy to define cases of corruption. To see how the formal/legal definition can serve to clarify our decisions, let's apply it to the "tough cases" cited at the beginning of this section.

John Kennedy's appointment of his own brother as Attorney General broke no laws and hence, by the formal/legal definition, was not corrupt; those who charged corruption on grounds of Robert Kennedy's limited trial experience were employing an implicit public-interest notion of corruption. The case of the university's accepting a mural as a gift from a construction contractor is a bit tougher. If the contractor had offered the mural as a gift, or if the university had solicited similar "gifts" from competing bidders *before* the contract was awarded, then laws regarding bidding on state construction projects might have been broken, and corruption could have occurred. If, on the other hand, the mural was a spontaneous good will gift, given after the contract was awarded, then no corruption occurred. In practice, of course, these would be difficult standards of judgment to apply, for they would involve questions of intent and of the timing of the offers and transactions.

The case of the young woman who made money as a go-between is an example of the multiple standards of conduct that exist in society. It is a documented fact that many people earn a substantial living in just this manner. They operate openly in every city, and they have even formed state and national associations to pursue their interests. They are called real estate agents. No one would argue that their doings are corrupt, because they operate in the private sector of the economy. But the same sort of conduct *in a public role* would be a different story. If the young woman were a bureaucrat and took a 6% cut every time the government bought paper clips or fighter planes, her conduct would surely be termed corrupt. Corrupt conduct must be viewed in its context if it is to be reliably identified and understood.

Corruption was indeed involved in the secret bombing of Cambodia and Laos, but not necessarily at the Presidential level. Waging an undeclared war violates the letter of the Constitution, but the Nixon administration could and did reply that the bombing was justified as part of an effort to *end* an undeclared conflict started by a predecessor. "Private-regarding gains" were not at stake for Nixon and company, unless one regards favorable public-opinion polls as a private-regarding gain. But those officers who falsified flight records or ordered others to do so certainly broke formal standards of conduct. To the extent that they did so in order to maintain or enhance their images (and promotion chances) in the eyes of the White House or top brass, they could perhaps be said to have sought private-regarding gain. One could certainly argue that the Nixon bombing strategy was *morally* "corrupt," but what formal/legal corruption there was took place in the ranks of the military.

Finally, the case of the under-the-table inspection sticker shows that corruption is not just the province of elected or appointed government officials. The owner of the service station, in performing state-mandated auto inspections, is for the moment acting in a public role, even though his is a private business and he holds no actual government office. His formal duty is to inspect automobiles fairly and impartially, according to safety standards set by the state. By accepting money to certify a car falsely, he has deliberately chosen not to perform the formal duties of his public role. He and the motorist have entered into a corrupt transaction and each has realized a private-regarding gain. Corruption does not always revolve around large sums of money and great issues:

$20 and an inspection sticker are hardly the stuff of grand intrigue. Still, the motorist has engaged in corruption to circumvent the expensive requirements standing between him and what he wants from government—in this case, permission to drive his car. He has used illicit influence to break through a legally imposed bottleneck.

TYPES OF CORRUPTION

We have arrived at a definition of corruption based on formal standards of conduct in public roles. Within the scope of that definition fall many types of corrupt behavior. Let us identify those types of corruption that will be the primary focus of this analysis.

Looked at in detail, each instance of corruption is in some way unique. Even at a general level, there are many types of corruption, ranging from bribery and extortion to election fraud to outright theft from the public purse. We can appreciate something of the diversity of corruption if we classify types of misconduct by two criteria, although this is by no means the only possible classification. The first criterion is the *purpose* of a corrupt act. Is its purpose to attain or augment power, or to obtain material benefits such as money? The second criterion is the *execution* of the act. Is it *unilateral*, involving only public-role holders acting on their own behalf, individually or in concert; or is it *transactional*, involving direct dealings between people who do and people who do not hold public roles? Table 1-2 uses these criteria—which are a good deal less precise in practice than in theory—to reveal some of the diversity of corruption.

In the chapters to come I will touch upon many of these forms of corruption, and I believe the analysis I will develop offers insights into most of these forms, if not all of them. My primary focus, however, will be those forms of corruption that fall into the lower half of Table 1-2: corrupt *transactions* entered into for

TABLE 1-2. Types of corruption compared on criteria of purpose and execution

Execution	Purpose	
	Attaining or augmenting power	**Obtaining material benefits**
Unilateral	"Cover-ups"	Outright theft
	Falsification of data, records	Diversion of resources, services to personal benefit
	Vote fraud (stuffed ballots, phony absentees)	Fraudulent financial schemes
Transactional	Illegal patronage practices	Bribery
	Nepotism	Extortion
	Vote buying	Kickbacks

purposes of *power* or *material gain*. I will emphasize these sorts of corrupt acts because they are the most varied and challenging to analyze and because these sorts of dealings, perhaps more than the other types, spotlight corruption as a problem in the analysis of public policy. They are a major influence upon program administration and effectiveness, upon service delivery, and upon the determination of which groups get what out of the policy process. They are a major issue in the design and restructuring of policy and institutions. Finally, these sorts of corruption are examples of the very real difficulties of reconciling public power with private interests in a system designed and operated by fallible human beings.

As noted above, I do not intend to ignore the other sorts of corruption. Each will come in for discussion at several points, and in Chapter 5 I will take up the Watergate scandal, which was really a congeries of problems of all four sorts. The chapters to come cannot explain all possible permutations of corruption in complete detail, but I hope they will offer a useful analysis of the many manifestations of political corruption as it has been here defined.

EXPLAINING CORRUPTION: THREE PERSPECTIVES

There are as many possible explanations for corruption as there are incidents and observers. Just as there are common types of corrupt practices, however—bribery, extortion, nepotism, and other sorts of favoritism—so too do our explanations of corruption tend to fall into recognizable categories. In this section I will introduce three of these general types of explanation: the personalistic, the institutional, and the systemic.

Rotten apples: Personalistic explanations

Are the causes of Watergate buried in Richard Nixon's psyche? Did the Korean bribery cases occur because unfit individuals were thrust into positions of public trust? Can we decisively clean up our politics by "voting the scoundrels out"? The personalistic explanation of corruption suggests that the answer to all these questions is yes.

Corruption is the work of people, and when individuals or small groups are found to have broken the rules governing public roles, it is tempting to search for causes in the personal qualities (real or imagined) of those involved. Politicians and bureaucrats, after all, are just as human as the rest of us (indeed, current public opinion often will not give them even *that* much credit for honesty). Hence, we often regard bribery or extortion as the work of unethical individuals, and Richard Nixon's mind has become a popular focus for psychological speculation.

Personalistic explanations hold that corruption is simply a consequence of "human nature," that we all are subject to greed and rationalization. This perspective has its attraction, for it poses the ever-interesting question of why people in similar situations act differently. It brings the patterns and mechanisms of interpersonal influence into close focus and compels a consideration of just what sorts of people we should place in positions of public trust. The personalistic approach can at times help us study why certain kinds of corruption take the course they do, as I will discuss in the Watergate chapter. Although Watergate was not merely the extended shadow of some Nixonian neural pathology, some of the ex-President's characteristic ways of defining problems and acting out solutions may have influenced the development of the scandal in important ways.

There are several drawbacks to the personalistic perspective. One is that corruption does not seem to be the exclusive domain of any particular type of individual. All sorts of people—educated and illiterate, pious and unchurched, Democrat and Republican, members of all ethnic groups, races, and classes—have turned up at the heart of corrupt doings. Civil-service testing and education requirements have not done away with corruption. Similarly, residents of many cities have voted out machine politicians, thinking they have slain the machine dragon, only to find that two or four years later the same machine, perhaps with new individuals on the ticket, sweeps back into office.

Another problem with a focus on individuals is that it may actually place us too close to the problems we wish to understand. Flaws in our institutions or fundamental political dynamics can put strong corrupting pressures on certain public roles regardless of who holds them at any given time. Consider, for example, the potential pressures bearing upon even the most honest building inspector to overlook code violations. A focus solely on personalistic factors would miss these more general causes of corruption. And if greed and other aspects of "human nature" cause corruption, how do we account for those humans who are *not* corrupt? In any event, we can only know who has been involved in corruption *after* the fact, if even then. If there are no especially "corruptible types," our explanations of corruption will tend to be more or less unique from case to case, to be *post hoc* in nature, and to rest on the attributes of the specific persons found to have been involved. As a result, it will be very difficult to predict where corruption will break out next or to reach other general conclusions about corruption and its causes.

In the end, to base explanations of corruption solely on the personal attributes of the guilty, or on the terms of some notion of "human nature," is to take the easy way out. To accept this sort of explanation is to ignore more difficult questions about imperfections in our laws and institutions or about basic problems and contradictions within our collective experiment in democratic government. The personalistic view typically is an exercise in blaming individuals, not explaining political processes, and frequently tells us little about more basic problems of corruption. Although personalistic notions will be found helpful at several points in the chapters to come, they can at best be only a part of a more general outlook on corruption.

Rotten barrels: Institutional explanations

Another common explanation for corruption holds that corruption is often the consequence of loopholes, hidden dynamics, or unintended side effects inherent in our institutions and laws. Institutional problems that could cause corruption might involve mundane matters of administration, such as lax auditing procedures or uncertain communications among the sections of a large organization. Less obvious but more interesting as possible causes of corruption are incentives or strategies emerging as by-products of institutional and legal arrangements. For example, the partisan ballot and the election of city council members by district, rather than at large, have frequently been suggested as causes of machine politics by reformers and scholars.

Like the personalistic approach, the institutional explanation of corruption has definite strengths. It can help us regard corruption as a deep-seated problem, rather than merely as the doings of a few bad individuals. Institutions and laws do indeed shape individual choices and behavior, in part because that is precisely what they are designed to do. It is entirely possible that this shaping is not always positive—that at times it leads the holders of public roles into corrupt behavior. People engage in corruption, institutions as such do not; but a full understanding of corruption should include some conception of how people and institutions fit together.

Another advantage of this approach is that it can point to institutional remedies for corruption. If partisan elections by district are an institutional cause of machine politics, these conditions can be changed. Indeed, nonpartisan, at-large elections were near the top of the reformers' list of anti-machine prescriptions. These remedies can at times get at the heart of persistent corruption problems because they deal with long-lasting arrangements and procedures governing the use of public power and resources and may thus be more effective remedies than personalistic reforms. On the other hand, because institutional remedies *can* alter basic aspects of politics and administration, misguided "cures" can be worse than the original disease. This possibility will be discussed further when we examine such reforms as "sunshine laws," some campaign-finance reforms, and the anti-boss reforms of local government.

The major drawback of the institutional focus is that it leads us to analyze laws or organizations in isolation from their wider political context. Governments, their subunits, and the laws and procedures they enact and implement are all matters of great concern to various parts of the general public. Those who feel they have a stake in government decisions may try to influence those decisions. These efforts can take many forms, legitimate and otherwise, and it is far from impossible that basically honest people, working in well planned and tightly managed agencies, can be drawn into corrupt transactions by forces from without. The extent to which these external demands and pressures have an effect within agencies is no doubt partly a function of the conduct of individuals and of the way agencies are constructed and operated. But we still must pay direct attention to the relationship of government to its environment if we are to understand the full dynamics of corruption.

The big picture: Systemic explanations

Governments, as we have just noted, almost never act in isolation. The pressures, demands, and influence brought to bear upon government by interested individuals and groups are important forces in shaping actions and decisions and are essential to democratic politics. The systemic view of corruption sees the origins of corruption in this interaction between government and public. In the systemic approach, corruption is regarded in a "neutral," analytical manner—as a form of influence, rather than as a failing of individuals and institutions. Regarded as just one of many types of political influence, corruption can be studied with familiar tools and compared to influence of other sorts. Systemic analysts may well conclude that corruption is frequently damaging to democratic values, institutions, and processes, but this judgment is a conclusion based on analysis, not an initial assumption.

More will be made of this view in Chapter 2, for it will be the approach I will rely upon through most of this book. But a brief assessment of its strengths and weaknesses is in order. On the positive side, it is the most comprehensive explanation of corruption. Because it regards corruption as a form of influence *within* the political system, rather than as some sort of despoiling force from without, it can best account for the difficulty we have had in eradicating corruption. People engage in corruption in the face of the law and public opinion, this view suggests, because they stand to benefit from it. The systemic view, in fact, at times points to cases of fairly widespread benefits from corrupt practices. A systemic focus fits nicely with the formal/legal definition of corruption because it regards the law as an important source of benefits and sanctions. The law is shaped by political influence, and it serves as a channel for efforts at influence. Because it entails an understanding of the whole political system, the systemic perspective can link the study of corruption to other lines of theory and inquiry into politics and administration. Another strength is that, because it offers no simple explanation for corruption, it does not delude us into searching for one-shot "quick fixes" for the corruption problem. Finally, it is essentially an analytical approach, not a moralistic one, in keeping with the notion that the first thing we need to do about corruption is to understand it.

Problems with the systemic view include the possibility that its analysis of a given case can almost be *too* complete, including so many systemic forces—as well as institutions and individuals—that it may suggest few clear causal linkages or manageable remedies. We may thus get the idea that corruption is inevitable, which it is not. And, as the systemic view reveals instances when corruption has been beneficial to large segments of society, there is a danger of confusing analysis with romanticism and concluding that we should never be concerned about corruption. The images of the old big-city boss as the benevolent head of a friendly social-service agency—his machine—and of the contemporary Mafia as merely an extended-family brotherhood dealing in "victimless" vices are examples of this danger. So too is the view that Richard Nixon was the innocent victim of a media–liberal conspiracy. Although machines, the mob, and Watergate are best understood in the context of wider systemic trends and pressures, to see their actions as totally justified by their situations is to ignore serious wrongdoing and social costs.

Three disclaimers are in order at this point. First, to see corruption as systemic in origin is not to contend that a whole system is totally corrupt. Political systems are the means by which humans conduct their collective affairs; no perfect way to do this has ever been devised, and in fact pointing out the faults of a system may be a good way to make it better. Second, to rely most upon the systemic view is not to discard totally the individual and institutional perspectives, for they can be of value if employed within a broad systemic understanding. Thus, even though I will contend that Watergate had systemic roots, I will find individual and institutional factors helpful in explaining the path the scandal took. Third, by attributing corruption to deep-seated systemic problems, I do not wish to imply that efforts at reform are doomed but rather that they can be successful only if they are conceived and implemented with the complexity of the whole political system in mind.

THE DATA PROBLEM

We should recognize that data represent a basic problem in any study of corruption. Corruption may be fascinating, but it is also elusive: parties to corrupt transactions normally have an interest in keeping their activities secret. Other corrupt activities, such as bribery and extortion in urban police departments, may be well known to people who are not directly involved, but for a variety of reasons these people may decide to look the other way. Exposés of scandals may produce indictments and convictions, but it is safe to assume that most malefactors are never caught. Even when corrupt behavior does come to light, it is difficult to decide just how corrupt a given agency is, for offenses come in many forms and involve the exchange of many sorts of goods, both tangible and intangible. Finally, as I argued earlier in this chapter, it is often difficult to decide whether certain actions are corrupt at all.

Many sections of this book will thus suffer from a data problem. I have managed to gather some evidence on the use of patronage and on the number of corruption convictions in federal courts. And I will be able to discuss widely observed and often repeated patterns of corruption (as in machine politics and police corruption), or specific individuals and events (as in the case of Watergate). But sophisticated measures of corrupt activities, or of amounts of money and other benefits involved, are beyond the scope of this work.

This book represents my efforts to think systematically about corruption and to assemble the available evidence into useful perspectives on corruption as a policy problem and as a form of influence. My analysis grows out of a firm conviction that corruption must be understood before it can be judged—that moralism is a luxury bought only by careful analysis. My reluctance to condemn corruption and its perpetrators immediately should not be taken as approval of all corruption; nor should my critical remarks be taken for total disapproval. Finally, to contend that corruption grows out of the basic dynamics of our political system is not to argue that Americans or their institutions are inherently corrupt. With these comments in mind, we can begin to examine the place of corruption in political systems.

SUMMARY

In this chapter I have set out competing definitions of corruption and alternative ways of understanding it. The accompanying discussion has been aimed at revealing the complexities of what may seem like a fairly clear-cut political problem. In chapters to come I will employ a formal/legal definition of corruption, and I will rely most heavily on systemic explanation. The systemic view needs further elaboration; questions remain as to the techniques and resources underlying the use of political influence, corrupt or otherwise. The dynamics of government's relationship with society also need further description, as do the characteristics of political systems that affect the types and amount of corruption that occurs. These issues are the subject of Chapter 2.

Notes

1. Allan Temko, *Norte Dame of Paris* (New York: Time Incorporated, 1962), p. 111.
2. Larry L. Berg, Harlan Hahn, and John R. Schmidhauser, *Corruption in the American Political System* (Morristown, N.J.: General Learning Press, 1976), pp. 14–16. A number of studies of the history of corruption in America are listed in the Selected Bibliography at the end of this book.
3. Joseph LaPalombara, *Politics within Nations* (Englewood Cliffs, N.J.: Prentice-Hall, 1974), p. 403.
4. James C. Scott, *Comparative Political Corruption* (Englewood Cliffs, N.J.: Prentice-Hall, 1972), p. 3.
5. Hazel Erskine, "The Polls: Corruption in Government," *Public Opinion Quarterly*, 37:4 (Winter, 1973–74), p. 632.
6. Wallace S. Sayre and Herbert Kaufman, *Governing New York City: Politics in the Metropolis* (New York: W. W. Norton, 1965), pp. 538–548; Martin Tolchin and Susan Tolchin, "How Judgeships Get Bought," *New York* magazine, March 15, 1971, pp. 29–34; and Raymond E. Wolfinger, *The Politics of Progress* (Englewood Cliffs, N.J.: Prentice-Hall, 1974), pp. 90–91.
7. Daniel Elazar, *American Federalism: A View from the States* (New York: Thomas Y. Crowell, 1972), Chapters 4 and 5.
8. J. S. Nye, "Corruption and Political Development: A Cost-Benefit Analysis," *American Political Science Review*, 61:2 (June 1967), p. 416. The final clause of the definition is from Edward C. Banfield, *Political Influence* (New York: The Free Press, 1961), p. 315. Scott, in *Comparative Political Corruption*, also employs this definition and provides a useful discussion of its merits and faults. Scott, op. cit., pp. 3–9. For an excellent discussion of a number of competing definitions, see Arnold T. Heidenheimer, Ed., *Political Corruption: Readings in Comparative Analysis* (New York: Holt, Rinehart & Winston, 1970), pp. 3–9.
9. Scott, pp. 4–5.
10. *Ibid.*, pp. 6–8.

Corruption in Political Systems

2

We can best focus on political corruption as a form of influence by examining its place in political systems. In this chapter, I will discuss what political systems are, the uses of authority and influence within them, and the way routine policy processes in a complex social environment create built-in tensions that can lead to corruption. I will point out the characteristics of systems that affect types and amounts of corruption, and I will conclude with a section on the many and wondrous properties of money as a political resource.

WHAT IS A POLITICAL SYSTEM?

Politics involves elections and formal governmental institutions, to be sure, but it is much more than that. Most important political decisions actually take place outside the arena of elections and elected officials—in the courts, in the bureaucratic and regulatory agencies, and in the activities of lobbyists, organizations, and pressure groups. Beyond this more or less organized political sphere lie other important political actions and sentiments, such as public controversies over taxes or the growing embitterment of a minority group. Politics, broadly defined, includes the entire range of activities that influence "who gets what, when, (and) how," as Harold Lasswell so succinctly put it.[1]

For our present purposes, then, a political system can be defined as a *regular and persistent pattern of action and institutions, rewards and sanctions, through which public policy is made, influenced, and executed*. "Public policy" here includes decisions to regulate, spend, tax, reward, punish, proscribe, prosecute, or decisions *not* to do any of these things—in short, the whole range of governmental action. Not everything we do in life is "politics," but our definition makes it clear that there is much more to a political system than just the institutions of government. Understanding "who gets what" in such a large and complex system entails more than just an analysis of what goes on within formal institutions; we will also have to look at relationships between those institutions and their environment.

At their simplest, these relationships are of two types: actions of the environment upon government, and actions of government upon its environment. The former category can be thought of as "demands and supports"[2]: letters to Congressmen, electoral mandates, protests, and the whole range of activities through which people and groups attempt to communicate with those who govern. The latter includes all the actions I have already termed "public policy." A highly simplified diagram of this process appears in Figure 2-1.

This diagram, of course, oversimplifies the political process. In practice, there is not just one government, but many, at all levels (there were 79,913 units of government in the United States in 1977[3]). Moreover, the distinction between the political system and the rest of society is hardly as clear in practice as the diagram suggests. All phases of the process are in motion at any given time as countless numbers of groups pursue diverse goals, so the neat cause-and-effect linkages suggested by the diagram become difficult to pinpoint in actual cases. Only rarely can we say, for example, that the influence of group or individual X "caused" policy Y. But Figure 2-1 does illustrate the way influ-

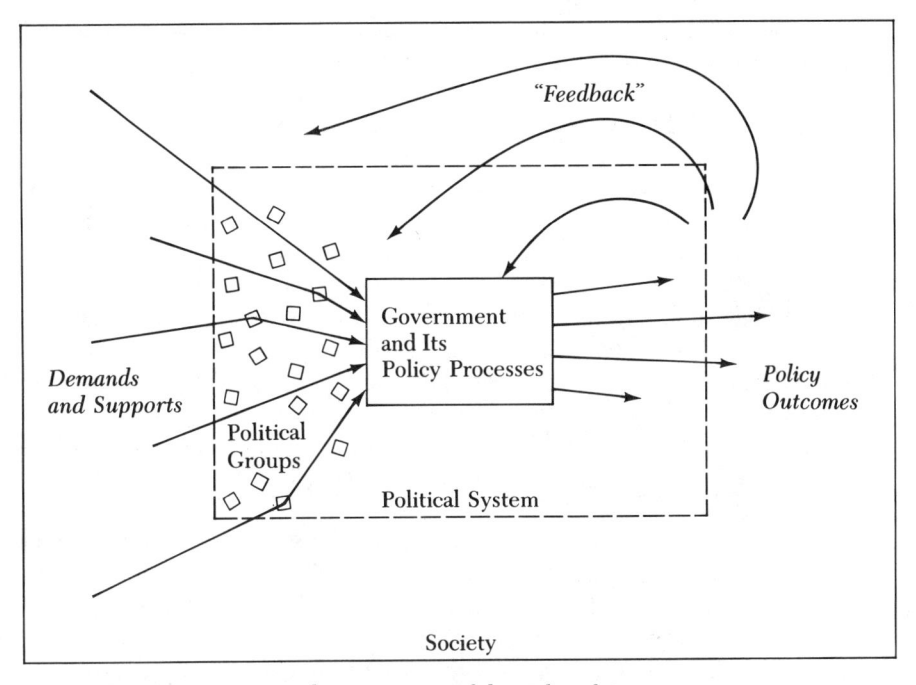

FIGURE 2-1. A Schematic View of the Political System

ence is brought to bear on government from many quarters in order to shape public policy and the way the government's actions "feed back" to produce new demands or give new impetus to old ones.

Exercising influence in the political system

Much of the foregoing is fairly obvious; how does it help us understand how systemic forces create an environment that encourages corruption? The answer to this lies within three characteristics of the governmental process:

1. The fruits of governmental action are often extremely valuable (or, in the case of penalties and sanctions, extremely costly), with demand for benefits frequently exceeding supply.
2. These benefits and sanctions often can be gotten or avoided only by dealing with government.
3. The routine process through which benefits and sanctions are conferred is time-consuming, expensive, and uncertain in its outcome.

Each of these systemic factors contributes to corruption.

Value of government benefits

Government is a big-time enterprise in the United States. The federal government annually spends half a trillion dollars or more on goods, services, and transfer payments. States, cities, counties, special districts, and other lesser governmental entities all add their own shares to this total; in 1977, state and local government spending was an estimated $321 billion.[4] Governments employ millions of people, buy countless commodities ranging from paper clips to aircraft carriers, and annually award contracts for services worth billions.

In addition to direct expenditures, governments confer benefits in the form of licenses, permits, concessions, and grants of authority of great value in the private sector of the economy. An entrepreneur may have a sure-fire idea for a restaurant, but before the restaurant can ever open its doors, the entrepreneur must obtain a number of important things from government: a favorable zoning decision, a building permit, occupancy permits, a restaurant license, a liquor license, health and sanitation inspection certificates, a sales-tax collection license, and more. These pieces of paper have no value in themselves, but the privileges they confer can be worth hundreds of thousands of dollars to the would-be restaurateur. Legislative enactments are another important kind of government action: a small change in the tax laws can add millions to corporate profits.

The other side of the coin is that government also has the power to level penalties and sanctions. Regulatory decisions are a good example: if the Occupational Safety and Health Administration sets new health and safety standards for farm workers, the cost to citrus growers could be immense. Law enforcement is another example: a police chief's choice to commit scarce resources to arresting numbers runners rather than to chasing purse snatchers can have a significant impact on the profits of organized crime. Government can impose cash penalties and prison terms, pursue anti-trust cases, and deny contracts to businesses that fail to meet certain policy standards. The "value" of these sorts of sanctions is large, in the sense that people will often go to great lengths to avoid them. As a result, even after policy has been made, people may seek to exercise political influence—legitimate or otherwise—upon the enforcement or implementation process. It is not uncommon for a business to put up little resistance to the passage of unfavorable regulatory legislation and to concentrate instead on cutting the heart out of the law at the implementation stage.

The point is that, because government actions can be quite valuable or costly, people and groups devote large amounts of time, effort, and resources to influencing decisions. This is true of both the multinational corporation seeking defense contracts and the individual who sets out to win a government job by working his precinct for the mayor. In many cases the demand for government benefits exceeds the supply available. Thus, tremendous amounts of pressure and influence are brought to bear upon public officials and upon the routine and legitimate processes through which they make their decisions.

Government as "the source"

Political pressure on decision-makers is all the more intense because many of the benefits they hand out can be gotten only from government. A firm that builds nuclear submarines essentially has only one customer; even sales to other governments must have federal approval. The restaurateur mentioned above must get his permits and licenses from government; if the permits are denied, he can't go get them at Sears. An employer who is caught violating safety and health standards cannot "go shopping" among several regulatory agencies in search of the lightest penalty.

Government's monopoly on many valuable decisions and benefits, then, serves to focus all the more pressure upon the routine tasks and procedures of decision-making. When the stakes are high, and when only one source of reward exists, efforts at influence are apt to become most intense.

Costs and uncertainties of decision-making

Between the people and groups seeking to influence governmental action and the rewards they seek stand the hurdles and delays that comprise the legitimate policy process. Political scientists currently are devoting much attention to this process, trying to understand how public agencies choose courses of action. Results of such study have often been mixed and have shown above all else that the policy process is most complex and difficult to understand.[5] But to someone seeking influence and a favorable outcome in a decision of importance a few things are quite clear: the policy process is time-consuming, expensive, and uncertain in its outcome.

That government decisions take time is often a good thing. Quick decisions are not always good decisions. Some delays and time-consuming procedures, in fact, are required by law and administrative regulation. For example, if a city needed to buy a few dozen police cars, the quickest course of action might be for the purchasing director to call up his brother-in-law, the Ford dealer, and place an order. But there would be no assurance that the city would get suitable vehicles at a good price. So instead, specifications are drawn up and published, stating what the city needs; a bidding period then ensues, and after bids are opened the city may take a while to study them before awarding a contract. All of this takes time, and many may regard the delay as bureaucratic red tape; yet in the end the city will probably make a much better deal.

From the standpoint of those awaiting favorable government action, delay may seem intolerable. The classic example is the death-row inmate awaiting a call from the governor as midnight draws near; a more pertinent case might be that of bidders competing for a construction contract. In a time of high inflation, every week or month lost means higher costs and lower profits; still, work cannot begin until the government acts. There is a built-in temptation to search for ways to speed up the action.

Influencing the policy process can be expensive as well. Lawyers, lobbyists, consultants, and other experts do not come cheaply; yet they are essential even in many seemingly minor matters. If one chooses to wine and dine key officials, the cost goes even higher. There is thus a basic predicament for those seeking favorable decisions: spending more money on attempts to influence a decision through normal channels might make a favorable outcome more likely; but, even if it does, it can substantially reduce the net profit from the governmental deal. Departing from legitimate procedures, on the other hand—channeling a little cash directly to decision-makers instead of to middlemen such as lawyers and consultants—may not only be an effective form of influence; it may also be quicker and cheaper.

Finally, established decision-making procedures are uncertain in their outcome. Even once a decision has finally emerged, it can be nullified, recalled for reconsideration, or substantially modified. This sort of uncertainty can cause anguish and a prolonged shortage of cash for a person seeking a job. It can be even more serious for a would-be defense contractor, who may have millions of dollars invested in an aircraft design that will never earn a cent if a contract is not awarded. Here again, a form of influence that can reduce uncertainty and make a desired outcome more probable is most handy indeed, even if it does bend or break a few rules.

Government as "bottleneck"

The sum of these observations is that because government benefits can be so valuable, because they can often be obtained only from government, and because the legally sanctioned policy process is so arduous, government and its standard procedures stand as a "bottleneck" between what people want and what they get. *The bottleneck effect will be a characteristic of the policy process, at least to some extent, regardless of the ethics and training of public officials, and despite any good intentions underlying the laws and institutions within which they must work.* The bottleneck will be present both in active governments and in those performing only "bare bones" services. It is a basic aspect of the relationship between government and its environment.

Corruption is an informal kind of political influence that can break through this bottleneck. Corruption by definition cuts across the established standards of official conduct, which stand as expensive, time-consuming obstacles to those seeking the benefits of public policy. It can speed things along, make favorable outcomes much more likely, and cost less than legitimate forms of influence. Institutional and personalistic factors will have a bearing upon whether or not corruption takes place in particular cases. But the basic pressures and tensions that make corruption so advantageous and tempting are products not of the kinds of people to whom we entrust public power, nor necessarily of flawed institutions, but rather of government's basic relationship to society.

My comments thus far may give the impression that corruption is always initiated by private citizens or groups competing over the stakes of public policy. This, of course, is hardly the case: the public officials who make the decisions and hand out the goods can and do exploit their strategic roles. Spiro Agnew was alleged to have demanded and gotten sizable cash payments from contractors and engineers doing state business during his term as governor of Maryland; similar cases have taken place in many other states and cities. The distinction here is essentially one between bribery (corrupt transactions proposed by those seeking government benefits) and extortion (corrupt transactions demanded by public officials), and in practice the two are difficult to distinguish.[6]

Corruption, then, is a form of political influence. Despite its illegality and informality, it can and should be studied in its place within the political system, just as we would study any other form of political influence, such as voting. That corruption breaks the laws and formal standards of the political system does not mean that corruption takes place "outside" the system, or that it is somehow a unique phenomenon; rather, it suggests that corruption and the law are two opposing forms of influence within the same system.

By regarding corruption as a form of influence, I assume something of a neutral stand for the moment on its costs and benefits. Clearly, *someone* always benefits—or perceives a plausible chance of benefiting—from the exercise of corrupt influence. And, if it can be shown that one's corrupt influence has channeled benefits away from others, then obviously someone is the loser. But whether the rest of society always "loses" because of corruption—or indeed, whether it is substantially affected at all—is not always clear. Some instances of corruption might be beneficial, at least in some small degree, to the majority of a polity's citizens. Political machines, for example, built their strong electoral majorities in part by handing out small favors and benefits of all sorts. People working as illicit "go-betweens" in centrally planned economies such as that of the Soviet Union make a handsome (if illegal) income by expediting economic transactions and finding ways to adapt production schedules without incurring the wrath of economic planners.[7] These deals may be corrupt, but they probably benefit many people and groups, consumers as well as producers.

A more indirect case is that of Pittsburgh's late Mayor David Lawrence. The clout he wielded as head of a powerful Democratic machine—some of whose basic processes were corrupt—enabled him to build an alliance with such strategic local business leaders as Richard K. Mellon. Together they were able both to win passage of tough smoke-control legislation and to enforce it, greatly improving the quality of the city's air. They also enlisted enough business, labor, and community backing to get a massive downtown redevelopment program rolling. It is difficult to imagine a mayor who relied only on the formal powers of office being able to achieve such results.

With corruption, as with any other form of influence, we must examine the substance of actual cases before engaging in blanket condemnation. Any form of influence that can make government decision-making less expensive and time-consuming holds out potential benefits for *someone*. Corruption does not necessarily undermine the established order; indeed, by informally resolving serious tensions between political demands and governmental performance and perhaps even hastening economic growth, it may calm potential disorders and increase popular support of existing institutions. The converse of this, however, is that corruption may also "prop up" regimes and institutions long past their time. Whether or not corruption ultimately has a "good" or "bad" impact will thus depend upon the relative merits of the systems being undermined or preserved. I will argue later that corruption definitely has its costs, but the most serious of these costs involve long-term questions of justice and popular attitudes toward government. By short-term standards, we may find some types of corruption widely beneficial.

CORRUPTION AND CHARACTERISTICS OF POLITICAL SYSTEMS

Systems and societies are not all alike, of course. The bottleneck is a part of any government's relationship with its environment, but each case will have its own colorations and tendencies. These characteristics affect the type and amount of pressure brought to bear upon the governmental bottleneck. They have much to do with who exerts the pressure, and toward what ends; and they influence the outcomes and "feedback" implications. These system characteristics can be ordered into three major categories[8]:

1. Social attachments and customs
    a. political culture
    b. popular attachment (or lack of it) to government
    c. popular customs
2. Attributes of the policy process
    a. speed of the process
    b. persistent patterns of influence and exclusion
    c. anti-corruption laws and their enforcement

3. Economic arrangements
   a. level of economic development
   b. relative size of the public sector

A brief examination of these system attributes will suggest some of the reasons why corruption varies, in type and amount, from case to case.

Social attachments and customs

The ways people and groups seek political influence are affected by how they understand their ties to government and to each other. Traditions, customs, and widespread political attitudes all influence corruption; for the sake of convenience I have sorted them into three categories.

Political culture. Political culture is a general term referring to an enduring set of values, norms, and dispositions defining the individual's relationship to the collectivity. Though its significance may vary somewhat from issue to issue and year to year, political culture is generally regarded as a deep-seated attribute of a collectivity, one that changes only very slowly because of basic social and economic developments. We might contrast the political cultures of, say, France and Indonesia, examining individual orientations toward authority to reach a better understanding of how people in those nations exercise forms of influence.

The most provocative recent analysis of political culture in the United States has been developed by Daniel Elazar.[9] He holds that three political cultures, diffused by waves of migration and settlement, set the tone of politics in various states and regions. These political cultures—the individualistic, moralistic, and traditionalistic—not only reflect "regional flavors" of politics but also can account for important variations in policy and patterns of influence.[10] In individualistic areas, Elazar contends, politics is regarded as a marketplace—just another arena in which people contend over benefits and positions of advantage. For many in this political culture, winning benefits is more important than obeying the rules of the game for their own sake. The moralistic political culture, by contrast, regards politics as that potentially noble process through which people build "the good community." *How* this exalted state is reached is of great importance in the moralistic culture, for policy questions are infused with dimensions of right and wrong, and one distinguishing mark of a good community is the way it treats its citizens and conducts its business. Regions with a traditionalistic political culture represent yet another kind of politics. Here, politics and control over policy are regarded as primarily the province of a traditional—perhaps even hereditary—elite. Popular support of this elite, or acquiescence in its rule, is generally high, and popular participation in governance is correspondingly low. Northeastern states such as Pennsylvania and New Jersey, Elazar tells us, tend to be individualistic. Many Midwestern states, such as Minnesota and Wisconsin, qualify as moralistic, and much of the South—for example Louisiana, with its Long family—is broadly traditionalistic.

To the extent that political culture has an influence on corruption, we might expect individualistic areas to have relatively high levels of corruption and moralistic areas to have relatively low levels, or at least rather strict popular standards of official conduct, as suggested by the Minnesota "highway scandal" mentioned in Chapter 1. The traditionalistic culture yields a less clear prediction about corruption, though we might find relatively low levels of corruption involving the mass citizenry and somewhat higher levels among the traditional elite. These notions, and the general concept of political culture, will be examined further when we discuss the political beliefs and orientations of machine politicians and their followers.

Popular attachment to government. The loyalties people feel (or do not feel) toward their government, and the ways they regard its policy processes, will also influence how they go about winning its benefits or avoiding its sanctions. If people and groups feel strongly attached to a particular regime—whether for reasons of the government's longevity, a belief that its processes and institutions work well, or even an emotional commitment to a particular leader—we might expect them to be less likely to break the law in pursuit of benefits. On the other hand, if people regard the regime as foreign to them, as contemptuous of their values and wishes, or as capricious, arbitrary, or plainly corrupt in its policy processes, they might feel that the ends of politics justify the means and pursue government benefits with little regard to legality.

Popular attachment to government and its processes might be so deep and widespread that it becomes part of the political culture, especially in systems where the government has enjoyed a long and widely supported reign. But in systems experiencing an influx of people without much attachment to the current government, in colonized or newly independent areas where government itself is a newcomer, or in systems where government has ceased to "deliver," weak popular attachments might well encourage corrupt influence.

Popular customs. This category includes the full range of social arrangements and traditions that influence people's decisions on how to act in certain situations. These customs need not be explicitly political in origin to have an impact on politics: traditional gift-giving customs, for example, have been advanced as explanations for bribery of judges and other public officials in West Africa.[11] Other customs might be so comprehensive in scope that they provide an alternative set of standards for public officials. A bureaucrat in a nation with strong traditions of kinship obligations may be faced with some difficult decisions if a nephew is among those seeking a job or license. As noted, the term "popular customs" includes a tremendous range of attitudes and behavior, but in general, those customs that pose standards of popular or official conduct directly contrary to law will be most directly relevant to corruption. Hence, we would look more toward kinship obligations than to dietary customs as possible sources of corruption. Other social customs will be discussed in later chapters.

Attributes of the policy process

Speed of the process. How rapidly or slowly decisions are made can have much to do with the amount of corruption in a system. "Speed" is a somewhat slippery concept when applied to policy-making. It can be subjectively "measured," perhaps, in routine cases: if it takes six months for a state board to decide on an application for a liquor license, the applicant may conclude the process is too slow, even though board members may feel they are making decisions as fast as they can. For non-routine policy processes, the concept of speed may drop out entirely if participants see the goings-on as a set of open-ended conflicts rather than a fixed set of hurdles to be crossed. But to the extent that a process is regarded as fast or slow by key participants, and remembering that these perceptions may vary widely, I would suggest a curvilinear relationship between speed of the process and corruption, as presented schematically in Figure 2-2.

A slow process can indeed lead to corruption—a little money put into the right hands can move things quickly. This sort of "speed money" transaction can be initiated by either civil servants or their public clients. Clients may offer bribes, or civil servants may deliberately drag their feet until a client gets the message, thereby extorting a gift or gratuity.

Although corruption is probably more often used to speed things up, it can also be used to delay decision processes. A client who feels that unfavorable decisions are about to be rammed through might spread around a little bribe money, literally to "buy time"; conversely, public officials can use the threat of such quick decisions as a tool for extortion. Perhaps the best example was the tendency of boss-controlled legislatures in New York and other states to threaten utility and railroad companies with rapid passage of "soaker" laws, which usually involved large tax increases and nuisance regulations. These bills were mysteriously tabled after the firms made large campaign "contributions."

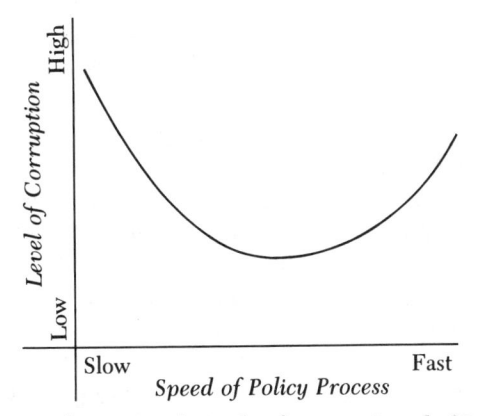

FIGURE 2-2. Schematic Relationship between Speed of Policy Process and Levels of Corruption

Patterns of influence and exclusion. [12]   The governmental bottleneck is costly, time-consuming, and uncertain in outcome for all who seek benefits through its routine processes. It is even less responsive to groups that, for reasons of law, custom, or the predilections of the ruling regime, are excluded from positions of political influence. If excluded groups have reasonably coherent, non-revolutionary goals and the political resources to pursue them, they might get around the barriers to influence through corruption. Those who cannot come in through the main entrance may still gain access through a basement window.

Excluded groups are of many sorts. Social and economic developments may create factions possessing significant political resources but lacking a niche in established policy processes. For example, Scott argues persuasively that the outright sale of royal offices in Stuart England came about, in part, because a newly emerging business class was banned from established arenas of influence for want of hereditary title.[13] Because they commanded a significant political resource—money—they were able to "buy into" the system. Another sort of exclusion can result from more abrupt political developments. If a socialist regime takes power in a political system, formerly powerful business elites might quickly find themselves on the outside, looking for a way to get back in. The same might be true for ethnic or regional minorities, or for traditional elites adapting to a new government whose political base lies elsewhere.

Groups that follow this informal path to influence will likely be seeking relatively specific, short-term policy benefits, rather than complete revolutionary change (although a credible threat of violence or secession might well make existing elites all the more receptive to under-the-table deals). These groups must have significant political resources, such as money or organized numbers of people. Blacks were formally excluded from influence in the Jim Crow South, but they could not have attained corrupt influence even if they had wanted to—they hadn't the money. The resources needed for corrupt influence can be of many types, but Scott notes that wealthy elites will be the most able to counter exclusion with corruption.[14] Even in contemporary American politics, where paths of access for moneyed individuals and groups are relatively open, governmental regulation of the economy, coupled with the fact that demand for the benefits of public policy frequently exceeds supply, means that at least some moneyed elites will likely feel excluded (if only temporarily) from influence over important decisions. Non-wealthy "excluded groups," by contrast, are not likely to be so well endowed with political resources, and many non-monetary resources, such as kinship or ties to a patron-client network, carry less political clout here than in other nations. Hence, much corruption involves the use of money as a political resource. The special political properties of money will be the subject of a later section in this chapter.

Anti-corruption laws and their enforcement.   Simply passing laws against corruption will not make it go away. But the sorts of laws we pass and the ways we enforce them can have an effect on the amount and types of the corruption that does occur. Anti-corruption legislation typically is of two kinds: outright prohibitions of certain kinds of behavior (for example, laws against bribery or nepotism) or—less frequently—laws aimed at easing the "bottleneck" conflict between government policy and people's wishes. An example of this latter kind of legislation would be laws legalizing prostitution, or other sorts of vice, in order to reduce bribery of police officers.

The effectiveness of the first strategy—that of simply outlawing corrupt behavior and transactions—rests on several immediate factors. One factor is the scope of the laws: Do they prohibit a wide or narrow range of activities? Do they focus directly on corrupt behavior (by, say, prohibiting officials from accepting gifts), or are they more indirect (requiring periodic disclosure of personal finances)? Here there is an important trade-off: broad-scale laws may cover more corrupt activities, but "direct" prohibitions may go more effectively to the heart of a particular pattern of corruption. At any rate, either will be difficult to enforce—the former because of their very scope and the latter because getting to the heart of corrupt activities requires long painstaking investigation.

Another factor in the effectiveness of proscriptive legislation is the stakes involved. If the perceived benefits of corruption are great, and the probability of getting them is high, corruption may go on in the face of all sorts of legislation. In the same vein, lax penalties or a low probability of being penalized may do little to deter corruption. Finally, the accessibility of legislators or enforcers to those wielding corrupt influence is also important. If legislators can be bribed, anti-corruption laws may never be enacted; if enforcers can be bought, laws that are passed may have little effect.

The effectiveness of the second kind of law—that intended to reduce the bottleneck effect—is more difficult to predict. The most important question is whether the legislation truly makes legitimate routes to influence more attractive, or less arduous, than illegitimate routes. A good example of this sort of law is the proliferation of state lotteries in the East and parts of the Midwest. Lottery advocates commonly argued that lotteries not only would raise badly needed revenue but would also strike a blow against organized crime, its illegal numbers games, and the bribery of police that so often accompanies them. Remove government prohibitions against small-time gambling, it was suggested, and people would no longer have to play the mob's game.

The problem with this argument is that the objectives of raising revenue and undercutting organized crime are contradictory.[15] Setting payoffs to bettors high enough to compete with illegal numbers games would mean very low revenue returns to the state; taking a larger state share would reduce payoffs. Most states, hard pressed for funds, have chosen the latter route; as a result, payoffs from state lotteries usually are less than those from illegal games. Moreover, state lottery winnings must be declared as income for tax purposes; illicit winnings, by contrast, amount in practice to tax-free income. Hence, this effort at encouraging people to pursue their wishes through legitimate channels has met with limited success. The illegitimate channels remain more attractive. There is no evidence I know of suggesting that state lotteries have cut seriously into illegal gambling, or that they have reduced the bribery of police.

Thus, the effects of anti-corruption laws hinge upon a number of factors, and even the general comments I have just offered will not always be accurate. My generalizations about laws prohibiting corruption, for example, assume that wrongdoers act on rational cost-benefit estimates of the consequences of their actions, and that they make these judgments separately for each corrupt transaction. Many people engaged in corruption, I would guess, have neither the information nor inclination to act in so calculated a manner. And, if the Watergate cover-up has taught us anything, it is that pressures and temptations to break the law can be cumulative—reflecting, in the Watergate case, increasing amounts of illegal conduct that had to be concealed. Still, a system's efforts to control corruption can be a major factor influencing types and amount of corruption. More will be made of this in Chapter 6, which takes up the problems of reform.

Economic arrangements

Level of economic development. Not long ago many people assumed that corruption was mainly a phenomenon of economically underdeveloped areas. Watergate and corporate bribery of public officials in many of the most developed nations have disabused us of this oversimplistic notion, but it is still true that a nation's level of economic development can have an important effect on a system's political corruption.

Scott points out that low levels of economic development emphasize government's role as a source of jobs and benefits and create a wide "status gap" between public officials and the general citizenry. The former factor means that the pressure on the governmental bottleneck will be extremely heavy. People's needs for benefits will be greater, due to mass poverty, and the supply of government benefits will be smaller. The poverty of the private sector of the economy may also mean that for many people, jobs, money, and goods will be completely unavailable if government cannot supply them. The government, meanwhile, may be faced with few (if any) countervailing forces from the private sector—mass political parties, trade unions, and organized interest groups capable of influencing decision-makers. It may thus dispense its benefits arbitrarily and capriciously, bringing about more extortion and bribery.

The "status gap" between officials and citizens can lead to corruption in more subtle ways. Scott explains that citizens in more economically advanced systems have grown accustomed to dealing with public employees who are people much like themselves, but that their counterparts in developing systems often must approach functionaries who far outrank them in social, educational, and economic status. In the former instance, citizens are aware of their own rights and of the general rules governing public employees' conduct. Citizens are more likely to recognize that public employees' authority is not their own but rather derives from an institutional mandate. But in the latter case, citizens may see a public employee's power as personal in nature and may resort to flattery or even outright bribery in order to ingratiate themselves with this distant and powerful figure. The public employee in this latter situation may also feel much more free to extort money or gifts from the thoroughly intimidated client.[16]

Much of the private economic activity that does take place in underdeveloped nations often is under the ownership or control of outside interests such as multinational corporations. These interests, it seems safe to assume, have relatively little attachment to the government and its routine procedures; in fact, they may often regard the local government as simply an irritation to be dealt with as self-interest may dictate. The absence of countervailing private powers, the often tremendous assets of outside interests, and their ability to blackmail economically marginal states by threats of withdrawal or reprisals can combine with these weak attachments to make outside interests a significant corrupting force in developing nations.

Relatively affluent nations, though, have their own dynamics of corruption. As economic and technological activity accelerates, public-policy benefits can increase in type and number. Government contracts can become larger and more valuable, and taxes and regulations can become more bothersome in the face of real chances for larger profits. Further, as domestic concentrations of wealth increase, more groups with more resources may be competing over political access and benefits than ever before.

The point is not that economically developed systems are inherently more or less prone to corruption; they are neither. Rather, the point is that there may be differences in the types of, and participants in, corrupt activities. In less developed economies, dealings between traditional social groups (tribes, kinship, and patron-client networks) and government may involve much petty bribery and extortion, nepotism, and other sorts of favoritism; what major bribery there is probably will come from external interests such as the multinationals. Increasing economic activity may not actually reduce the amount of nepotism and petty corruption, but these activities may be overshadowed by more major and extensive corruption involving emerging domestic wealth elites. In time, the direct corrupt transactions between individual citizens or small traditional groups and government may be aggregated into political machines, which can also strike up alliances with business interests (see Chapter 3). Finally, in highly developed economies, citizens' most pressing needs may be addressed by the private economy or by routine government services: instead of having to bribe a hospital functionary in order to see a doctor, a sick person may get government-guaranteed payments or services-in-kind. The total amount of corruption will not necessarily diminish in a highly developed system, but significant corrupt influence will largely be the province of wealthy groups and individuals from inside or outside the system. Not only do wealthy elites have a sizable interest in policy; those seeking corrupt influence based on kinship or small amounts of wealth simply cannot compete with the "big boys."

Relative size of the public sector. Finally, the larger the public sector of the economy—by which we mean government institutions, enterprises, and services—the more corruption there will be. This observation is not merely predicated on the existence of governmental inefficiency, although inefficiency will make the bottleneck effect even worse. It is based on the fact that, as the public sector grows in relation to the rest of the economy, more and more types of human conduct become issues of public policy. Extension of land-use controls may mean that building a house—once a purely private endeavor—now requires permits and licenses. With these new rules, of course, come opportunities and temptations *to break* the rules. More corruption is the likely result.

The number of public roles increases with the growth of the public sector as well. When a nation nationalizes its steel industry, for example, the same individual may be in charge of purchasing coal as before the takeover. But the purchasing agent is now a government employee. When a coal company deals with the agent, it no longer sells to another private enterprise, but to government. Informal deals executed when the two were both in the private sector—discounts, gifts, rebates, and the like—may now be construed as bribes, extortion, and kickbacks, because a different set of standards governs the transactions. In this regard, recall the distinction made in Chapter 1 between a realtor taking a commission and a defense department employee "skimming" a percentage of a contract. Much the same would be true if *both* the steel and coal industries became part of the public sector.

Part of the correlation between large public sectors and higher levels of corruption is simply a consequence of our definition of corruption, which emphasizes formal standards of conduct in public roles. Thus, observers who point to upsurges of corruption in recently nationalized industries, and who regard this as evidence of some inherent defect of centrally planned economies, should ask themselves whether anything other than the formal rules of the game has really changed. Being sensitive to the difference between private and public roles can also help us understand black markets and administrative corruption in nations such as the Soviet Union. A nut-and-bolt manufacturer in the United States who faces a shortage of steel may remedy the problem simply by offering a premium price for any available steel. The manufacturer in Omsk, however, may not be legally allowed to depart from a planned price for steel, so perhaps he must "persuade" a planning bureaucrat to ignore steel purchases that exceed planned prices. Neither transaction is inherently more or less efficient, if in the end the nuts and bolts are manufactured on schedule. The difference lies in the existence of differing public- and private-sector standards of conduct.

In this section we have examined several aspects of political systems that can affect types and amounts of corruption. None of the relationships described should be regarded as an ironclad law; rather, they are descriptions of general tendencies. Real political systems possess a mixture of attributes, some making for more corruption, some for less. Understanding the corruption in any actual system will be a complex and demanding task, even with these generalizations in mind. But if these propositions have any empirical validity—a matter requiring further inquiry—they suggest that understanding corruption in terms of the broad character and structure of political systems will be more rewarding than looking just at individuals or at flaws in institutions. One of these general tendencies—the role of wealthy elites in advanced economies such as our own, and in particular the uses of money as a political resource—is the topic of the concluding section of this chapter.

MONEY AS A POLITICAL RESOURCE

The relationship between wealth and political influence has been an issue in American politics since the earliest days of the colonies, when ownership of property was frequently a requirement for taking part in public decisions. It continues to be a concern today—witness our recent efforts to regulate campaign finances. Whether or not wealthy elites call the tune in American politics—openly or covertly—has been the subject of much debate among political scientists. I cannot resolve the debate here, but in this concluding section I will discuss money's extraordinary versatility as a political resource. What are money's political properties, and how do these properties make it especially useful in corrupt transactions?

People and groups employ a remarkable variety of political resources in their quest for influence and benefits. Votes are an obvious political resource, but there are many more: time, education, and information; connections, both to elites and to large numbers of ordinary citizens; organization (both formal, such as an association of milk producers, and informal, such as Eugene McCarthy's army of doorbell ringers); weapons, protest, strikes, and violence or credible threats of violence; and money. Each resource has its advantages and drawbacks, and each is more effective in some situations than in others; but the handiest and most versatile of these resources is money.

Money is effective partly because it is *convertible*. Money can buy any of the other resources listed. Other resources are not so directly convertible. Money also *can be used on a continuing basis*.[17] One need not wait for an election or time of general upheaval to put it to political use; money is welcomed at any time, especially by politicians who must pay for the last campaign or build up a war chest for the next. Alternatively, money *can be stockpiled* for an advantageous moment. By contrast, a voter who does not like any of this year's mayoral candidates cannot save the vote and vote twice next time. Money is *mobile:* it can be dispatched to jurisdictions far away from one's home or place of business, to jurisdictions where, for reasons of citizenship, one cannot vote or hold office. Money *can be given or spent anonymously,* if need be, in the form of cash; or, *it can be given with the name of the donor clearly understood,* so that a politician or bureaucrat knows clearly to whom he or she is indebted. Votes and much political work, by contrast, are more anonymous. Money as a political resource thus allows interest groups, corporations, and other entities to "vote."[18] Further, money has been, until recently, one of our *least regulated* political resources: we have devised elaborate precautions to prevent skid-row drunks from voting several times, and the departed from voting at all, but we have only lately begun seriously to regulate the use of money in politics. Finally—and most important—time and votes are distributed evenly throughout the population, but money is *distributed unevenly*. Some people and groups have many times more money than others; these inequalities are probably even greater when we compare amounts of truly disposable income. And one can donate as much money as one has to use, distributed among causes pretty much as one wishes; there are no absolute limits to the political uses of money.

We need not contend that money always calls the political tune in order to observe that these qualities make it a most useful political resource. Candidates with little money do win elections, letters to Congress carry definite weight, and protest has at times been a most effective tactic for the poor. But it is clear that money's flexibility and convertibility make it an effective tool of influence in any situation; and its suitability for continuous, anonymous, hard-to-trace uses make it especially well suited for corrupt influence.

These qualities, together with money's unequal distribution in society, have important implications for the issue of who benefits and loses because of corruption, a question upon which we shall touch in Chapter 7. I will contend that although we can point to cases in which corruption has benefited the vast majority of a system's citizens, the logic of money-in-politics more frequently means that corruption will benefit the wealthy. This undemocratic bias, I will argue, is one of the greatest costs of corruption. It is an informal but highly effective form of influence through which the "haves" can appropriate the benefits of public policy, and stave off legislation and reforms that might benefit the "have-nots."

SUMMARY

In this chapter I have sketched out a very general picture of corruption as it fits into the larger political system. Corruption originates in the relationship between government and its environment. Personalities, laws, and institutions may well explain why corruption does or does not occur in a specific instance and may help us understand the directions it actually takes. But the ultimate dynamics of corruption lie in the bottleneck between what people want from government and what they get. I have discussed several characteristics of political systems that can affect the types and amount of corruption in actual cases. Finally, we examined the way money—a political resource which can be put to use continuously and anonymously—is well suited to the exercise of corrupt influence.

These observations constitute a framework for comparison of political systems and the corruption we find within them. But a detailed understanding of corruption and its causes can only come by seeing these tendencies in action and by examining the ways specific personalistic and institutional factors are woven into the larger dynamics of whole systems. The case studies in the next three chapters will present such an analysis; and it is the first of these—a chapter on political machines—to which I now turn.

Notes

1. Harold Lasswell, *Politics: Who Gets What, When, How* (New York: Meridian, 1958).
2. This is a fairly classic conception of the political system; it draws upon David Easton, *A Systems Analysis of Political Life* (New York: Wiley, 1965).
3. The figure is from the U.S. Census of Governments, 1977, as reported in U.S. Bureau of the Census, *Statistical Abstract of the United States: 1979*, 100th ed. (Washington, D.C.: U.S. Government Printing Office, 1979), Table 471, p. 283.
4. *Ibid.*, Table 483, p. 292.
5. See, for a recent example, George D. Greenberg, J. A. Miller, L. B. Mohr, and B. C. Vladeck, "Developing Public Policy Theory: Perspectives from Empirical Research," *American Political Science Review* 71:4 (December 1977), pp. 1532–1543.
6. The bribery-extortion distinction is often disregarded by the courts altogether, on the grounds that requiring explicit agreements or demands by officials as evidence of extortion would enable authorities to capture only the small-time operator who is beginning an extortion racket by making explicit demands, while preventing the prosecution of major extortion figures whose dealings are so pervasive and well established that no explicit agreements or demands need be made. See Herbert J. Stern, "Prosecutions of Local Political Corruption under the Hobbs Act: The Unnecessary Distinction between Bribery and Extortion," *Seton Hall Law Review* 3:1 (Fall 1971), pp. 1–17.
7. Colin Leys, "What Is the Problem about Corruption," *Journal of Modern African Studies* 3:2 (August 1965), p. 220. See also John M. Kramer, "Political Corruption in the USSR, *Western Political Quarterly* 30:2 (June 1977), pp. 213–224; and Hedrick Smith, *The Russians* (New York: Random House/Ballantine Books, 1976). See especially Chapter 3, "Corruption: Living Nalevo."
8. The following comments on system characteristics draw, at several points, upon James C. Scott, *Comparative Political Corruption* (Englewood Cliffs, N.J.: Prentice-Hall, 1972), pp. 9–35.
9. Daniel Elazar, *American Federalism: A View from the States* (New York: Thomas Y. Crowell, 1972), Chapters 4 and 5.
10. For some recent empirical applications of Elazar's formulations, see the articles presented in *Publius* 10:2 (Spring, 1980); see also Charles A. Johnson, "Political Culture in the American States: Elazar's Formulation Examined," *American Journal of Political Science* 20:3 (August 1976), pp. 491–509.
11. Scott, pp. 11–12 and 16–17.
12. The following discussion draws upon Scott, pp. 28–34.
13. *Ibid.*, Chap. 3. This process is an interesting example of what Scott terms "proto-corruption": political behavior, legal at a given time, that is later defined as corrupt because of changes in the law.
14. *Ibid.*, pp. 33–34.
15. I am indebted to Rafael Sonenshein for his comments on this point.
16. Scott, pp. 10–15.
17. Larry L. Berg, Harlan Hahn, and John R. Schmidhauser, *Corruption in the American Political System* (Morristown, N.J.: General Learning Press, 1976), pp. 38–41.
18. *Ibid.*, Chapter 2.

The Political Machine

3

In the early 1870s Thomas Nast, the famous New York political cartoonist, was searching for a symbol of machine rule to use in his epic battles with Tammany Hall. He eventually developed a caricature of boss William M. Tweed himself: a tall, heavy-set man, well dressed in a vested suit, often smoking a cigar, and sporting a diamond stickpin that grew larger and more ostentatious by the year. Nast's Tweed often wore an expression made up of equal parts of amusement and contempt for his political foes and the general public. His immense bulk suggested that he had prospered in the course of his "services" to the people of New York. With this caricature an image was born; even today, the term "machine boss" conjures up a Tweed-type mental picture.

Political machines have been part of American life since the Civil War.[1] Tweed and his Tammany Tiger were the most famous practitioners of machine politics, but there have been many others: Kansas City had its Pendergast organization, San Francisco its Boss Ruef, and Cincinnati, Boss Cox. Vare of Philadelphia, Frank ("I Am the Law") Hague of Jersey City, Crump of Memphis, and Boston's James Michael Curley all built strong organizations. The Chicago machine story—from William Hale Thompson's Republican organization through Democrats Cermak, Kelly, Nash, Daley, and now Byrne—continues today. Political machines have ruled whole states, including at various times New York, Pennsylvania, and Louisiana. Today, there are fewer classic big-city machines of the Daley or Tammany variety, but machines still rule in some middle-sized cities, and machine politics as a type of political practice is very much alive in many areas.[2]

Boss Tweed's physiognomy is not the only popular image we have retained from the machine era. We often think of machines as quintessentially American, thriving in the heavily Irish, Italian, and East European sections of big industrial cities, usually under the Democratic party label. But there have been rural machines, suburban machines, and machines run by Protestant Yankees.[3] Many cities had Republican machines long before the Democrats developed their urban base. Boss Ruef's San Francisco organization, in fact, flourished under the banner of the Union Labor Party.[4] And machines are not just an American phenomenon; they exist today in a number of nations, especially those undergoing rapid urbanization.[5]

There are two competing myths about the costs and benefits of machine politics. The first, and more common, myth is that of machine-as-octopus, putting a tentacle into every pocket in a never-ending process of graft, extortion, and outright theft. This machine monster rules by fear and views the legitimate needs and wishes of residents and businesses with contempt. The second myth is that of machine-as-benefactor, as a sort of extended family providing services for the poor and cutting red tape for businessmen. The Boss and his minions are seen not as cynical opportunists but as friends in time of need, providing food, clothing, business contracts, and jobs—and asking only for loyal support in return.

In reality, machines are both, and neither, of these things. Myths like these survive because they contain elements of truth. But the costs and benefits of machine politics are diverse, and sometimes intangible; frequently, one group's cost is another group's benefit. And while machines have a simple and durable structure, their internal political dynamics can be quite complex. Thus, machines are resistant to simple labels of good or bad.

This complexity makes machines interesting. The questions that machine politics and related corruption pose for public policy make the study of machines important. To rid our cities of bossism, we have set up whole new systems for elections and administration. We have fragmented public power, weakened executive officials, and placed important responsibilities in the hands of non-elected professional managers, all in the name of "good government." Have we improved urban life by "throwing the scoundrels out," or do machines perform important services and functions that we do not recognize until they are gone? Have our "cures" for machine politics proven to be worse than the disease? A careful analysis of machine politics can help provide answers to these questions.

MACHINES AND CORRUPTION

Not everything about machine politics is corrupt. Many of the boss' fundamental techniques—strong party discipline, capitalizing on divisions in the social structure, and vigorous efforts to turn out votes—are perfectly legal and often are used by the machine's enemies as well. But other aspects of machine politics *are* corrupt, and herein lies the connection between machines and the perspective on corruption proposed in Chapters 1 and 2. The strength of the machine rests crucially upon control of the policy process—upon the ability to use the "bottleneck effect" to its advantage. The ability to confer the benefits of public policy upon one's friends and to withhold them from one's enemies helps make the machine strong. Some instances of this preferential policy-making are corrupt, some are shady, and some are fully legal. But whether or not specific cases are corrupt, machine control of the policy process is calculated to take advantage of the kinds of relationships outlined in Chapter 2 between policy-makers and their social environment.

THE "IDEAL MACHINE": AN ORGANIZATIONAL ANALYSIS

Let us begin by imagining an organization that does not exist: the ideal machine. Machines vary from place to place, depending upon local political or economic factors and upon the personality and predilections of political leaders. For now, I am discounting these local variations and sorting out important attributes that machines have in common. This discussion will not describe any *one* case perfectly, but it should help us understand machine structure and operations.

A political machine is a *party organization within which power is highly centralized, and whose members are motivated and rewarded by divisible material incentives*[6] *rather than by considerations of ideology or long-term goals of public policy*. Divisible material incentives are rewards that have tangible value and that can be given to or withheld from specific individuals (hence the term "divisible"). Money, jobs, and contracts are divisible material incentives. Opening a park or declaring Martin Luther King's birthday a holiday might be political rewards, but they are neither divisible nor of direct material benefit. Bosses use divisible material incentives to build and reward organizations that obtain enough votes, legally or otherwise, to win and maintain control over public authority—in most cases, city government. Control over public authority is in turn a source of more incentives, such as city jobs, contracts, licenses, and discretionary law enforcement, which are used to strengthen the organization still further. Machines are thus complex political animals standing on three legs—votes, incentives, and control of public authority. As a result, the formal institutions of a machine-run city may represent only the tip of the political iceberg. The city charter may state—and many people may believe—that the city is governed by a mayor, a council, and agencies accountable to these elected officials. But the machine leadership really calls the tune, deciding who shall hold the formal positions in government, and it is often the machine's power that those officials use in making and executing policy.

Machines have dominated politics at one time or another in many cities and states, deftly bridging social divisions by playing off the money of the affluent (obtained in exchange for, say, franchises and business contracts) against the votes of the poor (won in exchange for small favors and gifts). Machines have survived and often thrived on waves of ethnic succession and economic change. In the face of the disruptive social forces that built our cities and continue to change them, machines have been able to "organize, centralize, and maintain in good working condition 'the scattered fragments of power' which are at present dispersed through our political organization."[7] The skilled use of divisible material incentives has enabled such organizations to do all of this so reliably that they truly have earned the name "machines."

Three characteristics of the ideal machine combine to make it strong and reliable: a widespread organization that can maintain electoral control in many sections of the city; a persistent imbalance in obligations between the boss and subordinates; and the fact that the vote-getting performance of machine members, and the divisible rewards they get, can be precisely assessed and compared.

Widespread organization

Citywide pluralities are constructed out of thousands of face-to-face contacts and individual favors. Responsibility for making these contacts is explicitly delegated down to the block level. Often the city's wards and precincts, or neighborhoods, provide a natural framework for delegating duties. The result is a pyramidal structure of authority and obligation, perhaps containing several tiers of leadership, as shown in Figure 3-1.

This structure allows each level of leadership to supervise a manageable number of subordinates; yet it still covers all of a city's neighborhoods. The structure also produces clear lines of authority and responsibility: individuals are each responsible to the person directly above them for delivering the vote in their area and for keeping track of political developments and constituent requests. Those who slip up at these tasks can readily be identified and disciplined; those who perform well can be considered for, and motivated by, possible promotion or extra rewards. The ideal machine can thus maintain an active, disciplined presence in every street of even the largest city.

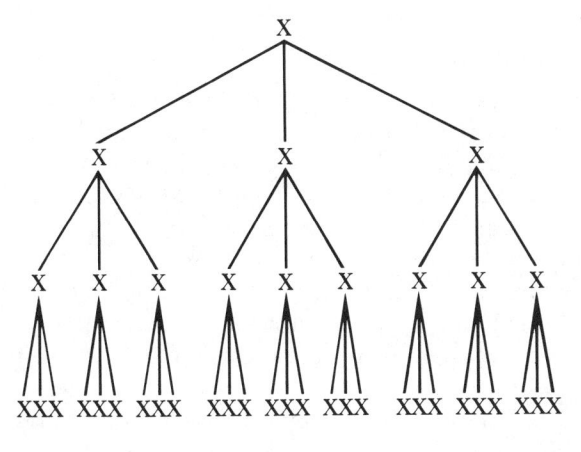

Top Leadership ("boss" or small group)

Major Subleaders (such as assembly district leaders)

Ward Leaders

Precinct Captains (who may in turn delegate people to cover specific blocks, or specific apartment buildings, etc.)

FIGURE 3-1. Structure of Ideal Machine Organization

Unbalanced obligations

Machines do not just spring up out of their social and political context. Someone must build a machine, and someone must maintain it. Someone with clear and centralized power must make and enforce tactical decisions. By controlling and carefully allocating incentives, a "boss" can create and hold such a position of power. This is so because the granting of rewards can create and discharge obligations.

The power of bosses is based on an *unbalanced* ("patron–client") structure of obligations. Simply put, most of the boss' followers feel they owe the boss something. Those not actually "in debt" may support the boss in hope of future rewards. The "something" owed to the boss is active support at election time and in times of factional fights. Often the debt is paid through year-round service to loyal supporters in their neighborhoods. This imbalance of obligations may seem puzzling: no boss has an unlimited supply of incentives, and even those with immense resources may have few rewards to shift around, since one can hardly confiscate benefits from long-time supporters to give to new friends. Supporters recruited recently, even active ones, may have to endure a probation period before being cut in on the spoils. Still, bosses can ensure that most of their followers are indebted to them. First, most of the rewards that hold a machine together can be gotten only through the boss' organization. Second, jobholders are reminded of their obligations with each paycheck, and voters' requests can be granted throughout the year; but the boss usually demands major efforts only on certain occasions—at election time, or in time of internal struggle. Thus, by foregoing immediate repayment and instead storing up obligations against the time they are needed, the boss maintains the imbalance.[8] Power is thus centralized within the organization, and the boss can make critical political decisions and count on a disciplined organization to carry them out.

Measuring performance and rewards

The third factor that makes our ideal machine strong and efficient is the ability to judge precinct and ward leaders' performance by an exacting standard—the number of pro-machine votes produced. Often ward leaders and precinct captains are required to set a target number of votes to be gotten from their districts. They are then expected to meet that goal. Obviously, precinct captains cannot set their target figures too high, for it is votes, not promises, that win elections, and they cannot afford to fall short. But neither can they set their targets too low, for exceeding them by too wide a margin opens them up to the charge of not knowing what is going on in their precincts and of leaving results to chance.[9]

Just as the machine can measure performance by vote production, it measures rewards through divisible material incentives. A boss can keep track of exactly how many patronage jobs have been channeled into an area and can adjust the distribution of these rewards as events dictate. These easily understood standards of production and reward allow precise accounting of obligations and performance. Whether or not such precise comparisons and adjustments are made in practice will be the topic of a later discussion.

The ideal machine is an efficient organization. It is in effect a business organization, run for the profit of its members, that must win elections from time to time. In return for divisible material incentives, it gets enough votes to win control of public authority. The astute use of public authority, in turn, yields more incentives for use in strengthening the machine. It is no wonder that where machines have taken control, they have proven difficult to beat.

THE POLITICAL BASE OF THE MACHINE

Where do machines get their support? Typically, they do well in poor and working-class districts, winning votes through generosity, manipulation, or both. But this is only half the picture. Machines often perform a delicate political balancing act over a chasm of class differences, winning votes from the numerous poor and money from the affluent few. These classes often clash over issues of policy, culture, and economic self-interest, but bosses can turn these diverse groups into complementary forces supporting the machine. In the process, machines help dampen potentially serious class conflicts.

Machines can help pave over differences because both business interests and the poor want things from the machine and the government it controls. Additionally, each group commands a resource that enables the machine to serve the other. Businesspeople want government contracts, licenses, franchises, and weak enforcement of regulatory laws, and they are able to use money as a political resource. Poor and working-class people need more modest favors—food, clothing after a fire, small amounts of cash.[10] In return, they can offer large numbers of votes. With the votes of the poor, a machine can control local government and thus furnish to business the desired benefits of public policy. The money of the affluent provides not only the major spoils for the top leadership but finances many smaller benefits channeled to the poor. We can examine these relationships in greater detail.

Small favors for the poor

In exchange for the votes of the poor, the machine provides a wide range of favors and services. Robert K. Merton gives us perhaps the most frequently quoted summary of these benefits:

> The machine welds its link with ordinary men and women by elaborate networks of personal relations. Politics is transformed into personal ties. The precinct captain is forever a friend in need. In our prevailingly impersonal society, the machine, through its local agents, fulfills the important social *function of humanizing and personalizing all manner of assistance* to those in need. Food baskets and jobs, legal and extra-legal advice, setting to right minor scrapes with the law, helping the bright poor boy to a political scholarship in a local college, looking after the bereaved—the whole range of crises when a feller needs a friend, and, above all, a

friend who knows the score and who can do something about it—all these find the ever-helpful precinct captain available in the pinch.[11]

Merton probably overstates the selflessness of the precinct captain. And we should remember that machines do not provide social services out of sheer goodness; rather, gifts and favors serve political ends, and the scale of these benefits should not be overestimated. Nevertheless, ties with the poor and working classes built up through these sorts of favors can be strong and enduring. Precinct leaders help loyal supporters in times of need, and they do it without moral judgment or class-based disdain. Machine politics can also be a source of status and recognition for people—and even whole ethnic communities—who otherwise would get little.

Machine favors should also be viewed in light of needy people's alternatives. Before the New Deal, providing aid to the poor, the sick, and the unemployed was primarily the task of church and charitable groups. Their resources were limited, and help was often tied to well intentioned but demeaning efforts at "moral uplift." Since the 1930s, social services have been extended and formalized, but a large bureaucratic agency can still seem distant and hostile, especially to a poor person who may not speak English. Even after the New Deal, people turned to the machine for help because it was one of the few alternatives they had. If the machine's favors came at a price—minor benefits for a vote, perhaps a job for a long record of active support—this too must be judged in its context. Many early immigrants came from nations where mass suffrage was unknown, or where elections made little difference in the day-to-day struggle to survive. If this abstract thing called a "vote" could be traded for something of value—then, why not? Those more familiar with American politics knew that voting the issues could make a difference in the long run, but playing the machine's game could bring benefits far more tangible and immediate.

We should be careful, though, not to overestimate the scale of the machine's largess. It was never the case that immigrants fresh off the boat were greeted with open arms, told how to vote, and immediately given jobs. There are not that many jobs to be had; those that are available are reserved for people with long records of active support. Voting, in itself, wins only small favors in most cases, and those who do not even "vote right" are simply out of luck.[12]

It would also be wrong to assume that machines had an interest in fully assimilating whole waves of immigrants or lifting whole classes of people out of poverty. Some assimilation was necessary if immigrants' numerical strength was to be put to use: they had to be made citizens and voters, and they had to be tied into the organizational network. Beyond this there was no political benefit in aiding assimilation. Indeed, assimilation could be a liability if it lessened people's dependence upon the machine. Further detracting from the need for assimilation was the fact that many machines were built upon one ethnic group as their core; witness Mayor Daley's Irish-dominated Chicago organization. The "dominant ethnics" in the machine likely had no more affection for other groups than did anyone else. Succeeding waves of immigrants represented something of a drain on resources, a bloc of potential voters who had to be enlisted and controlled before someone else did it. Thus, Irish-led machines have taken best care of the Irish; Italian machines, the Italians, and so on. Even today, machine bosses practice balanced-ticket politics only as necessary, and subordinate ethnic communities often get less than their share of the spoils.[13]

As for lifting whole classes of people out of poverty, machines have neither means nor reasons to do so. Even the strongest machine has limited stores of benefits, most of them petty ones. Addressing the needs of whole classes would not only quickly exhaust the machine's resources and depart from the practice of emphasizing personal, divisible rewards; it would upset the machine's delicate balance between affluent and poor. There are also business interests to cater to, and the last thing business wants is to lose its reliable source of cheap labor. This relationship between machine and business is important, and it merits closer examination.

The "business connection"

Like the poor, business interests want things from government; unlike the poor, business can put money to use as a political resource. Hence, businesspeople and politicians involve themselves in a symbiotic relationship. Business interests need contracts and franchises from city government and may also wish to avoid various kinds of regulation, such as health standards for restaurants or safety codes for apartment buildings. Pursuing favorable decisions through routine channels means confronting the governmental bottleneck and its delay, uncertainty, and cost. Spreading some cash around in strategic places, on the other hand, can move things along quite nicely—and the machine has no misgivings about using the policy process to raise money. Thus, the "business connection" is a natural.

Many large cities and political machines grew up together. The heyday of machine politics, running roughly from the Civil War years until World War II, was a time of explosive growth in many cities. Growth offered a number of chances for businesspeople and politicians to help each other. In the early 1800s, government and business pretty much went their separate ways in many cities. Governing often amounted to little more than collecting taxes and hiring a night watchman. Few businesspeople played significant roles in politics.[14] But by the final third of the century, government and business were interacting on an increasingly intimate basis, for each stood to benefit from the needs and resources of the other. With urban growth came the need for capital improvements—bridges, streets and highways, sewers and aqueducts, and the like. Technological developments enabled cities to award lucrative franchises for gas, electric, telephone, and transit systems. Taxes were levied, building codes enacted, and laws passed regulating weights and measures, labor conditions, and purity of food. In the process, new relationships between government and business were created.

Bribery, graft, and extortion often were parts of this new relationship. Payments by an entrepreneur to a machine could win a franchise or a construction contract, and politicians could skim off a percentage of the revenues. Building inspectors could demand payments in exchange for winking at violations. Business did not cause all local corruption, nor did the machine ruthlessly exploit the entire private sector; but growth in business and government activity did increase the stakes of action for both sides. Members of both sectors simply "seen their opportunities and took 'em."[15] At times, it became difficult to tell the businesspeople and politicians apart. Dahl points out that, in New Haven at least, rapid business and urban growth roughly coincided with the emergence of entrepreneurs at the forefront of local politics.[16] Martin Shefter has shown that business figures were important in key phases of the development of the Tammany machine.[17] Likewise, there was little to stop politicians from going into business, if they had not already done so. Tammany stalwart George Washington Plunkitt, for example, made an interesting distinction between "honest and dishonest graft." Outright theft from the public treasury, he said, was dishonest graft. But "honest graft"—putting one's political information and connections to work in the business world—was just one of the legitimate perquisites of political power.[18]

The business-machine partnership is still with us today. It is not at all uncommon, for example, for politicians to go into the insurance business. Nearly everything a city does involves insurance, and since rates are often set by state government there normally is no competitive bidding. So why not channel the business to a crony? Real estate offers similar opportunities to politically connected people. And business figures are still involved in electoral politics: a list of contributors to any machine-supported incumbent's campaign (a list one is apt to see only where state law requires it, and not always even then) bears the names of many contractors, architects, legal and consulting firms, city suppliers, and labor leaders. All of them are interested in doing business with the city.

The money generated through the "business connection" is put to a variety of uses. Most important is simply enriching key figures in the machine. Money is also used to reward ward and precinct leaders for meritorious service or simple loyalty, and there is always a need for "street money" during campaigns. Poll-watchers, drivers and canvassers must be paid, and cash must be sent to certain ward leaders to "remind" them of the need for a big push on election day. Machines have even been known to buy a vote or two now and then, and to bribe election officials. All of this costs money. Finally, money is always needed to maintain neighborhood headquarters and to finance gifts and aid to loyal constituents. Money is the most versatile, sought-after divisible material incentive in machine politics, and without the "business connection" there would be a lot less of it to go around.

THE ORIGINS OF THE MACHINE: THREE THEORIES

Machines grew out of a definite social context and then showed a remarkable ability to adapt as that context changed. In this section I will discuss the social/political situation from which machine politics first emerged. Then I will spell out three alternative perspectives on *why* the machine emerged: a personalistic view, emphasizing the political culture and other attributes of immigrants and their leaders; an institutional perspective, which points to electoral laws and governmental structures as a cause for machine politics; and a systemic approach, which examines the opportunities and demands of the wider situation—from which astute leadership fashioned a new kind of political organization.

Social and economic preconditions

Three developments after 1840 set the stage for the emergence of machine politics. They were (1) rapid immigration, (2) rapid urban and industrial growth, and (3) chaotic electoral and administrative systems in local government. These developments did not in themselves cause machines to develop, but they did provide a particular environment of resources and constraints within which political entrepreneurs could begin to build the first machines.

Rapid immigration. In October 1845, the Irish potato crop failed. Troubles were not new to rural Ireland; agriculture had been in a state of gradual collapse since the early 1800s as harsh tithes and "rack rents" drove peasants off the land. Irish farm workers earned about ninepence a day, and potatoes were the staple of the diet. Life under Britain's Penal Code only served to deepen the despair. The famine lasted five and one-half ruinous years; whole regions were virtually emptied of people by death and emigration. In just a few years Ireland's population dropped from 8 million to 6 million.[19]

As famine pushed the Irish out of old homes and old ways, developments that would pull them into such cities as Boston, New York, and Philadelphia were underway. Urban expansion and industrial growth increased the demand for cheap labor. Hours were long, wages low, and working conditions brutal, but immigrants by the millions took pick-and-shovel jobs. A contemporary report had it that "There are several sorts of power working at the fabric of the Republic—water power, steam power, and Irish power. The last works hardest of all."[20] This demand for cheap labor was the "magnet" that drew immigrants to the city.

More than 1.7 million Irish came to the United States between 1840 and 1860.[21] They were followed, of course, by waves of immigrants from many other nations—Italians, Poles, Russians, Central and East Europeans. World War I industrialization, and restrictions on foreign immigration that made it more difficult for employers to recruit cheap labor from abroad, produced an internal migration: between 1910 and 1930, a million Blacks left the rural South for the urban North. In the 25 years after 1940 another 3 million came north to join them.[22] The migration process for all of these groups was strikingly similar—they were pushed out of their old homes by economic and political factors, and pulled into American cities by industrial and urban growth.

Wherever they came from, these millions of poor people amounted to a bonanza for political entrepreneurs. Concentrated in a city's "arrival neighborhoods," they were a potential army of voters the size of which had never before been seen. Their poverty and unfamiliarity with local customs made them dependent upon the first opportunities they could find. If help came from a politician skilled in trading small favors for those unfamiliar things called votes, then an important political alliance could be the result. As we have seen, it would be wrong to suppose that every poor immigrant was welcomed with open arms by a friendly, helpful precinct captain; but the machine's strong poor and working-class support, particularly in ethnic communities, did get its start during the great migrations.

Rapid urbanization. Immigration was closely tied up with a rapid expansion in the scale of many American cities. Boston was a town of 43,298 inhabitants in 1820; by 1865, its population was more than 140,000, and by 1900 it was 561,000. Chicago grew from a prairie village of 4000 in 1840 into a metropolis of 1.7 million in just 60 years; New York's expansion was even more dramatic.[23] In these places the pace of life quickened, factories and business establishments multiplied, and acres of farmland were covered up by tenements almost overnight.

Feverish expansion opened up many opportunities for the politically astute. If policemen and firemen were needed, why not hire political supporters? If there were contracts and franchises to award, why not put them to political use? Better yet, why not make kickbacks and graft routine parts of all city business and require public employees to "contribute" a percentage of their salaries to their political benefactors? A political entrepreneur willing to play this sort of game could quickly build a powerful organization, one capable of taking and holding power amid the chaos of urban growth.

Chaotic electoral and administrative procedures. Modern administrative procedures in budgeting, hiring, contract-letting, regulation of commerce and industry, control over land use, and sanitation were unknown in machine-era local governments. Indeed, many of the procedures local governments employ today were devised much later, as "cures" for machine politics, as we shall see when we examine structural reforms. Nowhere was governmental chaos clearer than in the administration of elections. Elections were held at odd hours in odd places, including bars and brothels. Voters seldom were informed of their franchise, and there was frequent intimidation of voters whose loyalties were suspect. Ballots were printed up by parties and political organizations, in distinctive sizes, colors, and shapes. Candidates who wanted to elbow their way onto the ballot simply had stickers printed up with their names on them and urged voters to put the stickers in the appropriate place on the ballot. Little systematic effort was made to control who voted. Those who did come to the polls were met by a small mob of candidates and party workers thrusting ballots at them and urging their support. To top things off, ballot boxes often were stuffed before the election or came equipped with false bottoms, where marked ballots could be hidden.[24]

The advantages of such chaotic electoral and administrative procedures to ambitious politicians are obvious. Those with a small following and the will to play political hardball could win power easily in such a system. They then could manipulate elections to their own advantage. Once in office, they would find many opportunities to amass power and money and few administrative safeguards.

Thus, three factors—immigration, urban expansion, and chaotic elections and administration—set the stage for the emergence of machines. For an explanation of *how* this emergence took place, let us look at our three theories: the personalistic, the institutional, and the systemic.

The personalistic theory: Values, attitudes, and political culture

The personalistic perspective suggests that political machines developed because of the presence of certain kinds of people in our cities. The idea is not a new one: writing in 1890, Andrew D. White tied the rise of bossism at least partly to immigration. Contending that the governance of American cities was "the worst in Christendom," White added: "Under our theory that a city is a political body, a crowd of illiterate peasants, freshly raked in from Irish bogs, or Bohemian mines, or Italian robber nests, may exercise virtual control. How such men govern cities, we know too well; as a rule they are not alive even to their own most direct interests. . . ."[25]

Many of those most active in the fight against the machine in the late 19th and early 20th centuries, in fact, were also supporters of anti-immigration laws.[26] Commenting on the council-manager plan, a major anti-machine reform, Banfield and Wilson note:

> In its early years, the plan appealed to a good many people as a convenient means of putting the Catholics, the Irish, the Italians, the labor unions, and all other "underdogs" in their places. When [the city of] Jackson, Michigan accepted the plan in 1938, for example, the new council first celebrated with a reception in the Masonic Temple and then replaced most of the Catholic city employees with Protestants.[27]

Part of this antipathy grew out of the fact that high-status Protestants represented the very stratum of society that had been pushed out of power in city after city by machines and their immigrant followings. Language, customs, religion, and the changing ethnic composition of neighborhoods also were sources of resentment. But the most telling link between the rise of immigration and the growth of machines, in the eyes of nativist critics, lay much deeper, at the level of basic conceptions of politics. Richard Hofstadter spells out these conflicting conceptions in *The Age of Reform:*

> Out of the clash between the needs of the immigrants and the sentiments of the natives, there emerged two thoroughly different systems of political ethics. . . . One, founded upon the indigenous Yankee-Protestant political traditions, and upon middle class life, assumed and demanded the constant, disinterested activity of the citizen in public affairs, argued that political life ought to be run to a greater degree than it was in accordance with general principles and abstract laws apart from and superior to personal needs, and expressed a common feeling that government should be in good part an effort to moralize the lives of individuals, while economic life

should be intimately related to the stimulation and development of individual character. The other system, founded upon the European background of the immigrants, upon their unfamiliarity with independent political action, their familiarity with hierarchy and authority, and upon the urgent needs that so often grew out of their migration, took for granted that the political life of the individual would arise out of family needs, interpreted political and civic relations chiefly in terms of personal obligations, and placed strong personal loyalties above allegiance to abstract codes of law and morals.[28]

For the immigrant, then, economic life and political life were one. Politics was a struggle for survival and for advancement. Its wins and losses were calculated in material terms rather than in terms of some vision of the common good. Today, as much as in the 19th century, machine supporters—many of them the great-grandchildren of the immigrants—are motivated and rewarded by divisible material incentives, and machines are built upon strong personal obligations. One can discount the pronounced prejudices of the old nativists and still see clear links between immigrant political ethics and the dynamics of machines. Values and perceptions do influence political behavior, and knowing the way certain people understand politics can be of much value to a political entrepreneur seeking their support. Perhaps the origins of the machine lay in these political values.

At least two notable efforts have been made to use these systems of values to account for types of political behavior. Neither was specifically advanced by its authors as an explanation for the rise of the machine, but both expand upon the contrasts Hofstadter described above. Daniel Elazar, as noted briefly in Chapter 1, contrasts what he terms "individualistic" and "moralistic" political cultures. Some years earlier, Banfield and Wilson suggested the existence of two kinds of "political ethos"—the public-regarding, and the private-regarding.

Elazar suggests that, in the moralistic political culture, the political system is seen as a commonwealth; in the individualistic culture, it is seen as a marketplace. Politics, for a moralist, should serve the common good; for the individualist, it is an arena for competition and self-advancement.[29] Public-regarding people, Banfield and Wilson contend, support candidates and proposals "for the public good" even when they themselves stand to pay most of the costs. Private-regarding people, on the other hand, weigh political questions on the basis of "what's in it for me."[30]

Both Elazar and Banfield and Wilson point to distinct variations in political values from group to group and region to region. "Old immigrants"—the primarily Protestant English, Scots, Scandinavians, and other North Europeans—brought moralistic, or public-regarding, values to their new communities. The "new immigrants" of the post-1840 era—mostly Catholic Irish, Italians, Poles, and Central and East Europeans—spread the individualistic culture and private-regarding ethos where they settled. Because of the complexity of settlement patterns in such a nation as the United States, no area will have a pure ethos or political culture. But Elazar does suggest that political culture can account for important political contrasts between, say, more moralistic states such as Minnesota and Wisconsin, and more individualistic ones, such as New York and New Jersey.

Elazar's political cultures, Banfield's and Wilson's types of political ethos, and Hofstadter's immigrant and native political ethics are not identical notions, but they have important similarities. Immigrant ethics, private-regarding attitudes, and an individualistic political culture do seem consistent with the dynamics of machine politics, and anti-machine "reformers" indeed seem to embody native ethics, public-regarding attitudes, and a moralistic culture. Can we, then, attribute the rise of the machine to the values that the immigrants and their descendants brought to our cities?

At first glance, there seems much to recommend this idea. The rise of machines did roughly correspond, in many cities, with the era of heavy immigration. Machines traditionally have been at their strongest, organizationally and electorally, in the "ethnic wards" of large cities. The anti-machine reform movement, by contrast, was heavily native. Machines play up ethnicity through balanced tickets that accord recognition to many communities. And machines would seem to flourish naturally in any area where people look at politics as a business, as a way to get ahead.

Strong as these consistencies may be, however, I do not feel such an individualistic perspective can account adequately for the rise of machine politics. There have been "Yankee machines"—organizations with little immigrant support, at times even built in reaction to the rising tide of immigration. Boss Thomas Platt's statewide machine in New York and the Rhode Island machine of "Blind Boss" Brayton are examples.[31] Some southern and western cities experienced heavy immigration without developing machines. Other cities, such as Minneapolis, experienced heavy immigration from "moralistic" sources such as Scandinavia, yet still underwent periods of corruption and machine rule.

Another detraction from the personalistic view of the use of the machine involves the way values and attitudes are passed on from generation to generation. My great-grandfather Michael Ryan, who came here from Ireland, probably held the sorts of "immigrant values" discussed previously. But this does not mean that his descendants necessarily feel the same way, or that if they do it is because of his attitudes. Parents do pass values and attitudes on to their children, but this process is never perfect: changes in economic and educational status, subsequent political events, and the simple fact that the later generations think and make choices for themselves all contribute to changing ethics and attitudes. Michael Ryan and I would likely disagree on a number of issues.

Still, we must reconcile this passage of generations with the fact that machines do draw much support from later-generation "ethnics," and with Hofstadter's, Banfield's and Wilson's, and Elazar's characterizations. Perhaps we should ask, does a distinctive ethos or political culture preserve machine politics, or does machine politics help preserve the ethos? In practice, both are probably true; with later generations of ethnic machine backers, the latter may well be more true than the former. If an Irish precinct captain in Chicago has a political ethos much like his great-grandfather's, he probably learned it as much through dealing with the machine as from his older relatives.

Finally, a straightforward argument that political values caused machine politics suffers from a "linkage problem." However consistent a set of political values may be with the existence of machines, moving from attitudes to a fully operational organization is a great leap indeed. Organizations do not just spring up out of society; nor are they simple extensions of people's attitudes. Rather, they are built by people who must judge the political resources and constraints in a given situation and act accordingly. There is nothing automatic about the process; usually it proceeds by trial and error, with the overall design of an organization becoming evident only after its construction is well along. Thus we need to know how the gap between attitudes and organization is bridged. Who builds the machine?

Often the machine builders differed in many ways from the people who made up their following. Leo Hershkowitz points out that New York's Boss Tweed was not a poor Irish or German immigrant; his was a family of English extraction that had been in New York for years, and it was not poor. San Francisco's Abraham Ruef was a law school graduate. Boies Penrose, who for many years bossed Philadelphia and most of Pennsylvania, was a graduate of Harvard. Not every boss fit this sort of mold; some, such as Richard J. Daley, worked their way through the ranks to take over existing machines and were genuine up-by-the-bootstraps types who embodied the essence of private-regarding, individualistic politics. But the people who took the key steps in establishing this distinctive kind of politics did not necessarily do so because they embraced the political values of the immigrants. To be sure, they were acting in an individualistic manner, seeking gain through the "business" of politics, and they definitely took advantage of the private-regarding attitudes of others. But they operated within a complex social and political setting, one in which many forces influenced their choices.

Finally, the immigrants and their descendants were not the machine's only constituency—indeed, not even the main one. The poor and their votes were only a means to an end: the control of public authority, which could then be used to raise money. Money is the whole point of machine politics, and those who are willing to spend money politically are in a sense the most important machine constituency. Money spenders were a key force in the development and persistence of machine politics, and they hardly fit the immigrant mold.

We should not totally discount personalistic factors. It is easy to see how large numbers of people delivered to the polls in a disciplined fashion would be a formidable weapon in any election. If these people shared political values that made them receptive to material favors in return for support, then the opportunities for a would-be machine builder would seem all the greater. Enterprising elites, not "political culture," built the machines. But immigrants, their descendants, and their political values were definitely *sustaining* forces behind the machine once someone got it started.

The institutional explanation: Wards, parties, strong mayors, and spoils

Institutions and electoral laws are not merely the playing field and neutral rules of the political game. They often have a coloring impact upon the game's progress, scoring, and outcome. Certain types of institutional arrangements may consistently favor the interests of some people over others. Institutional factors may also favor the growth of certain kinds of political organization and practice—in this case, the political machine. The powerful reform movements that began to emerge in the 1880s were built on this institutional supposition. In many places, these movements were successful, and today thousands of local governments—especially in smaller cities and in the Midwest, West, and South—bear the stamp of institutional reform.

Partisanship—the presence and activities of political party organizations whose labels appear on the local ballot—was a prime target of reformers. Party labels, they felt, divided the citizenry along artificial dimensions, leading citizens to be loyal not to the whole community but rather to the party alone. Where parties competed with each other, they compounded the problem by buying people's support with promises and favors. Parties had a way of making all sorts of "non-political" concerns—class, race, ethnicity, the conduct of city business—into political issues. Perhaps the worst thing about parties, from the reformers' standpoint, was that they were so handy at winning elections. The party label on the ballot gave voters with little knowledge of civic duty, local politics, or even of the English language, something to hold on to. Many would vote for the label regardless of the candidate's abilities or convictions. By slating representatives of various ethnic groups and sections of the city, parties played up the very concerns that reformers felt had no place in politics. And, of course, a party is an organization that can dominate politics and deliver the goods from the block level all the way up to City Hall. Whoever bossed the party could boss the whole city, and civic virtue would be the loser.

Election by wards and precincts, reformers argued, made the evils of partisanship even worse. Dividing the city into districts encouraged voters, candidates, and parties to think in terms of narrow neighborhood interests rather than in terms of the whole public interest. Wards and precincts provided a natural organizational framework for the machine and invited the sort of neighborhood bossism, operating out of saloons and other shady establishments, that first brought many people into contact with the machine. District elections enabled bosses to tailor their slates to fit various neighborhoods, running a Ryan in an Irish area and a Dombrowski for the Poles. This not only strengthened the ethnic connection, which reformers thought had no place in politics, but also made it easier for representatives of the poor to win public office, supplanting those "leading citizens" who were best able to govern.

Once in office, these politicians controlled a form of government that to many reformers was bossism incarnate. Strong-mayor government placed a potential boss or a hand-picked minion in control of the entire mechanism of government. Professional management and "the public interest" would lose out to party interest as guides for decision-making. Other city officials would have little power to resist the strong mayor, even if they were so inclined, and the boss' control over a legislative branch filled with machine followers would be practically absolute. If partisanship and district elections allowed machines a toehold in the political arena, many reformers felt the strong-mayor system virtually gave the machine the deed to City Hall.

Last, but perhaps worst of all to reformers, was the "spoils system." City government's activities were a source of jobs, and control of the city meant that bosses could hire anyone they saw fit, for there was nothing in the law or administrative system forcing them to do otherwise. The spoils system, reformers felt, not only strengthened the machine by making the public payroll a source of political rewards, but also entrusted important public services to the incompetent, the dishonest, and the politically opportunistic. Many machine appointees were "no-shows," working full time at party tasks. Education, past job experience, and other qualifications for city jobs were ignored in favor of strengthening the machine.

The reformers' institutional conception of the dynamics of the machine led to specific institutional remedies. Nonpartisanship took the place of the partisan ballot, and in many cities council elections were changed to an at-large (or mixed) format. The spoils system was replaced by civil service codes. The old strong-mayor form of government gave way to weak-mayor, commission, or council manager systems, particularly in cities outside the Northeast. A full description and analysis of these institutional reforms is beyond the scope of this chapter,[32] but I will offer some observations on the consequences of these reforms in a later section.

Institutions: Channels, not causes. Did the laws and institutions of local government, in themselves, cause machine politics? I think not. Machines did grow up in many cities with unreformed institutions, and there is some correspondence between these institutions and the dynamics of machines. It is also true that some non-reformed cities *did not* develop machines; still others experienced boss rule only intermittently. New Haven, for example, had unreformed institutions and a spoils system for almost a century before it finally developed a centralized machine in the early 1960s. Conversely, there are cities, such as Kansas City and Pittsburgh, that have had strong machines in spite of significant structural reforms. Perhaps the best example of this sort is "reformed" Chicago, with its nominally nonpartisan election of Aldermen, its "weak mayor" form of government, and (until 1976) its model civil-service laws. There is no clear-cut pattern of machines existing only in unreformed cities.

Neither is the fit between unreformed institutions and the internal dynamics of the machine as neat as it may seem. Parties whose names appear on local ballots are not necessarily machines, and machines can survive a lack of party labels quite well. Machine structure often does parallel ward and precinct lines, but nothing inherent in district or at-large elections makes it inevitable that a machine will or will not form. Strong party bosses can hold awesome powers in a weak-mayor city (Chicago, again), and if bosses control the city council they may be able to hire and fire "non-political" city managers at will. Conversely, strong-mayor charters do not necessarily make mayors strong: New York City strengthened its mayor's powers in the late 1950s, but its mayors did not become bosses. Indeed, they had a great deal of difficulty accomplishing anything at all.[33] And although civil service laws can in theory cut the heart out of machine patronage, in practice they can be circumvented. On the other hand, the absence of such laws does not make patronage politics inevitable.

Unreformed institutions did not "cause" the machine, and reform did not always smash it, because *machines do not derive the bulk of their power and vitality from the formal powers and institutions of government*. Control of public authority—using the governmental bottleneck in politically advantageous ways—is indeed critical to the machine. But this control is won and exercised through a strong *party* organization; governmental institutions become an appendage of that organization. Public authority is, in turn, only one of the three legs the machine stands on; money from the "haves" and votes from the "have nots" also make the organization strong. To argue that unreformed institutions gave rise to the machine is a little like saying that the structure of the Supreme Soviet is what makes the Communist Party powerful in the USSR.

The one aspect of formal authority most important to the machine was neither created by unreformed institutions nor fundamentally altered by reform: the bottleneck effect described in Chapter 2. Local government is an important source of rewards and punishments whether it is reformed or not. People exercise influence in pursuit of these benefits no matter what local structures may be. Some sorts of institutions may be more hospitable to machine politics than others, and some reforms, such as civil service, were based on an accurate understanding of how machines work. But reformed structures can be adapted to or circumvented; as long as the bottleneck effect exists, powerholders willing to bend or break the rules for political advantage will always find takers.[34]

The systemic perspective: Stalemate and opportunity

In this section I will offer a view of the rise of the machine that is systemic in two ways: first, because it starts with the great social and economic upheavals of the era in which machine politics was born; second, because it examines the pressures upon the policy process that grew out of those changes. I will suggest that the bottleneck effect, and the more general situation within which certain strategic people and groups confronted it, made it possible and advantageous for the pursuit of political power to take the form of machine politics.

An "explosion of interests." The "social preconditions" of machine politics described earlier did not in themselves cause the growth of the machine. But two of them—massive immigration and rapid urban and industrial growth—did give rise to a kind of "explosion of interests," in which new and strong demands were brought to bear upon the legitimate policy process. The third precondition, chaotic local administrative and electoral systems, virtually guaranteed that these new political demands would not—indeed, *could* not—be satisfied by then-routine policy processes.

Massive immigration and urban and industrial expansion produced a whole new set of demands upon the policy process, demands unprecedented in their strength and diversity. The poor needed food and shelter; industrialists wanted land, water, and cheap, reliable labor; entrepreneurs wanted street car and utility franchises. Existing services such as police and fire protection needed to be made formal, streets and bridges had to be built and improved, and so on. Many city governments, founded during much simpler times, were overwhelmed by the tasks at hand. Some of the problems—such as the survival needs of poor immigrants—had never been regarded as matters of governmental responsibility. Others, such as the need for new streets, bridges, and water supplies, were of an unprecedented scale. And still other problems—the demand for business franchises and concessions, and later the licensing, inspection, and regulation of commerce and industry—brought government and business together in situations where the ground rules were far from clear. Robert K. Merton has argued, in an influential essay, that this combination of new political demands and a socially sanctioned governmental structure incapable of addressing them gave rise to machine politics. As he put it, *"the functional deficiencies of the official structure generate an alternative (unofficial) structure to fulfill existing needs somewhat more effectively*. Whatever its specific historical origins, the political machine persists as an apparatus for satisfying otherwise unfulfilled needs of diverse groups in the population."[35]

Bosses won the support of many different sorts of people because they could deliver what others could not or would not. This view captures several important aspects of the rise of the machine—the organization's mixture of informality and effectiveness, the way it derived much of its strength from the weaknesses of the very government it controlled, and the delicate balancing act of catering to "diverse subgroups." Above all, Merton makes it clear that machines were neither historical accidents nor the casual tools of evil men; instead, they were intimately related to the workings and changes of entire political and economic systems. Still, some questions remain. Why did this new structure take the particular form of the machine? Do we know of cases where similar deficiencies have generated functionally equivalent structures other than machines? Indeed, how do we know that needs actually exist, or know what they are, until structures are created to fulfill them? And if we are forced to infer needs from the generation of new structures, are we really explaining anything? Further, if we argue that deficiencies "generate" structures, the word "generate" becomes a blanket for a whole range of actions, choices, and decisions by real people struggling with real situations. These political actions are far from inevitable; thus, we may be concealing the most interesting—and most political—parts of the rise of machines.

It is that sense of *political* dynamics that we need to complete the systemic explanation. "Diverse subgroups" were being left unsatisfied because of a *po-*

litical stalemate, born of extreme fragmentation. New interests, problems, and potential constituencies were injecting new challenges and demands into politics, and no one had the political power it took to get things done, to impose some sort of stable order over the situation. Politics was a fluid, formless game of individual aggrandizement, built upon personalized followings and played with no holds barred. While structural deficiencies are "solved" by the "generation" of new or changed structures, political stalemates are resolved through political action. If we can trace the origins of machine politics to this sort of political action, we can explain political developments in political terms.

Martin Shefter offers such a theory as an explanation for the rise of Tammany Hall in New York City.[36] He contends that the organization was not "generated" spontaneously overnight but instead was painstakingly built in distinct stages over a 40-year period. The first of these stages, during the years before 1871, was a time of "rapacious individualism." Politics was unstable, complex, and highly factionalized:

> On the governmental level the most important political formations were shifting legislative combines, groupings that coalesced, collapsed, and reformed with remarkable rapidity. In the electoral arena party factions also were loosely structured. Major politicians were essentially independent political operators, whose influence was a function of the size and strength (often, literally the physical strength) of their personal followings.[37]

The next stage in the rise of the Tammany machine was a period of "consolidation of power," spanning roughly the 1870s and 1880s, when political competition took place among a few major factions of the Democratic party. Politics was still a rough-and-tumble game, but the factions were becoming considerably larger and better organized. Finally, after about 1890, a mature Tammany machine ruled New York. It resembled the "ideal machine" described at the beginning of this chapter and as such was a clear contrast from earlier political organizations.

How was a powerful, tightly disciplined machine assembled out of the chaos of rapacious individualism? Shefter examines the interests and actions of key elites in both the political and business worlds. Political elites had an interest in attaining and holding power in the most reliable and profitable ways possible. This meant moving away from politics based on brute force and continuous, expensive bribery of one's own followers and instead toward a political device that could reliably control the mass electorate and command subordinates' loyalty. Business elites' motives were more complex; fiercely individualistic speculators and entrepreneurs gave way to a generation of organizers and oligopolists, who in turn were succeeded by a new class of "business professionals" and managers. The entrepreneurs were quite at home with a Boss Tweed and the politics of rapacious individualism, but the organizers and empire-builders wanted predictable dealings with a more stable political leadership, one that could take care of increasingly massive investment interests in return for financial contributions. Many of these "organizers" ran for office themselves; the high-water mark of their political activity corresponds, in Shefter's analysis, with the era of "consolidation" during which strong party leaders such as John Kelly built ever more disciplined organizations. Finally, Kelly's successors (such as Richard Croker) were able to crush opposing factions at the polls and bring New York under the control of a single, centralized machine. This machine, with its highly developed structure and monopoly over public authority, could finance its own activities and reward and discipline its members internally. As a result, business figures not only were no longer needed in the party's top ranks but indeed could now be threatened and exploited like any other group. An emerging class of business professionals, seeking to expand on a nationwide scale through efficient corporate management, could hardly be expected to stand for such treatment; many ended up in the anti-machine movement. But only at this stage—*after* the emergence of the mature machine—did the ethnic/machine versus native/reform political cleavage become as pronounced as the individualistic theory would have us believe.

Thus, the creation of the machine was the work of people pursuing their various political interests within a specific systemic context:

> In the New York case the creation of a centralized machine was grounded upon the formation of a coalition between a set of party politicians and members of the city's upper class who had a common interest in controlling a tumultuous mass electorate, subjecting rapacious ward politicians to a reliable system of discipline, and insulating the political system of discipline from the influence of businessmen who were prepared to bribe low level public officials to secure favors from the city government.[38]

Shefter's scenario was not necessarily reenacted in every machine city, but it yields a systemic explanation for the rise of the machine. The explanation is systemic because it includes the "big picture" of social and economic trends in urban society, and yet it remains a *political* explanation, linking these changes to the machine through the actions and interests of political elites. Machines were made, not born, and they were made in a trial-and-error fashion by real people grappling with system-wide political situations. Personalistic and institutional explanations have their points of interest, but a systemic view gives us the most exact and comprehensive account of where machines came from. And, as the following section will show, it provides the best framework for an understanding of machines in action.

MACHINES IN ACTION

Let us begin to examine the ways actual machines have operated by raising three main questions:

1. How do machines actually hand out their patronage rewards?
2. How well do machines govern cities?
3. Who benefits and who loses in machine politics?

Handing out the spoils

Machine bosses, of course, do not go around announcing to the public which of their supporters gets what, and why. Indeed, James Q. Wilson has rightly observed that "So much secrecy is maintained in city politics that no exact data on patronage may ever be obtained in cities of any size."[39] Not long ago, however, information became available on the way the Democratic machine in New Haven, Connecticut handed out 675 jobs in 1974.[40] The jobs were created under Title I of the Comprehensive Employment and Training Act (CETA) to provide work experience for the hard-core unemployed. Evidence suggests, though, that they were used as patronage by the Democratic machine leadership.

I have analyzed this job allocation by counting the number of jobs in each of New Haven's wards. New Haven is not divided into precincts, so wards and their Democratic organizations were the building blocks of the machine. By comparing job allocations to past voting patterns, to the social and economic composition of the wards, and to tentative information about the job recipients themselves (gathered through a short mail survey), I found an interesting picture of how this one form of patronage was distributed.

Analyzing the job distribution. There are several possible explanations for the way the jobs were handed out. *First,* it is possible that the jobs were not used as patronage at all but were instead distributed according to the intent of CETA Title I. *Second,* patronage might have been used to maintain and strengthen the machine organization. This could have meant handing out jobs according to various standards of vote production, such as: (a) an ideal distribution, in which each job would yield an equal number of votes wherever it was allocated; (b) a distribution based on past vote production; or (c) efforts to develop new areas of support. Another way of strengthening the organization would be to use the jobs to recruit new political workers on an individual basis. *Third,* ethnic loyalties might play an important role: since the machine built its political base in Italian neighborhoods, perhaps jobs were channeled to Italians in order to maintain that ethnic base. These three ideas are more distinct in theory than in practice: rewarding active Democrats, for example, would entail rewarding many Italians. Still, it was possible to test these ideas statistically to see which ones best accounted for the way jobs were handed out.

Ethnic loyalties, it turned out, were the most important consideration in distributing the jobs. Tests showed that CETA's intent must have carried little weight in the job allocation; the heaviest concentrations of jobs were in mostly White, middle-class areas. Poor and Black districts got many fewer jobs than one would expect if fighting unemployment had been the goal. Vote production came only slightly closer to accounting for the job allocation. The "ideal" distribution was neither achieved nor likely intended; wards varied widely in votes-per-job. And no new support for machine candidates emerged in areas given many jobs; if anything, the best-rewarded ward organizations could be said to have faltered when post-1974 vote totals were compared to earlier figures. Black wards would have been a logical target for a "new support" effort, since they had strongly backed a Black primary challenger in 1969 and 1971 who had since come back into the machine fold. But they got only a handful of jobs, suggesting again that patronage was not used to seek new support. Job allocations *did* correspond fairly closely to patterns of past support, but even this correlation was imperfect at best; in fact, there were some cases in which machine opponents' vote totals corresponded more closely to the way jobs were handed out.

Mail-survey data suggested that the patronage allocation did not produce significant numbers of new workers for the machine. Job holders who responded reported very low levels of political activity both before and after hiring. More than 80% reported that they never voted before being hired, and levels of other kinds of activities (such as wearing a button, poll-watching, or donating money to candidates) were even lower. Post-hiring increases in political activity were modest at best; 57.6% said they *still* never voted.

Ethnic loyalties seemed to account best for the way jobs were handed out. My analysis suggested that the Italian-led machine distributed jobs mostly to Italians and did so out of proportion to considerations of organization maintenance. The job pattern followed very closely the distribution of the Italian population: the higher the Italian percentage, the more jobs given to a ward. Of the 675 persons hired, 386 (57.2%) had Italian surnames; New Haven was about 35–40% Italian at the time. Italian-American respondents to the questionnaire reported slightly higher levels of political involvement than non-Italians both before and after hiring, but their levels were still very low. It is thus unlikely that the jobs went to active Democrats who happened to be Italian.

The most telling evidence of the strength of ethnic loyalties came during the 1975 mayoral elections. The machine's incumbent mayor lost a bitterly contested primary to a White reform Democrat, who then narrowly won the general election over an Italian-American Republican. The machine boss actively aided the Republican, who thus ran the strongest Republican race in years. What makes these events interesting is the fact that the new Republican support gained with the boss' help correlated more closely with job distribution than any other single factor. Vote production for an Italian candidate endorsed by an Italian boss—*not* production on behalf of Democrats per se—was evidently the key standard of productivity. Ethnic loyalties in politics are nothing new; the Irish and other groups have engaged in similar practices. But in the New Haven case these ties were strong enough to cross party lines, and strong enough to outweigh and even redefine some of the seemingly most basic considerations of organization maintenance. This seems remarkable indeed.

Accounting for the New Haven results. It is unlikely the machine allocated the jobs as it did because of confusion or ineptitude. Instead, it seems that patronage-based machines don't run as smoothly in practice as in theory. Jobs, as incentives, are awkward and inflexible tools for maintaining an organization. There are only so many to hand out, and once they are distributed it can be difficult to reallocate them. Jobs as instruments of patronage are probably better suited to starting a new machine than to maintaining an old one. Networks of obligation are much more complex in practice than in theory and are based on multiple standards of exchange—differing mutual expectations between the boss and various machine factions. And machines tend to age, just as people do[41]; long-standing alliances and patterns of reward may not adapt well to new social and political realities.

The seemingly puzzling New Haven patronage allocations, then, grow directly out of inherent complications in machine politics. These complications, in turn, raise questions about other, more general issues. We are sometimes told, for example, that despite their problems machines at least "make cities work," and that because they traded material goods for political support, machines were the friends of the poor. But are these blanket statements warranted?

"Making cities work": Machines and urban management

The notion that machines "make cities work" is actually a fairly recent one. For many years people felt that machine politics was just an elaborate form of theft. But during the 1930s, and especially after World War II, this view was reconsidered. Machines might not be all bad, it was suggested; at least those who controlled them had the power to "get things done." Strong, centralized power was not necessarily evil if used to pursue worthwhile ends. Machine backing helped Pittsburgh's David Lawrence enforce tough smoke-control legislation in the face of vigorous opposition. In New Haven the backing of a strong organization was essential to Richard Lee's monumental redevelopment and antipoverty efforts. Mayor Daley's accomplishments in Chicago, by some accounts, are just this side of legendary: improved mass transit, new expressways, a downtown "skyscraper boom," and the world's busiest airport. If an observer of today's urban problems, reflecting on cities' political fragmentation and paralysis and on their lack of clout at the state and federal levels, begins to yearn for a strong boss, this is certainly understandable. The question is whether this yearning amounts to anything more than misplaced nostalgia.

I feel that though there *is* much nostalgia in such a view, machines are not a totally evil influence. In fact, I will argue that machines do not necessarily make for good *or* bad government. They are instead means for winning and holding on to power. As with any other kind of politics, the ends to which that power is used will depend much upon the people who use it and the circumstances they confront. I will also contend that in many ways reform "cures" have turned out worse than the machine "disease."

Cutting through the nostalgia. Once upon a time, it seems, American cities were great places to live. Populations were growing, business and industry were expanding, and cities were places of excitement and innovation. People could walk the streets at night, send their children to a good school, and not have to fight traffic jams. A melting-pot society offered opportunity to all, and various racial and ethnic groups got along without much tension or conflict. Who could resist wanting to live in such a city?

The only problem, of course, is that no such city ever existed. Modern cities have always been dirty and crowded; they have always had areas that were unhealthy and dangerous. They have always attracted the poorest and most desperate migrants from rural regions, here and abroad, and typically have not treated them kindly. Conflicts between racial and ethnic groups have always existed. As far as traffic jams are concerned, the automobile originally was welcomed as a clean and efficient alternative to horses, which were not only too numerous but also had a habit of messing up the streets.

It is equally inaccurate to romanticize the quality of urban management under the machine. Robert A. Caro notes in his biography of Robert Moses that between 1918 and 1932, Tammany mayors "Red Mike" Hylan and Jimmy "Beau James" Walker increased New York City's indebtedness by a rate of $100,000 per day, tripled the city payroll, and virtually bankrupted their own government.[42] The machine undermined the civil service codes, frequently appointing as architects or engineers men who lacked even high school diplomas. As a result, "forty public schools constructed during Walker's administration had to be closed for major repairs . . . within a year of opening."[43] At times, the quality of city services and planning sank to incredible depths:

> Although in 1932 the Queensborough Bridge had been open for a quarter of a century, the city had not yet gotten around to even marking lanes on it. . . . The city had created two additional lanes on the Queensborough upper roadway in 1931, but when the lanes were opened, it was discovered that there had been a slight miscalculation: the lanes were too narrow; cars were constantly skinning their tires on the granite curbs. The lanes had to be closed while workmen laboriously chipped away the edges of the curbstones—and the workmen would be chipping, and the lanes would be closed, for three years.[44]

Tammany's brand of mismanagement was not necessarily repeated in all machine cities, but it seems fair to say that machines never established a clear pattern of superior management. If Chicago really is "a city that works"—and I have yet to see this demonstrated—it may be due more to the importance of a few central personalities or to the very limited duties of Chicago's city government than to any inherent advantages of machine politics.

This is not to suggest, however, that structural reforms have worked any better. Indeed, they may have serious drawbacks of their own. Non-partisanship and at-large elections, for example, can work against poor and minority-group candidates. Instead of being able to campaign in a limited part of the city and to exploit group ties and geographical concentration of support, they must now run expensive citywide campaigns. They must seek support from many diverse groups, making it disadvantageous to emphasize the specific interests and issues of their own communities. They must compete against candidates embodying the values and enjoying the support of "mainstream" groups and institutions, and they must do it without the benefit of a familiar party label.[45]

Reform raises more general problems as well. During the 1960s, for example, Robert L. Lineberry and Edmund P. Fowler studied 200 reformed and unreformed cities. They found that, although these cities did not differ greatly in social composition, they *did* differ significantly in tax and expenditure policies. In unreformed cities policy tended to follow lines of social and economic division (such as wealth, ethnic, racial, and educational composition of the population) much more closely than in reformed cities. The more reformed structures a city had, the less its taxation and expenditures appeared to be influenced by its social composition and lines of conflict.[46] Looked at one way, the reform movement helped insulate public decisions from "irrelevant" influences. But from another viewpoint, reforms made local government less democratic, less able to respond to the diverse needs of different kinds of people.

Theodore Lowi has leveled an even more general charge against reform.[47] Comparing machine Chicago to structurally reformed New York, Lowi contends that in their pursuit of populism and efficiency as paramount values, reformers ignored or discounted the positive value of politics in governing cities. According to Lowi, reformers left us with cities that are "well run but ungoverned." They are well run in that there is less graft and bribery than before, fewer incompetent brothers-in-law getting city construction contracts, and fewer city employees dipping into the municipal till. But what of *governing*—the complex political process of conflict management, of imposing coherence and balance upon the full range of government activities? In Lowi's reformed city, one agency tries to lure commuters onto mass transit while at the same time, and without coordination, another builds expressways. A third builds parking garages honestly and efficiently, but without regard to the question of whether the city *needs* more parking, or whether it needs parking more than better schools. And groups for whom no agency exists—people supporting affirmative action, for example—may be heard by no one at all. In order to *govern* the city, someone must impose coherence and direction upon these "islands of bureaucracy." But who has the political power it would take? Certainly not the "weak mayors" reformers love so much.

It is fair to say that neither machine nor reformed government has done an outstanding job of governing our cities. It may well be that unreformed structures—not to be confused with machines themselves—may at least offer more possibilities for governing as well as managing. The reformist notion of a "nonpolitical" city government that simply provides services and maintains facilities in the spirit of a single overriding "public interest" is feasible only in the smallest of communities, and desirable in even fewer of them. Cities of any size are diverse; their social structures and politics revolve around any number of significant contrasts and conflicts. There may be no Republican or Democratic way to pave a street, but it is a highly political question whose street gets paved, when, by whom, and who picks up the tab. City governments thus must manage conflict as well as property and must provide political leadership in policy areas where managerial standards provide no clear guidelines for action. Providing such leadership takes a firm understanding of the highly political character of local government and not a little bit of political power. Unreformed governments have provided us with many cases of mismanagement and uninspired leadership and probably will continue to do so. But they have also provided examples of dynamic leadership based on an understanding of political power—the very thing reform governments were established to prevent.

Machines and democracy: Who benefits?

Were bosses and their machines really the friends of the working class, the champions of the downtrodden? Or did they serve the interests of the wealthy few, pacifying and buying off the potentially unruly masses with trivial gifts? In this section I will examine the distribution of the costs and benefits flowing from machine politics.

Neither of the characterizations above is wholly accurate, and different machines may work in different ways. But in general, the political machine is a conservative organization that channels its most significant benefits to some of the "haves" while exacting substantial costs from the "have nots." For affluent supporters, the benefits are immediate, tangible, and divisible; money, franchises, and weak regulatory policies are examples. For the poor, the costs are long-term, intangible, and shared; they include lost political opportunities, weakened group identity and solidarity, and a pervasive state of dependency. Machine politics preserves existing social, political, and economic alignments and defuses tensions and conflicts that could bring about change. We can understand why people who are cold and hungry trade their votes for petty favors, but we should also recognize that in the long run those favors come only at great cost. The thumbnail account in Table 3-1 illustrates this pattern of costs and benefits.

The machine performed its political balancing act by handing out something to almost everyone, but some got a great deal more than others. Machine politics, in this sense, is "regressive": a few affluent individuals and groups get more of the benefits and fewer of the costs than those below them on the social and political ladder.

There is a more subtle conservatism inherent in machine politics as well, one that proves significant in the long run. Machines must maintain their balance between rich and poor. They must protect the interests of affluent backers in order to get their monetary support, which means not only maintaining the ability to make favorable policies but also quelling unrest among the less affluent. The small favors channeled to poor and working-class areas serve both purposes admirably. The favors win enough votes for the machine to hold power, and by helping with basic needs in the short run while creating a dependency relationship in the long run, they placate the less affluent. But for the poor, the acceptance of immediate, tangible, divisible rewards has long-term, intangible, shared *political* costs that far outweigh the precinct captain's petty favors.

How did this regressive distribution of costs and benefits come about, especially if the machine brought "have-nots" into the political arena by the thousands? One answer is that what the "haves" *have* is money. Money is not only a wondrous political resource; it is the whole point of machine politics. Those

TABLE 3-1. Winners and losers in machine politics

Major beneficiaries		Minor beneficiaries		Minor losers		Major losers	
Machine leadership	(money and power, legal or otherwise)	Smaller businesses	(weak regulation, city business)	"Taxpayers"	(pay taxes for services they don't get, or get only on political grounds)	Class-, ethnic-based political movements	(low solidarity, lost opportunities, potential supporters "bought off")
Wealthy individuals, large businesses	(franchises, contracts, city business, privileged information, weak regulation)	Poor individuals	(small gifts, favors)	Able job-seekers	(turned down for work despite qualifications or need)	Poor as a class	(dependency, few sizable benefits, lost political opportunities)
Illegitimate enterprises, vice operations	(money and power, if able to prevent law enforcement through political "pull")	Patronage workers	(low-paying jobs)	People seeking policy benefits on merit	(loss of benefits to which they might otherwise be entitled)	Competing political parties, organizations	(machine hostility, city government harassment)
Favored banks, financial institutions	(deposits of funds, purchases of city bonds at favorable terms)					Competing social-service organizations	(machine hostility, city government harassment)

The Political Machine   63

who have money to spend politically can demand much in return. As I mentioned in my discussion of the personalistic approach, poor people and their votes are primarily a means to more lucrative ends.

A more fundamental answer to the question of how machine politics became regressive lies in the nature of the transactions between the machine and the poor. Machines do indeed bring large numbers of poor and working people into politics, at least to the point of voting. But by the time many of these people enter the political process, they have already incurred obligations to the machine. These obligations are highly personal, based perhaps even on a strong friendship with the precinct captain.[48] Personal or not, these obligations eliminate a poor person's political choices. Machines do not *mobilize* the political resources and participation of the poor. Machines *control* them.

In return for this political control, poor and working people get benefits no larger than necessary. A turkey at Christmas is nice, but in a few days it is gone; what remains is pervasive, long-term poverty. The boss' store of benefits is insufficient to wipe out poverty. Even if it *were* sufficient, no boss would ever use it to its full extent,[49] for the machine has no interest in making the poor less dependent. And with dependency comes a degree of political pacification. Loyalty to the organization is paramount: the title of Milton Rakove's fascinating study of the Daley machine, *Don't Make No Waves, Don't Back No Losers*, is good advice for anyone seeking a machine career. This is true not only in terms of subordinating one's personal wishes to the dictates of the machine; it is equally true when it comes to the interests of one's family, neighborhood, or ethnic group.

Thus, political leaders in poor communities may be forced to choose—either to accept the boss' petty benefits (and pay the price of losing political options) or to be excluded from the only game in town. Frequently, because of the need to deliver at least some benefits to their followers, they have chosen to back the machine and to place the machine's interests above all others. James Q. Wilson describes the case of the late Black Congressman William L. Dawson of Chicago. Dawson was once a "race man," a vigorous, independent advocate of Black interests. But when in the 1930s he became part of the Democratic machine, his style changed to reflect the new relationship. His ability to deliver the goods was dependent upon access to the machine's supply of rewards; and access to those rewards required playing the game on the machine's terms. But without an ability to deliver benefits, he would have no power. Dawson's militant style gave way to a much more accommodating political posture.[50]

Jerry Webman, in his study of Black leadership in Philadelphia and Detroit, showed that this pacification effect may well reach beyond the ranks of those directly involved with the machine to other community leaders. Webman analyzed opinion surveys of Black community leaders in Philadelphia—a machine city—and Detroit, a city without a machine. He found Black leaders in Philadelphia much less willing, as a group, to express militant or race-conscious political attitudes than those in Detroit. He reasoned that these contrasts in attitudes and political styles were at least partly the products of the presence or absence of a machine.[51]

This sort of pacification poses serious problems for poor urban communities. In a political system such as the United States', these groups have little to fall back upon except for strength in numbers and the credible threat of independent action—be it voting, strikes, protest, or violence. Machines take away both of these resources, the first through the appeal to individual interests by trading in small favors rather than in big issues, the second by making loyalty to the organization the paramount virtue. Leaders such as Dawson did deliver petty benefits to their followers; they may have had few political alternatives to backing the machine, if they wished to hold any political power in their communities. But the Dawson case, together with Webman's Philadelphia and Detroit data, suggests that the machine's political discipline and emphasis on small *divisible* material rewards can seriously undermine a poor community's efforts toward unified, independent use of the strength of numbers.

A final bit of evidence suggesting that the boss sought control and not mobilization is the hostility machines repeatedly showed others who sought to serve or organize the poor. Labor organizers bore much of this hostility in the late 19th and early 20th centuries. Not only did they compete for the loyalties of the poor, raise issues of collective action, and spread disenchantment with the status quo; they threatened the interests of the machine's business and industrial patrons. Bosses thus often fought the union movement, at times openly. Police were sent in to break up meetings and picket lines and to help strikebreakers get to work. This hostility was extended to the settlement-house movement as well; Allan Rosenbaum has commented on the bitter struggles during the 1890s between John Powers, boss of Chicago's mostly poor 19th ward, and Jane Addams' Hull House.[52]

In the end, the question of whether or not the machine was a true friend of the poor has not one answer but three. If by "the poor" we mean certain poor individuals, then the answer is clearly yes. History is replete with stories of people of modest means who won fortune and fame through the machine. If by "the poor" we refer to ethnic and racial groups, the answer could be either yes or no, depending upon which group we are talking about. Daley treated his Irish well, and the New Haven machine looked after the Italians; but if you were a member of another ethnic group, things might not have gone so well. Sometimes we are told that urban Blacks suffer because they don't have a friendly machine to help them out; it now seems clear that if a machine is to help Blacks, it had better be a machine led by Blacks. Finally, if by "the poor" we mean the poor *as a class*, the answer to our question must be no. Machine politicians never intended to lift whole classes of people out of poverty, for poverty and dependency helped secure their hold on power. Political pacification—especially when it extends beyond the machine to other community leaders—makes it most difficult for poor communities to put their political resources to independent use.

THE DEATH (?) OF THE MACHINE

When I began to write this chapter, I worried about the matter of tense. Should it be "machines are," or "machines were"? Machine politics has not vanished, contrary to what we often hear, but there are many cities where once-strong machines have given way to fragmentation, or even to clean politics. I have decided, though, that the present tense is still in order. Tweed-style machines may be less common now, but the basic *processes* of machine politics—distribution of divisible material incentives, patronage, conversion of public policy to private political advantage—are very much alive. And machines thrive in many poorer, rapidly urbanizing areas in Asia, Africa, and Latin America. Machines have had to adapt to circumstances and have at times suffered in the process. But at this point, an obituary for machine politics would be premature.

Many who argue that the machine has already died contend (1) that the boss' stores of patronage and favors have been abolished by law, have been superseded by "non-political" social service agencies, or have otherwise dried up; (2) that city dwellers today are so well nourished, clothed, educated, and blended into "mainstream" political values that there are few takers for what little the boss has left to offer.[53] Closer examination suggests that neither of these assertions is very accurate.

It is true that machines always have put informal social services to political use, and it is also true that much has been done to cut off the boss' supply of benefits and to put social services on a formal, professionally administered basis. Civil Service laws exemplify efforts to cut the supply of benefits; the move to a formal social service structure is demonstrated by the rise of the New Deal. But patronage and favors have not completely passed from the scene.[54] New Haven's CETA case shows that just one segment of one federal jobs program can channel 675 jobs into one city, jobs that a local boss then put to use. Civil Service laws can be circumvented in a number of ways. Patronage in the courts, such as easy and lucrative appointments for attorneys in probate cases, has not been significantly curtailed. Contracts and city business can still be channeled to friends, and Plunkitt-style "honest graft" abides.

Another sort of patronage flourishes *because of* the formalization of social services. Machines can act as middlemen between social service agencies and their clients. If you want to enroll in a jobs program, or get your family into public housing or onto the public assistance rolls, you might be able to get what you want by filling out the required forms, going through the routine channels, and waiting: this is the bottleneck effect all over again. But if your precinct captain can get you the same (or better) benefit faster, with less effort on your part, then he or she is doing you a significant favor.[55] The same is true if you can't read English well enough to fill out the forms, don't know which office to go to, or don't even know what programs exist. Even those services regulated by state and federal governments can be put to political use. These benefits, because of their greater magnitude and negligible direct cost to the machine, are if anything more powerful than the food baskets of old. For these reasons,

Bruce Stave has argued, the rise of machine politics in Pittsburgh during the 1930s was *aided,* not hindered, by the advent of the New Deal.[56]

The other half of the "death of the machine" argument suggests that, whatever favors remain, there are few takers left. A look at today's cities points up serious problems with this argument too. Despite all the economic progress of recent generations, there are still poor people in our cities. Indeed, suburbanization has made our big cities even more the haven of the poor than in years past. Other circumstances—the continuing deterioration of inner-city neighborhoods, the inability of cities and school districts to provide good basic services through conventional channels, and cities' loss of thousands of unskilled entry-level jobs—have kept the urban poor at least as dependent upon the favors of others as they ever were. Immigration from other nations has been reduced, until recently, by restrictive legislation. But Black migration from the American South brought more than 4.5 million people into northern cities over a 50-year period. Puerto Rican migration added hundreds of thousands more, and the recent Chicano influx has brought still more poor people to the city (there are sections of Los Angeles, for example, which have changed from mostly Black to mostly Chicano since 1970). Anyone who argues that economic growth has eliminated urban poverty is sadly mistaken.

The notion that a diffusion of "middle-class values" has made people less likely to accept political favors is equally suspect. Indeed, it has many of the problems of the personalistic theory discussed earlier. If private-regarding attitudes, the "immigrant ethos," and individualistic political culture did not give birth to the machine, it is hard to see how their alleged passing could kill it. Indeed, I doubt that our basic political values have really changed all that much or that "middle-class" political outlooks are so altruistic. The attitude upon which machines depend is the willingness to trade political support and other resources for the benefits of public policy, and this attitude has never been the monopoly of any class. Many bosses' supporters past and present have been high-status business and financial figures. Many more have been attorneys, contractors, realtors, and suppliers who are nothing if not middle-class. Machines have at times thrived in such thoroughly middle-class areas as suburban Long Island. People who express "middle-class" political values, I suspect, differ from others not in their willingness or unwillingness to pursue their self-interest through politics, but rather in their skill at expressing self-interest in "acceptable" terms.

Put simply, the boss' main clientele still exists. Millions of urban residents still need a helping hand. Millions more, whose basic needs may be less pressing, still play the political game to win. Enough of these people are willing to trade their support for divisible material rewards to enable a smart political operator to build a winning organization.

The classic, centralized machine has become less common—in the United States, at least—but the basic practices of machine politics live on. They flourish in *parts* of cities, at other levels of government (it is possible that in Pittsburgh the city's decaying Democratic machine may be giving way to a new one at the county level), and in other public organizations, such as public-employee unions and "non-political" public authorities. There are few Tweeds, Crumps, or Ruefs among us, and even their less colorful heirs, such as Richard Daley, are passing from the scene. But it is safe to say that a politics built upon organized self-interest and upon the conversion of public policy to private benefit will be with us for a long time, and that in many instances this sort of politics will involve the basic dynamics of the machine.

SUMMARY

Machines are tightly organized parties whose members and followers are motivated and rewarded by divisible material incentives, such as gifts, money, and favors. Votes, money, and control over public authority are the basic elements of machine politics; they are used in a mutually reinforcing manner to maintain political power and to channel the benefits of that power, in varying types and amounts, to machine members and backers. In the process, the machine plays off the money of affluent supporters against the votes of the poor.

Three possible explanations for the rise of machine politics were examined in the chapter: a personalistic explanation, emphasizing political values; an institutional view, pointing to factors such as partisan, district-based elections, the spoils system, and mayor-council government; and a systemic perspective, emphasizing the interests and actions of political elites and groups within the more general political environment. I have argued that the systemic view, while not perfect, yields the best explanation for the rise and persistence of machines. An evaluation of machines in action showed that in practice machines are more complex and unwieldy than "ideal" models suggest, leading to seemingly puzzling distributions of rewards. The evaluation showed that though machines do not always govern and manage cities in disastrous fashion, they do not necessarily do a good job either; yet reformed governments are often even worse. Finally, the evaluation showed that the machine is not a true political friend of the poor, helping them into the system and up the ladder, but instead perpetuates the status quo. A concluding section on the alleged death of the machine argued that, although the classic Daley-style machine may be less common in American cities now than in the past, the mass clientele for machine politics still exists, and basic practices of machine politics are very much a part of state and local politics in many places.

Notes

1. A number of useful works describing the development and history of machine politics are listed in the Selected Bibliography at the end of this book.
2. Raymond E. Wolfinger, *The Politics of Progress* (Englewood Cliffs, N.J.: Prentice-Hall, 1974), pp. 89–92.
3. Elmer E. Cornwell, "Bosses, Machines and Ethnic Groups," *Annals of the American Academy of Political and Social Science*, Vol. 353 (May 1964), pp. 28–29.
4. Walton Bean, *Boss Ruef's San Francisco: The Story of the Union Labor Party, Big Business, and the Graft Prosecution* (Berkeley: University of California Press, 1952). See especially Chapter II.

5. A useful introduction to machines in a variety of systems appears in James C. Scott, *Comparative Political Corruption* (Englewood Cliffs, N.J.: Prentice-Hall, 1972), Chapters 7–9.
6. James Q. Wilson, *Political Organizations* (New York: Basic Books, 1973), pp. 32–35, and *passim*. The analysis also owes much to Edward C. Banfield and James Q. Wilson, *City Politics* (New York: Vintage Books, 1966), Chapter 9.
7. Robert K. Merton, *Social Theory and Social Structure* (Glencoe, Illinois: The Free Press, 1957), p. 72.
8. The point here is not whether an outside observer would conclude that a voter or other client actually "owes" the boss, but whether the client believes he or she is in the boss' debt. An analyst might contend that voters who get a traffic light installed owe the boss nothing, since this is presumably a public good paid for through taxes. But if these voters perceive the traffic light as a favor from the machine, obtainable only through political support, I presume that at least some of them will acknowledge a political obligation and act accordingly. Of course, this perception is often reinforced by a friendly precinct captain who reminds the voters that the light was installed and that as a result support at the polls would be appropriate and much appreciated.
9. Milton Rakove, *Don't Make No Waves, Don't Back No Losers: An Insider's Analysis of the Daley Machine* (Bloomington, Ind.: Indiana University Press, 1975), p. 111. Presumably a precinct captain could set a high target and then, by tampering with absentee ballots, voting machines, or election judges, steal enough votes to reach the goal. How much of this actually occurs is, of course, difficult to know. But this possibility does not affect the "ideal machine" analysis much, for in the short run a successfully stolen vote counts just as much as an honestly won vote.
10. This is not to imply that small favors are all the poor ever need or want, but rather that they are often what is expected and what gets people out to vote.
11. From *Social Theory and Social Structure*, by R. K. Merton, p. 74. Copyright © 1957 by The Free Press. This and all other quotations from this source are reprinted by permission of Macmillan Publishing Co., Inc.
12. See, in this regard, William F. Whyte, *Street Corner Society* (Chicago: University of Chicago Press, 1955), p. 194.
13. Rakove, *Don't Make No Waves*, pp. 32–42. Also, on this point, see Matthew Holden, Jr., *The White Man's Burden* (New York: Chandler, 1973), Chapter VI.
14. Robert A. Dahl, *Who Governs? Democracy and Power in an American City* (New Haven, Conn.: Yale University Press, 1961), pp. 11–24.
15. William L. Riordon, *Plunkitt of Tammany Hall: A Series of Very Plain Talks on Very Practical Politics* (New York: Dutton, 1963), p. 4.
16. Dahl, *Who Governs?*, pp. 25–31.
17. Martin Shefter, "The Emergence of the Political Machine: An Alternative View," in Willis D. Hawley et al., *Theoretical Perspectives on Urban Politics* (Englewood Cliffs, N.J.: Prentice-Hall, 1976), pp. 25–33.
18. Riordon, *Plunkitt of Tammany Hall*, pp. 3–6.
19. Carl Wittke, *The Irish in America* (Baton Rouge, La.: Louisiana State University Press, 1956), p. 5; Oscar Handlin, *Boston's Immigrants: A Study in Acculturation*, rev. ed. (New York: Atheneum, 1972), p. 41.
20. William V. Shannon, *The American Irish: A Social and Political Portrait* (New York: Collier, 1963), p. 29.
21. *Ibid.*, p. 28.
22. Charles E. Hall, *Negroes in the United States 1920–1932* (New York: Arno Press and the New York Times, 1969), pp. 5–25; Stanley B. Greenberg, *Politics and Poverty: Modernization and Response in Five Poor Neighborhoods* (New York: Wiley, 1974), p. 15; Joel Aberbach and Jack L. Walker, *Race in the City: Politics, Trust and Public Policy in the New Urban System* (Boston: Little, Brown, 1973), pp. 8–10.
23. Stephan Thernstrom, *The Other Bostonians* (Cambridge: Harvard University Press, 1973), Chapter 2; Wesley G. Skogan, *Chicago Since 1840: A Time-Series Data Handbook* (Urbana, Ill.: University of Illinois, Institute of Government and Public Affairs, 1976), Table 1, pp. 18–20; Wallace S. Sayre and Herbert Kaufman, *Governing New York City* (New York: W. W. Norton, 1965), pp. 18–20.
24. See, for example, the description of young Abraham Ruef's first Republican caucus, in Bean, *Boss Ruef's San Francisco*, pp. 2–3.

25. Andrew D. White, "The Government of American Cities," *Forum* (December 1890), reprinted as "Municipal Affairs Are Not Political" in Edward C. Banfield, Ed., *Urban Government: A Reader in Administration and Politics* (Glencoe, Ill.: The Free Press, 2nd ed., 1969), pp. 271–274.
26. Banfield and Wilson, *City Politics*, p. 141.
27. Stone, Price, and Stone, *City Manager Government in Nine Cities* (Chicago: Public Administration Service, 1940), pp. 221–223; quoted in Banfield and Wilson, *City Politics*, pp. 170–171.
28. From *The Age of Reform*, by Richard Hofstadter, p. 9. (New York: Knopf, 1955). Copyright © 1955 by Alfred Knopf, Inc. Reprinted by permission.
29. Daniel J. Elazar, *American Federalism: A View from the States*, 2nd ed. (New York: Thomas Y. Crowell, 1972), pp. 90–97.
30. Banfield and Wilson, *City Politics*, pp. 235–240.
31. Cornwell, "Bosses, Machines and Ethnic Groups," pp. 28–29; see also Harold F. Gosnell, *Boss Platt and His New York Machine* (Chicago: University of Chicago Press, 1924); and Lincoln Steffens, "Rhode Island: A State for Sale," *McClure's Magazine* 24 (February 1905), pp. 337–353.
32. For a good summary and description of reformed and non-reformed systems of local government, see Demetrios Caraley, *City Governments and Urban Problems: A New Introduction to Urban Politics* (Englewood Cliffs, N.J.: Prentice-Hall, 1977), Chapter 4.
33. Theodore J. Lowi, "Gosnell's Chicago Revisited via Lindsay's New York," Foreword to Harold F. Gosnell, *Machine Politics: Chicago Model*, 2nd ed. (Chicago: University of Chicago Press, 1968), pp. xi-xv.
34. This may be true even in city-manager governments, where the public pretense of technical, non-political decision-making may leave little room for political give-and-take in the public arena. Bargaining and the use of influence, in these cases, may ironically be driven underground by the very ethos of "good government," into an informal bargaining process where deals can be made with relatively little risk of outside intervention. A critic of reformed local government might suggest that it is best to acknowledge the political nature of the issue in the first place.
35. Merton, *Social Theory and Social Structure*, pp. 72, 73.
36. The following discussion draws heavily upon Martin Shefter, "The Emergence of the Political Machine: An Alternative View," loc. cit.
37. *Ibid.*, p. 15.
38. *Ibid.*, p. 41.
39. James Q. Wilson, "The Economy of Patronage," *Journal of Political Economy* 69:4 (August 1961), p. 372 at n. 5.
40. A more complete account of this analysis appears in Michael Johnston, "Patrons and Clients, Jobs and Machines: A Case Study of the Uses of Patronage," *American Political Science Review* 73:2 (June 1979), pp. 385–398.
41. Eric L. McKitrick, "The Study of Corruption," in Seymour Martin Lipset and Neil J. Smelser, Eds., *Sociology: The Progress of a Decade* (Englewood Cliffs, N.J.: Prentice-Hall, 1961), p. 456; Michael Margolis, Lee Weinberg, and David Ranck, "Local Party Organization: From Disaggregation to Disintegration," University of Pittsburgh, Department of Political Science, mimeo, 1977; *passim*.
42. Robert A. Caro, *The Power Broker: Robert Moses and the Fall of New York* (New York: Knopf, 1974), pp. 325–326.
43. *Ibid.*, p. 328.
44. *Ibid.*, pp. 328–330.
45. For a cogent argument in favor of partisanship in local politics, see Willis D. Hawley, *Nonpartisan Elections and the Case for Party Politics* (New York: Wiley, 1973).
46. Robert L. Lineberry and Edmund P. Fowler, "Reformism and Public Policies in American Cities," pp. 97–123 in James Q. Wilson, Ed., *City Politics and Public Policy* (New York: Wiley, 1968).
47. Lowi, "Gosnell's Chicago Revisited," pp. ix-xiii.
48. It is interesting to speculate how much these obligations may have been reinforced and made all the more binding by private-regarding attitudes, immigrant political ethics, individualistic political culture, or whatever we should choose to call a value system that places great emphasis upon personalized obligations and ties. To the extent that this reinforcement may have occurred, our view of these values' role might change. They would look less like a particular orientation to politics that built powerful machines and won substantial benefits and more like

a set of perceptions that held people back by encouraging dependency and discouraging independent action. See, for a more extensive argument along these lines, Allan Rosenbaum, "Machine Politics, Class Interest, and the Urban Poor," paper delivered at the 1973 Annual Meeting of the American Political Science Association, *passim*.
49. The New Haven case, with the machine backing a mayor who vigorously pushed for anti-poverty programs, would seem a contradiction of this assertion, but in fact it is not. Lee, though a popular and powerful mayor, was not boss of the organization. His relationship with Arthur Barbieri, who *was* boss, became increasingly strained as Lee's programs developed and Barbieri's power grew. Lee's treatment of blacks, especially during the city's racial disorders of 1967, became an issue of open conflict between the two. After Lee left office, Barbieri elected a mayor who had little interest in redevelopment and anti-poverty efforts.
50. James Q. Wilson, "Two Negro Politicians: An Interpretation," *Midwest Journal of Political Science* 4:4 (November 1960), p. 356.
51. Jerry A. Webman, "Political Institutions and Political Leadership: Black Politics in Philadelphia and Detroit," Yale University, Department of Political Science, mimeo, 1973.
52. Rosenbaum, "Machine Politics," pp. 14–33.
53. An excellent discussion of the alleged death of the machine appears in Raymond E. Wolfinger, "Why Political Machines Have Not Withered Away and Other Revisionist Thoughts," *Journal of Politics* 34:2 (May 1972), pp. 365–398. More conventional arguments that the machine has passed from the scene can be found in Thomas R. Dye, *Politics in States and Communities* (Englewood Cliffs, N.J.: Prentice-Hall, 1977), and in Fred Greenstein, "The Changing Pattern of Urban Party Politics," *Annals of the American Academy of Political and Social Science*, Vol. 353, pp. 1–13.
54. Wolfinger, in "Why Political Machines Have Not Withered Away," lists a number of continuing sources of patronage, some of them a bit unusual; Wolfinger, op. cit., pp. 371–374.
55. See Paul Martin Sacks, *The Donegal Mafia: An Irish Political Machine* (New Haven, Conn.: Yale University Press, 1976), Chapters 1–3, for a description of imaginary patronage. Sometimes, just making people *think* you've done them a favor can place them in your debt.
56. Bruce M. Stave, *The New Deal and the Last Hurrah: Pittsburgh Machine Politics* (Pittsburgh: University of Pittsburgh Press, 1970), *passim*.

Police Corruption

4

A police officer and his partner stop for lunch at a small diner. Both in uniform, they sit at the counter and eat a full meal. When they are done, they wave at the owner and leave, paying nothing. Neither the owner nor the police officers give the matter much thought, for the owner routinely gives free lunch to the officers working the district.

A rookie patrol officer and his veteran partner investigate a break-in at a liquor store. When they arrive at the scene they find several other patrol cars, a broken window, and a ransacked store. The rookie notices that his veteran colleagues are taking a great deal of interest in the remaining liquor. Some of them are taking bottles back to their cars. One veteran hands a couple of bottles to the rookie: "Here kid, have yourself a party. It's all covered by insurance anyway." The young cop pauses a moment, then takes the liquor out to his car.

Several years of hard work in an inner-city precinct have finally paid off for a patrolman: he has been designated captain's bagman. On the first and 15th of every month, he makes the rounds of the book joints, speakeasies, and numbers writers in the district, collecting protection money. Back at the precinct, the money is divided into shares. The captain, lieutenant, and sergeant get the most, but even for some patrol officers the illegal take exceeds $1000 per month.

City police are charged with responsibility for enforcing the law. Yet at least some police officers, in almost every city of any size, break the law. All of the cases mentioned previously are examples of actual police misconduct. They vary in seriousness and the frequency with which they occur, but in each case department regulations and public laws are being broken.

In this chapter I will examine typical patterns of police corruption, their causes and effects, and some possible strategies for policing the police. As in the chapter on political machines, the analysis will be guided by three theoretical approaches. First, the personalistic perspective suggests that police corruption is either a "rotten apple" problem or a systematic one. In the "rotten apple" theory, a few dishonest officers spoil the image of a basically honest department. If the corruption is systematic, the personalistic perspective suggests that corruption is caused by the social background of police recruits, their motivations, and their personalities. Second, institutional factors affecting the development and persistence of corruption include bureaucratization of large police departments, the role of the police in the broader criminal justice system, and the difficulties of maintaining "police professionalism." Finally, the systemic view directs our attention to value and culture conflicts in society, particularly over vice and personal morality. The systemic view points to crime and vice as big business and to peer-group socialization processes through which veteran officers teach recruits how to resolve the dilemmas of police work. As with the analysis of machine politics, I will argue that the systemic approach is the most useful of the three. I will also suggest, however, that institutional factors are important as well, especially when viewed in the wider systemic setting.

POLICE IN THE CITY

Urban police officers live and work at that crucial pressure point where law and society meet. Their lot is one of tension, ambiguity, and conflicting demands from many segments of the community. They are isolated from the rest of the community by their work schedules, their uniforms, and the power and danger that go with the job. Police work quickly becomes an all-encompassing way of life for the officers and their families. Yet we depend heavily upon them. As August Vollmer put it in 1936, we expect our police:

> . . . to have the wisdom of Solomon, the courage of David, the patience of Job and the leadership of Moses, the kindness of the Good Samaritan, the strategy of Alexander, the faith of Daniel, the diplomacy of Lincoln, the tolerance of the Carpenter of Nazareth, and, finally, an intimate knowledge of every branch of the natural, biological, and social sciences. If he had all these, he *might* be a good policeman.[1]

When police go wrong, then, it is serious business. If we can no longer depend upon the police to protect us and our property, what happens then? If police powers of arrest, coercion, and violence are used in arbitrary and capricious ways, what happens to our rights and civil liberties? When police scandals are revealed, many citizens who have always trusted the police—frequently to the point of taking them for granted—respond with fear and bitterness. Life in the city becomes more dangerous and unpredictable when it turns out that the police officer is really *not* our friend.

Background

Police corruption emerged, it seems, almost as soon as there were police. Sherman notes that charges of corruption forced Henry II of England to relieve several sheriffs of their duties as early as 1170, and that the Paris police engaged in bribery, extortion, and active thievery from the end of the Dark Ages until the French Revolution.[2] The Sûreté of Paris, founded in 1817, recruited thieves as police, on the assumption that they could best catch other thieves. As Sherman explains, however, "The arrest of several Sûreté men for burglary showed that thieves as detectives were still thieves."[3] New York City authorities reorganized their police in 1845 but made the mistake of leaving the appointment of officers to elected ward representatives. Not only did police ignore election irregularities; often, they worked out lucrative crime-and-kickback schemes with ward officials and criminals. In 1857 the New York state legislature created a new police force accountable to the governor. The result was an actual battle at City Hall between the old and new police, with the army intervening to stop the mayhem. The new, state-controlled police force, once firmly in power, quickly developed corrupt practices of its own.[4]

Administrative reforms reduced police corruption somewhat in London and Paris beginning in the late 1800s, though both cities have had periodic outbreaks of scandal.[5] In New York, police corruption continues today. The Lexow Commission investigation in 1892 unearthed organized extortion, bribery, sale of office, and corruption in the enforcement of gambling, liquor, and prostitution laws. Seventy years later the Knapp Commission reported that many of these activities continued to flourish and that they had been joined by extensive corruption in drug-law enforcement.[6] Many observers, in fact, have noted that police corruption in New York seems to go through 20-year cycles of public apathy, scandal, investigation, "reform," and apathy again.

Other American cities have had police scandals. In the early 1960s, for example, corrupt activities—including active police burglary rings—were discovered in Chicago, Denver, and Des Moines. As of late 1979, charges of police misconduct were being investigated in such places as Atlanta, Miami, Nye County (Nevada), Chicago, Dade County (Florida), Miami Beach, Los Angeles, and New Britain, Connecticut. Allegations in these cases range from one officer's actively soliciting clients for an attorney (Miami) to a systematic graft operation involving the Chicago police motor pool.[7] Police corruption still flourishes and poses serious dilemmas for urban law enforcement agencies.

POLICE CORRUPTION: TYPES AND TECHNIQUES

Police encounter the full range of human activity in the course of their work, and as a result, police corruption assumes many forms. The seriousness of wrongdoing varies as well. The "free lunch" described previously is a common violation of departmental regulations and the law, but it is not as serious as the systematic bribery and extortion involving the captain's bagman. Corruption also varies in the number of officers involved and the degree to which it is organized. In this section I will set out some general categories of police corruption and then focus on bribery/extortion practices, which will be my primary concern.

What is police corruption?

Following the formal/legal definition of corruption employed in this book, I will define police corruption as *actions on the part of an officer that exploit the powers of law enforcement in return for considerations of private-regarding benefit and that violate formal standards governing his or her conduct.* "Actions" can include decisions *not* to act. "Private-regarding benefit" covers a wide range of rewards, tangible and otherwise, that accrue to the officer, colleagues, family, and friends. "Formal standards" can be public laws, departmental regulations, or both.

Obviously, our definition of corruption is a broad one. It puts free lunch into the same category as police burglary rings, at least for the moment. It does, however, distinguish corruption from other forms of misconduct, such as police brutality, and from such violations of department regulations as sleeping or drinking while on duty. The latter actions break laws or department regulations and could be said to yield certain private-regarding benefits, but they do not in themselves necessarily constitute exploitation of the role of police officer. They are the sorts of misconduct in which many people could engage.

Generally speaking, there are four major categories of police corruption:

1. internal corruption;
2. selective enforcement or non-enforcement of the law;
3. active criminality; and
4. bribery and extortion.

These categories blur considerably in practice. A motorcycle cop who takes a $20 bill in exchange for not writing a speeding ticket is engaging in bribery or extortion, depending upon who initiated the illicit transaction. The cop is also practicing selective non-enforcement. Moreover, the boundaries between many sorts of corruption and legitimate conduct are indistinct. There exist some situations in which selective enforcement is wholly legitimate. Still, these four categories of corruption enable us to catalog the types and practices of police corruption.

Internal corruption. Some kinds of police corruption do not directly involve the public but instead take place among officers or subunits of a department. In some departments radio operators routinely expect, and get, "Christmas money" from patrol officers.[8] Part of the motivation is simple good will, but radio dispatchers can also cover up for officers who go out of service for a time without authorization or who do not wish to take calls in certain neighborhoods. These special arrangements are against regulations and may produce slow or inadequate police service, but as corruption they are usually of minor concern. Another sort of internal corruption is the practice, found in some cities, of paying sergeants, lieutenants, and captains to secure choice assignments or to avoid disciplinary action. Officers may also give or sell portions of drugs confiscated in arrests to each other for use as evidence in other cases, for planting on suspects, for paying off informers, or even for personal use. The Chicago motor pool case—in which police cars were sold at cut rates to officers while still in good condition, forcing the department to buy new cars[9]—is yet another example of internal corruption. Just as the governmental bottleneck is the focus of corrupt techniques of influence because important decisions are at stake, a police department is a complex organization with internal bottlenecks of its own.

Selective enforcement or non-enforcement of the law. Discretion is the essence of good police work. Incidents rarely fall neatly into categories specified by the law. Officers must routinely make quick judgments as to what has happened and what, if anything, should be done. If police did not enjoy wide discretion, they would be highly ineffective and would quickly alienate the communities they are supposed to serve.

Legitimate discretion can, however, be abused or exploited. Traffic cops stopping speeders do not *have to* write tickets. They can issue verbal or written warnings. Many motorists know this, and some will offer a $20 bill to "aid" the officer in exercising discretion. Some officers, on the other hand, will use their powers of discretion to extort the money, thereby teaching the unsophisticated citizen that the law is often a matter of judgment and negotiation. Similarly, an officer who confronts small-time numbers runners or drug users can arrest them or let them go free. If they are freed, it makes a great deal of difference whether they were let go in exchange for valuable information or for money. Whether or not discretion is used corruptly depends, for analytical purposes, on whether or not the officer is pursuing private-regarding benefits. In practice, though, even this may be difficult to judge. An officer who aggressively uses her discretionary powers to get information from numbers runners may eventually arrest higher-ups in the operation and thus be doing a good job. But if she does this solely to win promotion to a plain-clothes detective squad where she hears bribe money comes easy, she is beginning to abuse her discretion for private gain.

Police discretion constitutes a particularly sensitive kind of bottleneck. Officers who detain citizens have them at their mercy, if only for a short time, for they can decide to use (or not use) significant powers of search and seizure, arrest, and violence. Abuses in these situations are difficult to detect because they happen quickly and are often concealed by both officer and citizen. Discretion is an essential part of police work, but it is also a root of the corrupt practice of selective law enforcement.

Active criminality. When allegations of an organized police burglary ring in Des Moines surfaced during the early 1960s, a story made the rounds that one of the physical-fitness tests for prospective recruits was how fast they could run the 100-yard dash with a television set under each arm. In point of fact, only a small percentage of any modern police force gets involved in the active planning and committing of crimes. But active criminality does take place, typically involving burglary and the sale of stolen goods. It is for many people a particularly disturbing type of police corruption.

Many of the powers and procedures that enable police to combat crime also enable them to commit crime. Police have access to all sorts of places, public and private, at all times of the day or night. Most of us do not question their right to be there. An officer trying the back door of a liquor store late at night is probably just making sure the lock is secure. But maybe something less honorable is going on. American police are armed, and they have two-way radios to keep track of the location and movement of other police. Both tools could be quite useful in pulling off burglaries. A uniform and a badge are symbols of trust, but they can also be used to deceive us or to allay our suspicions and caution. Most police use these powers in service of the law. Even those who are involved in other forms of corruption often regard active criminality as breaking the norms of "acceptable" misconduct.[10] Not all officers feel that way, though, and when active police criminality does come to light the result frequently is great public outcry. As the Des Moines anecdote suggests, people develop a widespread cynicism about all police—honest or otherwise.

Bribery and extortion. Bribery and extortion refer to practices in which law enforcement roles are exploited specifically to raise money. For analytical purposes, bribery is initiated by the citizen, extortion by the officer. In practice, the distinction is rarely clear,[11] for frequently these transactions are products of unspoken mutual expectations. In such an atmosphere, it makes little difference who initiates the deal. In fact, the systemic approach will suggest that often there are strong environmental pressures on both police and public to resolve potential conflicts through corruption.

Practices of bribery and extortion vary widely, ranging from a few officers who take whatever might come their way to systematic protection rings. Sherman divides these and other corrupt practices into three categories, based on whether or not they are pervasive and organized. He also outlines the typical "sources" of corruption present in each case, as shown in Table 4-1.

Type I corruption—non-pervasive and unorganized—includes departments in which most officers are honest, but where a few will take a bribe if the opportunity arises. There is no systematic bribery or extortion. If a contractor

TABLE 4-1. Sherman's three types of police corruption[12]

Type	Extent	Organization	Sources		
			Lone criminals	Public	Rackets
I	Small	Little	X		
II	Large	Little	X	X	
III	Large	Much	X	X	X

gives an officer a few dollars to ignore a truck parked on a sidewalk, the money is pocketed and the matter ends there. Lone offenders seeking to beat the rap on minor offenses are a major source of Type I corruption, as Sherman's table suggests. In practice, a Type I department is about as "clean" a police force as we could expect to find in a major city.

Type II corruption is no more organized than Type I, but it involves a majority of the department. Here too, officers take whatever a day's work may bring their way and keep it for themselves and partners. When a majority of a department "takes," however, opportunities to make money can become more frequent. Motorists may be more likely to try to buy their way out of tickets, for example, if they have reason to think that 70% of the police will go for the offer than if they think their chances are only 20%. The general public becomes a source of Type II bribery, particularly in nations where the police issue various licenses, permits, and certificates.[13]

Corruption in a Type III case is pervasive and organized. Money is taken on a systematic basis from persons engaged in gambling, prostitution, drugs, and illegal liquors in return for police "protection."[14] Other, perhaps less well organized shakedown operations may be directed at motorists, construction contractors, trucking firms who send overweight trucks through the city, bars, and restaurants. Money is collected monthly or every two weeks by a "bagman" and divided among all officers in the deal. Shares are awarded to patrol officers; a share and a half or a double share may go to commanding officers. A single share, called a "steady note" in some cities, can be quite sizable. The Knapp Commission heard of shares ranging from $400 per month per officer in quieter Manhattan districts to more than $1500 per month for some Harlem detectives. Because this money is tax free, it represents a sizable income supplement, exceeding in some cases an officer's legitimate take-home pay. New officers who want in on the deal may be put on a two- or three-month probation to test their trustworthiness. Later, if they leave the district, they may get that probation-time money as "severance pay." Ring members who find new protection clients frequently are given the first take from the new source as a "finder's fee." Discussions may be held on where to find new clients or whether or not to raise a client's regular assessment. A majority of a precinct's officers may be involved in the corruption. Those who are not involved know what is going on. Lone offenders and the general public are occasional sources of money for Type III bribery and extortion, but here two new and much more significant elements enter into the process—organized crime and vice. Many "protection" clients have direct or indirect organized crime connections. Vice is big business; substantial investments and big profits are at stake. Its scale, organization, and racket connections put Type III police corruption in a class by itself.

Scope of the analysis

Internal corruption, selective enforcement, active criminality, and bribery and extortion all pose serious policy problems and analytical challenges. My primary focus, however, will be the bribery/extortion problem, and, in particular, the pervasive organized practices of Type III cases. I will focus on bribery and extortion in part simply to cut the general subject of police corruption down to size. But I also focus on bribery and extortion because they are the most significant forms of police corruption. They are widespread and assume similar forms in many cities. More than other kinds of corruption, bribery and extortion are forms of influence, shaping the law enforcement service that society gets.

How much corruption?

No one knows the full extent of police wrongdoing. Normally, the parties to a corrupt transaction have an interest in keeping it secret. Even when police scandal is unearthed, we discover only part of the corruption. Albert J. Reiss' study of police behavior in four large northern cities, however, gives us some idea of the scope of the problem. Reiss' researchers rode with police officers—who knew they were being observed—for several weeks during the summer of 1966. The observers counted, among other things, all instances in which officers committed felonies and misdemeanors other than assault. They found that roughly 20% of the officers took part in criminal violations of the law.[15] These officers may not typify big-city police, and the precincts involved did tend to be high-crime areas. But if 20% of a group of officers *who knew they were being observed* indulged in some form of lawbreaking, how much police wrongdoing must there be overall?

Reiss' observers also found that small favors of the "free lunch" variety were commonplace. Thirty-one percent of the businesspeople surveyed in high-crime areas acknowledged giving free merchandise or special discounts to the police.[16] Many businesspeople extend these favors believing that they will receive extra police protection, an assumption Reiss finds generally unsupported by fact. Reiss' conclusions, based on his own and other data, give us an overall idea of the scope of police misconduct: "(D)uring any year a substantial minority of all police officers violate the criminal law, a majority misbehave toward citizens in an encounter, and most engage in serious violations of the rules and regulations of the department."[17]

What causes police corruption? The next section takes up this question, beginning with the personalistic approach.

PERSONALISTIC VIEWS ON POLICE CORRUPTION

There are three major personalistic explanations for police corruption. They all emphasize individual officers as the ultimate causes of police crime, but they differ in their degrees of rigor, in the variables they emphasize, and in the ends to which they are used by analysts and administrators. They are, first, the "rotten apple" metaphor; second, a recruitment perspective; and third, a "police personality" explanation.

"Rotten apples"?

Whenever evidence of police misconduct surfaces in a major city, someone is sure to bring forth the notion that corruption is merely the doing of a few "rotten apples" in an otherwise honest department. Typically, these assertions come from the police chief, followed by police commissioners, police union leaders, and the mayor or city manager. The "rotten apple" argument has a natural attraction for these people. It is in their interest that the public, prosecutors, and the press not regard the police as totally and systematically corrupt. Many citizens believe in "rotten apples" too, for the notion that all or most of our guardians cannot be trusted is a frightening one indeed.

"Rotten apple" metaphors, however, simply cannot account for significant cases of police corruption. In Type III cases they are wrong by definition, because a majority of the force is involved in systematic corruption. Even in cases involving only a few officers, "rotten apple" ideas are of little value. They assume that a few deviants indulge in corruption because of some defect in themselves. Yet the deviants typically turn out to be much like other cops—unexceptional in background, personality, and (with the exception of the wrongdoing itself) fairly typical in their career paths. Their motives for joining the force are much like other officers'. When they recount how they came to indulge in corruption, they often describe a gradual process of learning on the job.[18] "Rotten apples" are not corrupting the rest of the barrel; if anything, we ought to be looking at the barrel itself.

The "rotten apple" view rests on fallacies that are of more than theoretical significance. They are a distinct hindrance to understanding and—where necessary—combatting police corruption. "Rotten apple" arguments are often employed as an excuse for not vigorously uncovering corruption in a department; if only a few deviants are involved, why not just handle the problem on a case-by-case basis? Similarly, the excuse can be used to limit investigations already in progress, protecting important figures while passing off the dismissal of a handful of patrol officers as a systematic cleanup. This view diverts our attention from fundamental problems in department organization and in police work itself. Indeed, much police corruption may be not so much deviance as conformity. The "rotten apples" view shifts responsibility away from top administrators and covers up the uneasy relationship between the police and the rest of the criminal justice system. It implies that all we have to do to fight police corruption is to carefully recruit people who do *not* have certain "defects"—despite the fact that vastly improved recruitment standards have not prevented corruption.

Recruitment

Even if we discount the notion that isolated deviants are the cause of police corruption, it is still possible that personal traits shared widely within a department are at the root of corruption. If we found that police officers are recruited from social strata particularly susceptible to corruption, then we might have a more supportable personalistic explanation of police corruption than the "rotten apples" perspective.

Urban police officers are indeed recruited from distinct segments of the population. In the last 10 or 15 years, minority and women's organizations have made unrepresentative police recruitment a significant issue in many cities by citing problems of police brutality, police-community relations, and discrimination in hiring, firing, and promotion.

During the mid-1960s Arthur Neiderhoffer studied the New York City police to learn about the causes and consequences of what he termed "police cynicism." One of his concerns was recruitment: who became police officers, and what were their backgrounds? Not surprisingly, Neiderhoffer found the NYPD at the time almost exclusively to be a male preserve. There were, however, other distinctive patterns as well. Officers tended to come from White European (and frequently Roman Catholic) "ethnic" families. Neiderhoffer obtained data on membership in ethnic fraternal police organizations and found that of the more than 20,000 officers who belonged to one of these fraternal groups in 1965, 42% belonged to the Irish group, 25% to the Italian, and 5.4% to the Polish organization. These memberships are hardly a perfect indicator of police ethnicity, but the predominance of Irish and Italian officers is striking.[19]

Police recruits came from families of decidedly modest occupational and financial status, as Neiderhoffer observed: "For the past fifteen years (leading up to 1967), during a cycle of prosperity, the bulk of police candidates has been upper lower class with a sprinkling of lower middle class; about ninety-five percent has had no college training."[20] Data on the occupations of recruits' fathers revealed that 86.9% of the recruits came from the working class, broadly defined. Seven percent were sons of police officers. Police recruits tended in addition to be of average or better size and weight, above-average physical stamina and agility, and slightly above-average intelligence (mean IQ of 105). The percentage of applicants accepted in typical years ranged from 4% (Los Angeles) to 15% (New York).[21]

Some change in this picture has taken place over the last decade. Women, Blacks, and Puerto Ricans have joined city police departments in increasing numbers. Recruitment policies, height and weight requirements, and training procedures have been revised. It is not unusual today to see many sorts of people patrolling the streets. Still, changes occur only gradually; most police officers are still White males from working-class and lower middle-class families.

What does this have to do with police corruption? Maybe officers from low-status families are more likely to take a bribe. Strong desires to climb the status ladder might make these sorts of officers more receptive to making money whenever they can. Lack of advanced schooling and a rough-and-tumble adolescence might leave a young officer unaware—or even contemptuous—of standards of law and morality. Working-class origins are also sometimes presumed to produce certain attitudes, such as bigotry, authoritarianism, selfishness, and shortsightedness, any of which might lead to wrongdoing. Police recruiting procedures may be filling difficult and complex jobs with people who are all too ordinary, as Neiderhoffer suggests:

> The end result of the process of elimination (of potential police recruits) is to accentuate the medium and mediocre at the expense of the independent and exceptional. Working-class background, high-school education or less, average intelli-

gence, cautious personality—these are typical features of the modern police recruit. Only in his superior physical endowment does he stand above the world.[22]

When police scandal erupts, critics and concerned citizens often point to the social composition of the police force as a possible cause. Typical recommendations include stricter recruiting and training procedures and higher educational standards, such as two years of college or more. Are these prescriptions based on a sound explanation of police corruption?

I think not. It is true that many or most corrupt officers are White working-class "ethnic" males without extensive education. But so are most of the *honest* cops. Until recently there simply has not been enough variety in police officers' backgrounds for us to compare the corruptibility of differing types of recruits. It will be interesting to see whether the women and minorities now entering police work will turn up in the ranks of the corrupt. I am fairly certain that a significant number of them will. Even if they do not become as corrupt as established officers, it will not necessarily be because they are "less corruptible." Especially in Type III cases, suspicious old-style officers may simply be reluctant to let them in on the action.

I think it fallacy, too, that those from the classic police background are somehow more corruptible than the rest of us. Strong desires for status and financial and job security are hardly exclusive properties of the working class. If Watergate, white-collar crime, and illegal political contributions by businesspeople have taught us anything, it is that high-status people, too, will also bend or break the law to serve their private purposes. As for attitudes, Neiderhoffer's research on "police cynicism"—arguably an important part of an officer's decision to break the law—found that college educated officers were considerably more cynical than others.[23] It may even be that working-class recruits are *better* adapted to police work than, say, middle-class college graduates. Neiderhoffer suggests that they have been less insulated from street life and more thoroughly tested than their college trained counterparts.[24]

Whether or not Neiderhoffer's observations are correct is a question that must await future study. It seems unlikely, though, that an ethnic working-class background in itself makes a person more corruptible than others, or that stiffer entrance requirements will necessarily produce an honest department. And as a practical matter, if society decides it wants a college educated police force, it had better be prepared to pay for it. The recruitment and retention of college educated police will cost a lot more in salaries than we offer now.

Police personality

The "police personality" issue is partly a question of personal background, since the selection of applicants and recruitment standards influences the department's psychological makeup. But "police personality" can develop within the department, too, if training and on-the-job socialization perpetuate certain attitudes. There is such a thing as a police subculture in many departments.[25] There is evidence that applicants are judged in part on how well they are likely to fit in with the subculture,[26] and that they are further socialized into it as they learn the job.[27] *Is* there a "police personality," whatever its source? If there is, could it lead to corruption?

Controversy over police behavior during the last decade or so has spawned a great deal of research into personalities and attitudes of police officers. Joel Lefkowitz, in his very useful review of this research, notes that between the extreme views of police as heroes and police as ordinary people reside a number of images of police attitudes:

> Somewhere in the middle ground of informed opinion are those who feel that there exists a constellation of traits and attitudes or a general perspective on the world which particularly characterizes the policeman. This constellation is presumably comprised of such interrelated traits as authoritarianism, suspiciousness, physical courage, cynicism, conservatism, loyalty, secretiveness, and self-assertiveness. In addition these authors uniformly are of the opinion that these traits are fostered by occupational demands and do not especially characterize those who become police candidates before their exposure to the life of a policeman [citations omitted].[28]

Lefkowitz concludes that there *is* a "police personality".[29] Police officers tend to be somewhat more suspicious and defensive and feel more isolated than most people. They are not, however, especially cynical, dogmatic, or authoritarian in outlook, compared to many other occupational groups, and may be even less so than most lower middle- or working-class men. Police officers tend to be somewhat more impulsive, aggressive, and willing to take risks than people in other occupational groups. To some extent they prefer working under close supervision and are "more easily influenced by a status figure" than most other people.[30] As for the sources of these traits, Lefkowitz rightly observes that studies of police personality do not show conclusively whether the attitudes are brought to the force by recruits or learned on the job. Lefkowitz concludes that there is support for the notion that attitudes are learned in the process of police work, but he reminds us that police applicants are largely a self-selected group and come disproportionately from a social class that itself exhibits many of the psychological traits found in the police personality.

Does the police personality explain police corruption? I would argue that it does not. Many of the traits noted previously—aggressiveness, risk taking, willingness to take orders, even suspiciousness and impulsiveness—would seem to be *desirable* qualities in police officers. None of them seems inherently linked to corruption. If police attitudes are merely a reflection or distillation of the personality traits of a particular class, and if those traits are linked to corruption, then we might expect to find widespread corruption within that class. I am not convinced that in reality we would find such corruption. If on the other hand police personality grows out of police work itself, then—whether or not the attitudes seem tied to corruption—our attention is directed to the nature of the work and to its role in shaping behavior and attitudes.

This is where personalistic explanations for police corruption ultimately break down. Corruption takes place in actual police work situations. Pressures, opportunities, and frustrations are all part of the job, as are contacts with other people. Even if we could show that some personal or psychological characteristic somehow predisposes an officer to "turn corrupt"—a notion the evidence seems to deny—much would still depend upon pressures and opportunities growing out of dealings with other police, with the institutional workings of the police department, and with members of the public. This is especially true in the case of pervasive, organized bribery and extortion, my main concern here. The personalistic approach makes no provision for these pressures and opportunities and thus is an inadequate (or, in the "rotten apple" case, a downright pernicious) attempt at explanation. In the next two sections I will examine these pressures and opportunities in the dimensions of police work.

THE INSTITUTIONAL APPROACH

Urban police departments are awkward organizational hybrids. Chains of command are organized on a quasi-military basis, yet most of the force works beyond the reach of effective supervision. Administrators seek "professionalization," yet the majority of the situations encountered on the street require on-the-spot decisions for which established guidelines are little help. Police officers work at the intake point of the criminal justice system, where the standards of "justice" differ sharply from the vision pursued by the rest of that system. Perhaps it is the way we organize police work—rather than the specific people we recruit—that leads to blue-coat crime.

In this section I discuss a set of related propositions about police departments as institutions. They raise four major problems: (1) the organizational difficulties of policing urban areas; (2) the police role in the criminal justice system; (3) the tension between professional and bureaucratic standards of conduct; and (4) the role of commanders and administrators in spreading or preventing corruption. These institutional problems create the "bottleneck" in which the police work. They do not so much explain how corruption begins as point to *sustaining* factors.

Problems of policing the city

Sherman has discussed five problems in urban policing that can be regarded as institutional preconditions of corruption.[31] Some of them are inherent in the nature of the work, others developed in practice. They are wide officer discretion, low managerial visibility of police activities, low public visibility, peer group secrecy, and managerial secrecy. Each of these problems makes it easier for corruption to occur.

Wide discretion. Police officers do not simply "enforce the law." Every police encounter is a complex and possibly dangerous situation involving human beings, and often their property, health, and safety. Officers in many instances must act immediately and make critical decisions based on only the sketchiest information. This is true not just in service and emergency situations—rushing an expectant mother to the hospital, tending to the injured in a brawl—but in law enforcement encounters as well. Laws can be vague. What really constitutes "loitering," "creating a nuisance," or (one of my favorite legal locutions) "tippling and reveling"? There is a wide range of legitimate police responses. Officers must decide whether to arrest people or let them go, whether to write a ticket or give a verbal or written warning, whether or not to use force, how much to use. The rookie officer quickly encounters still more ambiguities. She may be certain that a man was an eyewitness to an event, but if he doesn't want to talk she will have to decide how much threatening or cajoling is in order to get the information. If the witness does talk, the officer must judge if what he says has any value.

Wide officer discretion is unavoidable, given the difficulties of dealing with people and the way we draft our laws. For the most part, it is desirable, too. But leaving that much room for individual judgment can also contribute to corruption. Officers can put police discretion to legitimate or illegitimate uses. The boundary between the two areas is anything but distinct. Many citizens are aware of this and will offer cash, gifts, and other favors to officers to help them exercise their "judgment." A traffic cop who accepts a speeder's promise to obey the limits and issues only a verbal warning may be acting legitimately; one who makes the same decision in exchange for a $20 bill is not. Or what of a patrol officer who has been buying auto parts from a store at a "police discount," and who does not ticket cars parked there illegally? The public is not hurt much, and nothing in officers' orders compels them to ticket every illegally parked car they see. Every officer ignores minor offenses at times to tend to more important business. These are probably cases of corruption, although minor ones, and wide officer discretion is a part of it. Discretion does not make corruption inevitable, but it enables an officer to conceal many illegitimate decisions. It can also foster belief among citizens and police that when the law becomes a matter of judgment, it goes up for sale. When this belief is widespread, corruption becomes safer and easier for all involved.

Low managerial visibility. Most patrol officers work on their own or with a single partner. They operate beyond the supervision of sergeants, lieutenants, and captains because they are dispersed throughout a district and are constantly on the move. Police officers are not soldiers. Despite the quasi-military chain of command and such innovations as two-way radio, the fact is that most police supervisors most of the time cannot know what their officers are doing. Sherman observes: "Since supervisors rarely observe line officers as they make decisions, controls on their use of discretion are relatively weak, and always after the fact."[32]

Low public visibility. If police supervisors have little knowledge of police activities, most of the public has even less. As frequently as we see police officers cruising down the street or writing parking tickets, we seldom see them investigating a crime or arresting anyone for anything more consequential than speeding. Much significant police activity takes place beyond the view of all but a few members of the public—those directly involved and perhaps a handful of bystanders. If we *do* see police in action we may have no way of knowing what is really going on. As noted earlier, if we saw an officer fiddling with the lock on a store late at night, we could not say for sure whether his or her motives were legitimate. Low public visibility, like low managerial visibility, offers many opportunities to conceal illicit decisions and behavior.

Peer group secrecy. Afficionados of police novels and movies have heard much about the ways police stick together and develop a distinctive belief system and vocabulary. Popular treatments of this "brotherhood" at times romanticize and exaggerate it for dramatic effect, but the police subculture is a fact, and along with it comes peer group secrecy.

There is nothing wrong or unusual about the growth of subcultures. Doctors and lawyers have them. So do college professors. But the police subculture stands apart from others in its comprehensiveness and strength. By "comprehensiveness," I mean that it seems to contain and teach a much more inclusive set of attitudes about politics, society, and self than do other subcultures. "Strength" refers partly to the effective socialization of newcomers. CBS's "60 Minutes," for example, televised a story in 1977 about a Florida sociologist and criminology scholar who took on part-time police work. In short order he became more police officer than sociologist in his activities, work schedule, and circle of acquaintances. Many of his beliefs and attitudes changed markedly, gravitating toward those of his fellow officers. "Strength" also refers to the sanctions and disapproval directed against those who threaten to break the rules of the subculture. These sanctions range from social ostracism to violence and can effectively bring "oddballs" back into line.

This is where peer group secrecy comes into play. The person most likely to see corrupt cops at work is another cop. Yet in many or most cases he or she will do nothing about it and will tell no one. Fear of retaliation plays a part in this, but so do bonds of friendship, an "us against the world" attitude toward the public and press, and the fact that an officer must ultimately be able to trust and be trusted by his or her colleagues. Outsiders and administrators will thus find information on corruption difficult to get. They will find it virtually impossible to get officers to testify against their colleagues. Honest officers may spend an entire career working with colleagues whom they know are "taking" and do nothing about it. Those who do try to fight corruption, such as detectives Frank Serpico[33] and Robert Leuci[34] in New York, will find themselves in grave danger.

It might seem that peer group secrecy and the police subculture are simply the aggregate result of personalistic factors. Peer group secrecy is, however, very much an institutional factor. It derives much of its special strength and comprehensiveness from the way police departments operate. The uniform, the gun and night stick, and the use of force separate police from civilians. Public resentment of police work (no one likes to be arrested or given a ticket), guidelines for police conduct laid down by the courts, and public controversy over police conduct and personnel policies have contributed to a cohesiveness that can approach garrison mentality. Police personnel work odd hours and rotating shifts (perhaps one six-day week on a "daylight" shift, one week of "nightwork," one week on the "graveyard" shift, and one week off), which means that most of their friends are apt to be other officers. Finally, the work itself involves long hours of tedium and paperwork, punctuated by short episodes of action and possibly great danger. These factors bind police together, make them feel isolated from and misunderstood by the rest of society, and encourage peer group secrecy.

Managerial secrecy. Sherman's fifth precondition for police corruption involves the values and actions of commanding and administrative officers. Most "top cops" are former patrol officers who have risen through the ranks. Though some change has occurred in recent years, few administrators enter a department at the top. All who have climbed the ladder are intimately acquainted with the patrol officer's lot and with the values of the subculture. Administrators and commanders are often reluctant to investigate and discipline officers on charges of corruption unless revelations of scandal and external pressure compel it. Even when they do take action, it is often less than vigorous.[35] Proactive strategies against corruption—active investigation and continuing efforts to stop wrongdoing before it starts—are rare in most departments.

Managerial secrecy also includes resentment of "interference" by the public, press, or politicians. Allegations by the press frequently are ignored. If a response is necessitated by the emergence of sensational evidence, the "rotten apple" explanation is revived and thrown out for public consumption. Formal inquiries, such as the Knapp investigation, are bitterly resented at all levels of the department. Similar resentment is found in many institutions—college professors, for example, do not like to have state legislators tell them what to teach—but in police departments managerial secrecy is strengthened by the values of the police subculture, by the anxieties that allegations of corruption provoke, and by the vigor with which the press often pursues the corruption issue once it has surfaced.

Sherman's five institutional problems are not in themselves a theory of police corruption.[36] They do, however, highlight institutional aspects of city policing that are preconditions to corruption. Each opens up opportunities for corruption and its concealment, and each is a more or less direct product of the way our police forces are organized. More will be said later about how these opportunities are converted into actual misconduct.

Police in the criminal justice system

Most of the cases entering our criminal justice system begin with some sort of police encounter. As noted at the outset, police work where law and society meet. They are "intake officers" for a complex social and institutional system made up of courts, penal institutions, parole and probation officials, lawyers, judges, victims of crime, and (at least indirectly) the public. How an officer acts in a given encounter—indeed, whether he or she acts at all—is of immense concern to all parts of the system. For a suspect, it may be a matter of freedom or imprisonment; for the public, safety or continued victimization; for the courts, a manageable load of well prepared cases or chaos; and for the officer, commendation or condemnation, safety or injury. All of these concerns weigh against each other in an environment of ambiguity and wide discretion.

The police officer's role in the criminal justice system creates two serious dilemmas. One concerns the means of providing justice, the other the ends. The dilemma of means involves conflicting professional and bureaucratic standards of police conduct. The dilemma of ends is one of differing conceptions of justice itself. The police officer resolves these dilemmas by making informal and unsatisfying compromises on behalf of a system to which he or she may have little commitment. This situation, I feel, is a cause of corruption.

Means of policing: Professionalism versus bureaucratization

Reiss has discussed the influence of professional and bureaucratic norms on police conduct. He suggests that in many situations these norms are irreconcilable—that an officer simply cannot satisfy both sets of demands. What are these conflicting standards, and where do they originate?

Reiss writes that a profession

> is commonly regarded as a special kind of occupation where technical knowledge is gained through long, prescribed training. The knowledge itself is regarded as a systematic body of theory and practice. The professional person adheres to a set of professional norms that stipulate the practitioner should do technically competent work in the "client's" interest. As Wilensky notes, at the core of professionalism is devotion to an ideal that ". . . the client's interest more than personal or commercial profit should guide decisions when the two are in conflict."[37]

The "professionalized" police officer, then, is a well trained, judicious decision-maker, able to handle authoritatively the many situations encountered on the street within a wide range of discretion. "Authoritatively" is an important word here, for professionals who have reached a decision based on their best judgment naturally wish to see that decision stick. "Professionalized" police departments emphasize education for officers, sophisticated crime-detection techniques, computerized data processing, and advanced communications systems. Professionalism as a managerial approach also allows and encourages commanders to insulate themselves from outside "interference." For the officer on the beat, professionalism is a source of status as well as of freedom to make judgments; the professional officer is not just the city's uniformed errand boy.

Bureaucratization poses a direct threat to professionalism and places the patrol officer in an acute dilemma. Reiss again:

> A *bureaucracy* requires the standardization of rules by a central authority in the expectation that universalism will prevail in the applications of those rules. This contradicts the concept that in a profession, the professional must be able to exercise discretion in the application of standards, particularly to meet the requirements of a particular case. A *command organization* threatens professional status because it

expects men to follow orders regardless of their judgment. The professional ideal holds that orders are antithetical to the exercise of discretion.[38]

Bureaucratization is a necessary aspect of urban policing, but the city police officer is still caught between the conflicting pressures of professionalism and bureaucracy. In most police encounters, the two cannot be reconciled. Consider the case of a narcotics detective who carefully cultivates a set of informants. Relationships here are delicate and based on a number of understandings. The officer may "have something" on the informant and use the threat of arrest to get information. Or she may trade drugs or money for tips and leads. Here is the dilemma: if the officer follows her department's regulations on dealing with informants—which may require her officially to record the informant's name and may prohibit exchanging drugs or money for information—she will quickly find she has no informants. The department also requires her to ring up a certain quota of drug arrests each month, and to get arrests she needs information. What does she do? In most cases she will disregard the regulations—and often break laws—to get information and make arrests. The tension between professionalism and bureaucratization often forces a "good cop" to break the law in order to produce arrests.

Ends of policing: What is justice? Police conceptions of justice often differ markedly from those employed in the rest of the criminal justice system, worsening the tensions of professionalism and discretion. The most visible of these value conflicts are matters of procedure. The U.S. Supreme Court's *Miranda* and *Escobedo* decisions, which laid down safeguards for the rights of the accused, were highly unpopular with most police. In the popular arena this was a "law and order" issue, but it also reflects more basic differences between the police and the courts. As noted previously, professionals seek to make *authoritative* decisions and do not welcome others' efforts to change decisions or to lay down rules of decision-making. Police often feel that legislators and courts create vague, unworkable, and hastily constructed laws and procedures while holding police conduct up to minute and arbitrary scrutiny. Officials in the court system may regard police as bumbling, overzealous in the use of force, insensitive to the subtleties of the law, and cavalier when it comes to the requirements of due process. The result, as Reiss points out, is sharply contrasting notions of procedural justice: "Matters that the police want defined by rules, the courts want to leave open to discretion. And what the courts want defined by rules, the police want to leave open to discretion."[39]

Contrasts exist, too, in conceptions of the substance of justice. Some officers might feel that legislators and the courts ask the police to apply unenforceable laws to activities such as gambling and prostitution, while violent crimes such as rape and muggings are ignored, their perpetrators freed by the courts on technicalities. Or, some might feel that the courts come down hard on the "ordinary guy" while letting the hardened offender and the affluent white-collar criminal off with a slap on the hand. Most frustrating might be the numerous cases in which an officer simply *knows* that a person has been committing crimes but that the evidence will not stand up in court. These conflicting substantive notions of justice are certainly debatable; when it comes to conflict between police and courts I find myself agreeing with the courts more often than not. But it is undeniable that many police officers feel their values of right and wrong, their hard work in putting together a case, and their first-hand knowledge of the community are constantly being disregarded and even repudiated by the criminal justice system they are asked to serve. The result is tension and resentment.

Two major consequences of these tensions can pave the way for police corruption. One is disillusionment with the criminal justice process and an accompanying lack of commitment to the standards defining police roles and conduct within that system. The second, more concrete consequence is that conflicting demands upon the police lead to actual police misconduct. "Misconduct" here refers not to corruption but rather to violations of law and departmental regulations that are more or less compelled by the conflicting pressures of police work. Police officers in many situations must literally break some laws if they are to enforce others.

One good example involves the enforcement of vice laws. One way police departments insulate themselves from the contradictory demands of other parts of the criminal justice system is by adopting a narrow definition of police responsibilities. For example, police departments regard a crime as "cleared" when an arrest is made, whether or not the accused is eventually convicted. Once the case has been "cleared" it is in the hands of the courts. Thus, when public outcry forces a crackdown on gambling, prostitution, or drug traffic, it is arrests and not convictions that department brass normally seeks. In New York City in 1970, Rubinstein reports, more than 9000 gambling arrests produced only 70 jail terms. During one period in the late 1960s, 73 numbers raids in Brooklyn resulted in 356 arrests. Of these cases, 198 were dropped, and 63 produced acquittals. Only 77 persons were fined. (The average fine was $113, mere pocket change for people involved in gambling.) Five went to jail and served an average of 17 days, 12 sentences were suspended, and one person went to prison for a year.[40]

The message to officers on the street is clear. To advance within the department, one must make vice arrests, and one must not worry too much about *how* one makes the arrest or whether it will stand up in court. As we have seen, making arrests requires information, and on the street, information is not just given away. Officers may buy vice information with money, drugs, or protection from arrest. They can extort it through violence or the threat of violence, or they can "steal" it through arrangements such as illegal wiretaps and entrapment. For years many members of New York's elite Special Investigating Unit carried bags of heroin wherever they went, for at any time they might have been able to use them to deal with an informant.[41] Looked at in one way, these practices are necessary parts of good police work. They may, however, also break the law.

Some officers may indulge in this sort of wrongdoing for years without ever "taking." For at least a few others, though, it seems plausible that conflicting pressures, weak and ambiguous standards of conduct, strong temptations, and the necessity to break laws in the course of duty might encourage corruption. These institutional factors can open the door to corruption for officers who, for whatever reasons, are already inclined to partake of it.

"Command corruption"

So far the discussion has focused on corruption among low-ranking police officers who work the streets. But a concern with institutional sources of police corruption naturally directs our attention to the command structure and to the fact that commanding officers themselves can be corrupted. Before we conclude our review of the institutional perspective on police corruption, let us briefly discuss corruption among commanders.

Everyone in a police department works for someone else. Even the chief or commissioner, despite his or her desires for political and professional independence, works for the mayor. A patrol officer, of course, is at the bottom of the heap. Knowing this, anyone engaged in an illegal enterprise who is being bothered by an honest cop can try to "get to" the honest cop's boss. Perhaps a sergeant, lieutenant, captain, or someone even higher up has already been corrupted, having risen through the ranks with old habits intact. Perhaps the superior is taking a "steady note" or is simply receptive to a good offer. Whatever the situation, a friendly commanding officer can do many things to get an honest patrol officer off your back. William F. Whyte, in his study of Boston's "Cornerville," reported a case in which a commander transferred an inconveniently honest officer to a cemetery beat. Similar actions might include assigning an officer to extra work without pay, posting him or her in a precinct far from home, assigning kinds of work he or she does not like, and even conferring or withholding promotions. "The threat of transfer," Whyte observed, "is particularly effective with those officers who become attached to the district in which they are assigned. . . ."[42]

Police commanders, then, can be of great help to someone who commands a gambling or other crime related organization. In fact, there are some significant similarities between police and crime organizations. Both have a stake in monitoring and controlling gambling and related vice activities, although their reasons for control are at least nominally at odds. Both have hierarchical command structures operated in a quasi-military manner. Each is a "brotherhood" of sorts, set off from outsiders. Both divide overall responsibilities into territorial jurisdictions; both have an interest in occupying that "turf," but neither wants to fight over it constantly. Both employ violence and coercion as needed, and—perhaps most important—both exist in the "no man's land" between society's public morality and its private vices.

Given these similarities, it is not surprising that Whyte found extensive cooperation between gambling "managers" and police commanders. In exchange for money, favors, and occasional political support, police commanders restrained anti-gambling activities. When, for public relations reasons, a raid had to be conducted, commanders would tip off their counterparts in the gambling organizations. That way, important individuals and large sums of money could be protected. Gambling bosses could even put these sporadic raids to disciplinary use by making sure troublesome subordinates would be on the scene to be arrested. This cooperation meant larger profits for gambling operators, extra income for police commanders, and a general reduction in conflict and violence between both.

Thus, we should remember that police corruption can occur higher up in the department. Not only does "command corruption" enable some officers to get in on the take and persuade other officers to wink at misconduct, it can also hinder reform if corruption is ever revealed. New York's Frank Serpico tried at first to fight police corruption by talking to his superiors, but he got little response. At least some commanders were involved in corruption themselves. Many more were reluctant to rock the boat. Actions of commanders, then, can be an important determinant of how much corruption exists; and as we shall see later on, they can be critical in determining the success or failure of efforts at reform.

The ways we have chosen to organize urban policing have, I think, a significant bearing upon corruption among the police. Aspects of police work such as wide officer discretion, low public visibility, and managerial secrecy open up opportunities for wrongdoing. Conflicting pressures of professionalism and bureaucratization create ambiguous standards of behavior. The department's uneasy relationship with the rest of the criminal justice system forces many good officers to break the law just to do their jobs. Commanding officers' behavior is significant throughout—a commander who is on the take can make life miserable for an honest officer, and a merely indifferent commander can make police corruption very difficult to detect and eradicate.

Institutional factors, however, do not provide a full explanation of police corruption. They do give us a description of the critical bottleneck that the police officer or commander controls through his or her power to make important decisions. The institutional perspective identifies conflicting sets of values and expectations that bear upon officers' decisions and that magnify the importance of officers as decision-makers. It also points out forces that sustain corruption once it has begun. What is still missing, however, is an account of how corrupt transactions are initiated—of how opportunities are turned into actual corruption. The institutional perspective explains why some police officers are "available" for corruption, but the sort of bribery and extortion that is my primary concern takes at least two parties. It involves the motives and actions of *private* parties—citizens who enter into corrupt transactions. Relationships between police and private parties are the subject of the systemic view, and it is to that which I now turn.

SYSTEMIC PERSPECTIVES ON POLICE CORRUPTION

Earlier in this chapter I suggested that one reason why the police are so interesting and why police corruption is so important is that police work where law and society meet. In the preceding section of this chapter I outlined some of the institutional pressures bearing upon that critical point. In this section I will look at pressures upon the police that come from the societal side. Institutional forces create the bottleneck that the police officer controls; the systemic view points to people and interests trying to get at things they want. If they want things that are illegal they must somehow neutralize the police officer's power to stop them. Corruption is a form of influence well suited to that task.

Vice and morals: Ambivalence or hypocrisy?

Systemic pressures that make for police corruption begin in our ambivalence about ourselves. Americans are particularly fond of turning questions of private conduct into matters of public policy. We regulate such matters as who may drink alcoholic beverages, what sorts of literature may be sold, and who may indulge in what sorts of sexual behavior with whom. Taking drugs of many sorts and most forms of gambling are illegal in most of the nation. Our public concern with others' morality and personal behavior has deep cultural and historic roots and has often reflected class, ethnic, and religious frictions. Prohibition, for example, was a native-versus-immigrant issue in many cities and was also proposed as a law that would force the improvident workingman to sober up and go home to the wife and kids. Behavior that one person enjoys often proves objectionable to someone else. In such cases we typically pass regulatory laws and send the police out to enforce them.

These laws create problems for both police and public. Vice laws are often arbitrary and vary widely from place to place. "Playing a number" at the drugstore is against the law; buying a state lottery ticket in the same store is not. A person of legal age can walk into any bar in Pennsylvania and buy a six-pack to go; a Connecticut bartender who sells beer to go can land in jail. In some states, liquor and other vice laws are matters of local or county option, further confusing the matter. For many people and police officers, vice laws are a nuisance.

A more serious problem is that many people simply do not obey vice laws. This is frequently true in cases of deep value conflicts, where one segment of a community has legally imposed its own morality upon others. Another difficulty is the fact that some citizens (and some police) regard many vice activities as essentially "victimless," unlike crimes of theft or violence. If someone wants to discreetly buy an after-hours drink, play a number, or buy a "dirty" book, the argument runs, who is being hurt? As long as people are people, there will be a strong demand for life's forbidden pleasures, and as long as people like money someone will be willing to supply such pleasures for the right price.[43] The result is the growth of illicit vice industries selling liquor, sex, drugs, and opportunities to gamble to the millions who wish to indulge. Many people underestimate the scale of these industries, assuming that vice is supplied by fly-by-night operators who can easily be driven out of business by the passage of an ordinance. This is not so; vice in America is a highly profitable multibillion dollar enterprise. It is supported and patronized by all kinds of citizens, not just a degenerate few. As Gail Sheehy demonstrated in her study of prostitution in New York, investments in vice come from, and a share of the profits flows back to, prestigious "mainstream" individuals and businesses.[44] Making prostitution, pornography, gambling, and other vice activities illegal does not make them go away; if anything, it makes them more profitable. Making these activities illegal also forces the police to stand between supply and demand and try to keep the two apart.

Society's ambivalence about vice creates strong incentives for people to break the law. It also encourages the police not to enforce the law because it is often so difficult. Vice laws govern activities in which people are generally involved of their own volition,[45] and—unlike crimes of theft or violence—in which none of the parties has a direct interest in seeing the law enforced. Completing this picture is the fact that participants in vice—sometimes the consumer, more often the entrepreneur or other police—will offer police bribes and other incentives to look the other way. Consumers caught gambling may put up cash to avoid arrest, fines, and embarrassment. Vice entrepreneurs have investments and high profits at stake; they make more than enough money to bribe the cops and may simply regard "protection money" as part of their overhead costs. They may spend several thousand dollars a month to keep the police at bay in the same way a grocer pays for heat and electricity. Especially in Type III cases, invitations to "take" will come from other officers, who will test young recruits to see if they are interested and "reliable."

These direct offers of bribe money and other incentives help convert passive opportunities for wrongdoing into actual corruption. Such pressures are systemic in that they emanate from interactions with the public, from society's ambivalence about vice, and from the workings of the underground economy that the ambivalence has fostered. In almost every police encounter with the public—and especially in contacts involving vice and the money it entails—there is a potential conflict over what the officer should do. One mechanism that neatly resolves this conflict is corruption.

Corruption benefits all of the direct parties to vice transactions, at least in the short run. The consumer procures his or her gratification, the entrepreneur buys protection, and the police officer makes some money. Corruption also does away with the need for violence or coercion. It is an attractive way of avoiding tasks that could never be accomplished anyway, such as the complete eradication of prostitution or of numbers games. There will always be vice, an officer may conclude, so what difference does it make if you "take" or not? The public need never know. Police can arrest a few minor lawbreakers to meet their quotas, vice entrepreneurs can keep their activities sufficiently discreet, and nobody has to talk about the money. Corruption is well suited to resolving the conflicts inherent in policing a complex society.

The systemic view yields a picture of the forces and actions that convert opportunities into corrupt behavior. It suggests that police corruption is rooted not in the kinds of people who become officers but rather in their interaction with society. Coupled with the pressures and contradictions of the institutional setting, this analysis creates a picture of the bottleneck situation out of which police corruption develops. Institutional factors define the bottleneck, systemic forces set up the pressures within it, and both drive the police officer toward corruption.

How to account for the honest cop?

The systemic and institutional perspectives are so all-encompassing that we are forced to consider why there exist any honest police officers at all. Many small and medium-sized cities probably have only moderate levels of police corruption, and frequently it is not well organized. Even the most corrupt big city departments have many officers who have never taken a dime. If systemic and institutional pressures have so much to do with police corruption, how do we account for those who remain honest?

This question, I think, has both many answers and no answer. Why any one officer does or does not get involved in corrupt practices may be impossible to say; certainly some officers will be more resistant to corrupting pressures than others. Not all officers, however, are exposed equally to these pressures. Vice activity is an integral component in the corruption problem, yet not all police are involved in vice work. Some may do traffic or communications duty, and others may serve the bureaucracy. A substantial share of the officers on the street work in quiet residential districts and may have little to do with the dilemmas of enforcing the vice laws. Some of those who do encounter systemic pressures as patrol or plain-clothes officers may decide to transfer to other sorts of work, and many more may not indulge in corruption themselves but choose to tolerate the corrupt actions of partners and colleagues.

One important factor influencing the way an officer will react to the pressures of the job is peer group socialization. We have already seen the kind of peer group secrecy that exists in police work, and it is also true that many of the most important norms of conduct are learned not in the Police Academy but on the job. These informal norms become crucial in high-pressure situations where formal standards of conduct are unworkable, ambiguous, or non-existent. It is in those situations that pressures making for police corruption tend to converge.

On-the-job socialization—the values and behavior a police officer learns from his or her colleagues—is a critical influence on corruption. New recruits and veterans alike need the guidance and support of others who understand:

> The policeman needs the support of his colleagues. It is not only that he needs them to come to his aid when his safety and well-being are threatened; he needs their understanding. They are the only ones who have "been there"; they are the only ones who know the ambiguities of the trade and require no lengthy explanations

and excuses in the recounting of his experiences. In exchange for the understanding, every man who chooses to remain a policeman will put up with a great deal.[46]

Much of this peer group socialization—especially that encountered by the new recruits—is of necessity negative in character. Many of the rules the recruit has learned in the Police Academy—dress and equipment regulations, paperwork procedures, the niceties of evidence, search and seizure, and interrogation processes—are widely disregarded out in the precincts. Some of these rules, as discussed previously, *must* be disregarded if an officer is to meet his or her arrest quotas. From more experienced colleagues young officers quickly learn what they can "get away with" and what minimal standards of activity must be met. Other attitudes are learned as well. Cynicism, authoritarianism, and a feeling that most people dislike the police have been suggested as attitudes learned from colleagues, though the evidence on this is far from conclusive.

Peer group socialization can lead to corruption in at least two ways. First, new recruits can learn an informal code of conduct that teaches that certain types of wrongdoing are widely practiced and thus acceptable. Wrongdoing within these boundaries will generally be kept secret by others, even if they do not take part in corrupt activities. The substance of the "code"—that is, which activities are or are not sanctioned—may vary from department to department and account for some variations in degree of corruption. The code is not a carte blanche to steal; it usually declares certain types of behavior off limits. Stoddard writes of an officer who first indulged in the sorts of shakedowns and bribery and extortion allowed by the "code" and then moved on to active criminality—planning and carrying out burglaries. He made this transition thinking that he was still within the code, and that he hence enjoyed the support of his colleagues. He assumed many of them were doing the same sorts of things. When he was finally arrested, he was surprised to learn that he had very little company: few fellow officers were engaged in active criminality, and most sharply disapproved of his conduct. Planning and carrying out burglaries was a violation of the code, and as a result few police officers got involved in it.[47]

The second way that peer group socialization can lead to corruption is through a process of "testing." Veteran officers may test a young recruit by offering him or her part of a take or by setting up situations in which the new officer must decide whether or not to join in questionable behavior (such as the hypothetical liquor store example outlined at the beginning of this chapter). Testing may be initiated by veterans actively involved in corruption who want to know if the recruit wants to join or will at least remain quiet. The testing may also be done by officers not deeply involved in corruption who simply want to serve notice that one's primary allegiance must be to one's colleagues on the street, come what may. New recruits are dependent upon veterans for knowledge, help in time of danger, and emotional support. Understandably, they very much want acceptance. In testing situations, then, we would expect many of them to go along with the deal, at least for the moment. It seems plausible to suggest that—for at least a few—this is where corruption begins.

Peer group socialization helps us understand how institutional pressures and systemic temptations lead to corrupt behavior in specific instances. Indeed, socialization may be the main mechanism through which new officers learn the full extent of institutional and systemic dilemmas—and the commonly accepted ways to resolve them. Some of these ways involve corruption, others do not. Perhaps certain kinds of socialization could even inhibit corruption; the Knapp Commission's recommendations for New York rested at least partly on this assumption.[48] This and other possible remedies for police corruption will be discussed later in this chapter.

So far I have laid out and discussed three general approaches to the explanation of police corruption. I have suggested that although the individualistic approach has serious flaws, institutional and systemic factors combined can give us a fairly clear and useful account of the development and persistence of police corruption. It is time now to examine the consequences of police corruption—to spell out its costs and possible benefits, to identify those who win or lose, and to speculate on its implications for law enforcement in modern society.

CONSEQUENCES OF POLICE CORRUPTION

Police corruption, like machine politics, is a regressive form of influence in its direct effects, benefiting "haves" at the expense of "have nots." As for the kind and quality of law enforcement a corrupt police force delivers, the answers are more complex. At the very least, police corruption poses questions about the kinds of laws we enact and about how we enforce them. Some analysts have suggested that police corruption even has some broadly beneficial latent functions.

Who wins, who loses?

Corruption of the police is a form of influence. All of us break laws at one time or another, and some of us get caught. Those who are caught—whether for running a red light or for dealing in heroin—presumably have an interest in avoiding a ticket, fine, or trip to jail. In some unknown percentage of these cases either the civilian or police officer initiates a corrupt transaction. Here is where the regressive consequences of police corruption begin. The currency of corruption is money, or things money can buy, such as meals or consumer goods. Some people can afford the cost of corrupt influence; most of us cannot. Police corruption, then, is in its most serious forms a kind of influence accessible to only a few.

These few are not necessarily the conventionally affluent, although a surgeon can probably more easily afford to fix a ticket than a waitress can. In pervasive, organized corruption, the "haves" tend to be those engaged in lucrative but illegal vice activities. Higher-ups in these fields frequently do become affluent. Less prominent figures, such as a petty numbers runner who may spend $200 a week or more on police protection, may simply depend on a large cash flow to buy off the cops. Both types are "haves" in the sense that they can devote much more money to illegal influence than can the rest of us. People who cannot or will not employ money and material incentives must rely on the call of duty and the law to influence police behavior. When they encounter officers who are "taking," they presumably have far less influence than those who make pay-offs. When corrupt officers comprise a significant portion of an area's police, people in the "have-not" majority lose in two ways. First, they are deprived of at least some of the police protection they are entitled to receive. Second, when caught in illegal acts they will likely suffer heavier sanctions than will those who pay, even though the latter are often engaged in far more serious offenses.

These inequalities and the central role of money in police corruption become more apparent if we make a rough accounting of the winners and losers in police corruption, much as we did for machine politics. This accounting appears in Table 4-2.

TABLE 4-2. Beneficiaries and losers in police corruption (gains and losses in parentheses)

Major Beneficiaries	Minor Beneficiaries	Minor Losers	Major Losers
Organized crime (*protection, money*)	Lone offenders who pay (*non-enforcement of laws*)	Area residents, "taxpayers" (*loss of services, possibly more crime*)	Inner-city neighborhoods, other vice locations (*stronger organized crime, increased vice and its detrimental neighborhood effects*)
Vice entrepreneurs (*protection, money*)	Individual police officers (Types I, II) (*money, gifts, "police discounts"*)	Businesspeople who cannot/do not pay (*reduced police presence, possible harassment*)	General citizenry (*loss of trust in an accountable police force*)
Groups of police officers (Type III cases) (*money*)	Vice "investors" (e.g., owners of buildings renting to vice operators) (*money*)	Lone offenders who cannot/do not pay (*relatively harsher law enforcement*)	Victims of increased crime (*crime losses, injury*)
	Businesspeople paying small incentives (e.g., free meals, "police discount") (*added police presence, non-enforcement of parking ordinances*)		
	Vice consumers (*opportunities to partake of vice*)		

The accounting is rough and tentative but reflects a consistent pattern. Major and minor benefits go to people who can pay the price; costs fall most heavily upon those who cannot or will not. Police corruption is a regressive and undemocratic form of influence. Table 4-2 also reflects the central role of money in the economy of police corruption. Corrupt officers sell protection for cash, and protection makes vice and other illegal activities more profitable. Some of the costs to the losers are monetary as well, though usually indirect and long-term. A businessperson who cannot pay, for example, may suffer higher crime losses, or loss of business due to vigorous enforcement of parking restrictions.

Corruption, the police, and society

What are the effects of corruption upon the quality of law enforcement and upon the more general role of police in modern society? Here the answers are not clear. One effect of corruption is that certain illegal activities are tolerated and made more profitable; in this sense the quality of law enforcement is diminished. I have also suggested (Table 4-2) that areas where vice operations flourish—particularly inner-city neighborhoods—suffer the adverse consequences of these sorts of activities. Society as a whole loses trust in its police, a critical factor when we consider their powers of search and seizure, arrest, and coercion. It is also possible that police corruption leads to increased crime, even in parts of the city away from the corruption and in types of activity not directly related to the bribery and extortion. For example, corruption may allow the drug trade to flourish, resulting in more burglaries by addicts. Or the presence of a corrupt and alienated police force that the public holds in contempt may encourage potential lawbreakers to act on their temptations. Solid understanding of these "ripple effects" must await further research.

As with machine politics, however, we should not dismiss police corruption out of hand as totally harmful. Some effects may be insignificant. The motorist who buys her way out of a speeding ticket with $20 has evaded formal "justice," to be sure; but she has also paid a fine of sorts and has suffered the unnerving experience of getting caught. The experience will probably make some people slow down, at least for a while. Others, of course, will go right back to speeding. Either way, speeders stopped by the police—whether they pay a bribe or take a ticket—make up only a small percentage of all those who break the speed limit. A possible positive by-product of corruption in the vice area could be a reduction in tension and violence if police and vice operators have worked out a *modus vivendi*.

Some consequences of police corruption may be neutral, or even beneficial. Dorothy H. Bracey suggests not only that police corruption has several important latent functions that help us understand why corruption is so persistent but that it "functions to fulfill societal and cultural goals, i.e., contributes to the maintenance of the social system."[49] How can this be? Bracey proposes several functional consequences of police corruption. Corruption can promote "solidarity, mutual trust, and *esprit de corps*"[50] in the ranks by creating a shared and secret pattern of behavior open only to police officers. This kind of solidarity presumably would develop only in cases of pervasive, organized corruption, Bracey notes. A small number of corrupt officers, or even many officers "accepting bribes unbeknownst to each other," she suggests, will not increase department morale and solidarity. Indeed, they may weaken it.

Bracey points out other latent functions of police corruption.[51] Corruption is a sort of "training device" or "rite of passage" by which veterans initiate and socialize young recruits into the "brotherhood." Corruption "reaffirms the status of superior officers at the same time that it increases their solidarity with their subordinates," and it is a "stabilizing factor" ironing out potential cultural conflicts over vice, morals, and regulatory laws. Corruption is a "facilitator of business," allowing licit and illicit enterprises to flourish despite a maze of arbitrary and often conflicting laws. The cost of bribing an officer, together with the information a good detective can extract by offering to ignore a criminal suspect's wrongdoing, make corruption a form of "para-legal law enforcement" and "crime control." Corruption in the form of small bribes enables people to obtain services otherwise unavailable, as in the case of a restaurateur who gets an escort to the bank with his day's receipts in exchange for free meals. It offers compensation for the low income and status of police work. Corrupt practices persist in part because they ease lasting problems of law enforcement. Any attempt to combat police wrongdoing must recognize this fact, Bracey tells us; anti-corruption programs must include alternative ways of addressing these problems. Bracey's analysis quite rightly suggests that police corruption must be viewed within its wider institutional and systemic setting and cannot simply be condemned without analysis.

Police corruption poses difficult questions about the quality of law enforcement the public demands and the kind of service it can legitimately expect to get. We have, I think, placed demands upon our police that are contradictory and can never be satisfied. We expect the police to regulate matters of personal morality while respecting the privacy and civil liberties of suspects. We expect them to crack down on clandestine activities while scrupulously obeying regulations on how they may obtain information and gather evidence. We hold them responsible for enforcing myriad regulations dealing with economic enterprise while somehow remaining immune to the pressures and temptations these laws inevitably create. We cannot have things both ways, and one result of these tensions and contradictions is corruption.

As long as we choose to police our cities and regulate individual behavior as we currently do, we will probably have to live with a certain amount of police corruption. Our options do not include having a crime-free urban society and a totally honest police force. We cannot have either one, let alone both. Our choices are instead more like cost-benefit calculations: what sorts of social behavior *must* we police, and what can we live with? How much police corruption is tolerable, and how much is too much? Might we not actually benefit from certain kinds of police corruption, and might there not be situations in which the corrupt cop is also the best cop? Failure to examine these questions in a realistic way may leave us in the sort of dilemma Robert Daley describes in New York, where extensive prosecutions had turned the narcotics detective force inside out:

> There came a day when Assistant U.S. Attorney Rudolph Giuliani, trying to put together a major narcotics investigation with new narcotics detectives newly assigned to him, realized that they were all inept. They couldn't tail a suspect without getting made (discovered). They couldn't conduct a surveillance without calling in that they were lost. They never played hunches.
> A great detective, Giuliani thought, should be a man of imagination and fearlessness. A man with a sense of adventure, a man not limited by procedure. In his new detectives, all these qualities were absent, so that he asked himself almost in despair: Where have all the great detectives gone? The answer that came back to him was this one: I put them all in jail.[52]

POLICE CORRUPTION: WHAT TO DO ABOUT IT?

I will discuss anti-corruption policies in fairly brief fashion, for a number of reasons. My purpose here is analysis, not prescription; and, as the preceding section suggested, I see a total eradication of police corruption as neither possible nor entirely desirable. Instead, our policy choices in the police corruption area must be tested against a wide set of goals and considerations involving competing conceptions of morality, due process, and the uses and limits of public power. Such a test is beyond the scope of this work. Anti-corruption programs have also been elsewhere proposed and analyzed in much greater detail than would be possible here.[53]

Many of the popularly discussed remedies for police corruption—revised training and recruitment, more intensive screening at the appointment and promotion stages, psychological testing, and the like—rest on an implicit personalistic theory of police misconduct. As I have suggested, however, institutional and systemic forces have more to do with the development and persistence of police corruption than do individuals' characteristics. Let us briefly look at the sorts of anti-corruption policies these theories might suggest.

Institutional strategies

Institutional factors define the bottleneck that police officers control. There is a limited amount we can do to change that fact; police officers, after all, are appointed to enforce the law, and that often means changing people's behavior and making unpopular decisions. It may, however, be possible to modify some of the institutional pressures bearing upon police behavior.

One institutional change might be the appointment of departmental inspectors with continuing responsibility for police corruption, but who are responsible to the mayor or city manager rather than to the chief of police. Inspectors' staffs could be a mixture of civilians and law enforcement officers, weakening some of the subcultural bonds between investigators and investigated, especially if the law enforcement veterans are hired from outside the department rather than from the ranks. A continuing investigative effort could also avoid the cycles of scandal, reform, and apathy that have occurred in many cities. This sort of investigative office, of course, would be extremely unpopular throughout the force and would evoke resistance similar to that in many cities against proposals for civilian review.

Another administrative adaptation might be to widen the range of salaries and work situations available to patrol officers; the higher salaries and better beats would be used as incentives and rewards for exemplary police work. In most departments today, patrol officers move up a fairly short ladder of salaries and work situations more or less on the basis of seniority rather than performance. As a result, there are few distinct incentives to excel and few penalties for substandard work, short of outright failure. Creation of a new rank of Master Patrol Officer, as has been proposed in New York and elsewhere, could confer added benefits on exemplary officers and serve as a clear message that good police work is rewarded. This step might be an expensive one, however, both in terms of direct salary payments and the bureaucratic burden of added evaluation of police performance. People who equate low municipal expenditures with efficiency might be unwilling to bear the added expense. Further, strict evaluation would run headlong into the problems of officer discretion and low managerial visibility, while wrongdoing might still be protected by peer group secrecy. It might also be very difficult in practice to decide who should be rewarded.

A third institutional strategy focuses on commanding officers. Sherman argues persuasively that commanders' commitment to fighting corruption is crucial to the success of anti-corruption policies.[54] This viewpoint is supported by most of the officers with whom I have discussed corruption. Clearly, if captains and higher administrators are involved in corruption themselves, if they discourage the efforts of would-be reformers, or if they simply decide to do nothing, the cause of corruption is aided. Conversely, a leadership committed to fighting systematic corruption can do a number of things. Commanders can support continuing investigations and create incentives for and offer protection to honest officers who will act against corruption. Commanders can cooperate with elected officials and the public in soliciting information and suggestions about police conduct in the city's neighborhoods. Such anti-corruption procedures must be backed up with strong leadership by example; notice must be served that certain kinds of behavior will not be tolerated. These leadership strategies will never eliminate all corruption, but they could have an influence on how new recruits resolve the dilemmas of police work. It is also true, however, that an intensification of command controls over police behavior may exacerbate the tensions between bureaucratization and professionalism, and between the police and the rest of the criminal justice system.

Related to the issue of commanders' behavior is that of command recruitment. As earlier observations on peer group and managerial secrecy suggest, commanders recruited through the ranks might be less likely to take a hard line on corruption than those hired from outside the department. Lateral entry has increased somewhat in recent years; a comparison of commanders' handling of corruption cases and their career paths might prove quite interesting.

Two other institutional strategies involve the department's relationship with the rest of the criminal justice system. First, perhaps we could reduce the gap in values, expectations, and procedures between the police and the courts. The police department could adopt a more general view of the vice business, for example. It could emphasize *quality* of vice arrests over quantity; the officer who nets a "big fish," or who prepares cases so well that convictions generally result, could be rewarded, instead of simply being asked to bring in a certain quota of arrests each month. Quota systems encourage bad arrests, falsification of evidence, and repeated roundups of "small fry" who are of little consequence in the vice trade. Police officers understandably can become cynical after years of this and may conclude that so long as they meet their quotas not much else matters. The courts, to reduce the value gap, could examine the difficulty of enforcing vice and other sorts of laws and revise their expectations and guidelines accordingly. This is not a proposal to "unleash the police," with all the dangers to civil liberties that might entail, but rather a suggestion that the officer's judgment and street experience be accorded greater credence.[55] Increased cooperation between the police and the courts, however, is much more easily described than accomplished. The obstacles to such coordination range from contrasting training to a wide gulf of social class differences.

The second suggestion concerning the criminal justice system grows out of the first. If officers must break some laws to gather the information necessary to enforce others, and if this sort of lawbreaking can lead to corruption, perhaps we should change the rules governing the obtaining of information. I am not advocating a wholesale repeal of restrictions on interrogation or a curtailing of civil liberties. I am suggesting, for example, that police departments be allowed to aid officers in paying and protecting informants, so that narcotics detectives would not get into the business of holding and distributing drugs to keep informants happy. Or, closer police relationships with prosecutors and the courts could reduce the necessity for detectives to wiretap illegally. We must move with great caution in this area of gathering evidence, for some restrictions are essential to our rights of privacy and the presumption of innocence. But squarely confronting the difficulties of enforcing some of our laws might enable us to reduce an officer's need to break others.

Systemic strategies

The systemic perspective suggests anti-corruption policies fewer in number but broader in scope. Foremost among them is to decriminalize many so-called "victimless crimes." If people partake of gambling, prostitution, pornography, and certain kinds of drugs of their own volition, and if enforcing the laws against them leads to corruption, then what good is the law? If police inspection of bars and restaurants fosters corrupt relationships, why not get the police out of the inspection business? Most of these "crimes" hurt no one, the argument runs, and the laws enacted against them do not so much protect society as impose one group's morality upon others. In any event, vice is big business. To try to stop these activities with laws no one believes in will never work, according to the argument. So why not decriminalize, license, and even tax these activities and take the police out of the bottleneck?

At first glance, this argument makes sense. Many vice activities *are* victimless in an immediate sense; doing away with laws against them might well reduce police bribery and extortion. Viewed in a broader perspective, however, vice is not really victimless at all. Gambling drains off income from many families and communities that can ill afford it. Hard drug abuse ruins lives and may cause crimes. Prostitution is accompanied by robberies and other crimes; many prostitutes are runaway teenagers recruited under pressure of financial need, drug habits, or violence, not by free choice. Feminist groups have recently contended that pornography engenders violence against women, though hard evidence has yet to be gathered. As for "nuisance regulations," many involve legitimate public interests, such as the maintenance of clean restaurants.

The costs and benefits of decriminalization are difficult to compare, if only because the costs are public and the benefits very much private. We might still decide to decriminalize some kinds of vice despite their ripple effects, whether out of libertarian conviction or the belief that the difficulties and futility of enforcing vice laws outweigh their presumed benefits. My point is that if we pursue decriminalization as an anti-corruption strategy, we should not delude ourselves that such a policy would have no costs. It might well reduce police corruption, but there would come a point beyond which its indirect costs would decisively outweigh the presumed benefits.

A related systemic proposal is to keep certain kinds of laws but assign their enforcement to someone other than the police. Why not let the health department license taverns and let the state police or FBI fight the drug trade? The problem here is fairly clear: police corruption might be reduced, but someone else would be put into the same kind of bottleneck. The locus of corruption would shift—tavernkeepers would now pay off the health inspectors—but the amount of corruption would not change. Indeed, the quality of law enforcement would deteriorate, at least for a time, as new authorities would be moving into new territory with almost no information to go on.

The final recommendation suggested by the systemic perspective is perhaps the most difficult of all, but it may hold some promise. The recommendation is that the public and its elected officials have a continuing and comprehensive concern and understanding for the complexities and contradictions of the police officer's lot. This involves careful thought about the laws we enact, the social and economic roots of crime, and the inherent conflicts involved in enforcing any law upon a highly skeptical and individualistic public. It even involves asking whether we could live up to the standards we impose on others. A former Denver police officer who resigned in disgrace during a police scandal made this sort of point when he was asked what should be done about police corruption: "Take an interest in the policeman, his family, his tensions, his fears, his standing in the community, and his future and you'll be buying yourself the best possible insurance policy."[56]

This approach would not necessarily make big-city police forces honest overnight, or indeed ever. It might, however, reduce the alienation and estrangement between ourselves and the people we have chosen as our guardians. Intangible as this strategy is, it might ease some of the systemic pressures that cause much of our police corruption.

SUMMARY

No one knows how much police corruption takes place, but we do know that it is a widespread problem. Departments vary in the pervasiveness and degree of organization of police misconduct. In some cities, only a few officers are involved, and they "take" only when an offer comes their way. In other cities, organized rings rake in thousands of dollars each month in effective and systematic schemes of extortion. Personalistic, institutional, and systemic explanations can be offered to account for police corruption; I suggest that the latter two in combination best account for blue-coat crime. Police corruption, like machine politics, is regressive in its distribution of costs and benefits, aiding haves at the expense of have-nots, but it also raises some fundamental questions about the kinds of laws we enact and the obstacles we place in the way of their enforcement. Total eradication of police corruption is probably neither possible nor desirable, but the institutional and systemic analyses offer at least a few suggestions for policy-makers concerned about corruption.

Notes

1. August Vollmer, *The Police and Modern Society* (Berkeley, Calif.: University of California Press, 1936), pp. 222.
2. Lawrence W. Sherman, *Police Corruption: A Sociological Perspective* (New York: Doubleday, 1974), pp. 40–41. A number of works on the general issue of police corruption are listed in the Selected Bibliography at the end of this book.
3. *Ibid.*, p. 41.
4. *Ibid.*, pp. 43–44.
5. *Ibid.*, pp. 41–43; V. O. Key, "Police Graft," *American Journal of Sociology*, 40:5 (March 1935), pp. 624–636.
6. New York City, Knapp Commission, *The Knapp Commission Report on Police Corruption* (New York: George Braziller, 1973). A useful summary of the commission's findings and principal recommendations appears on pp. 1–34.
7. *New York Times* Information Bank, July 1–October 1, 1979. The *NYT* Information Bank for the entire year 1978 contains more than 350 reports of police misconduct, not including reports from New York City itself.
8. Jonathan Rubinstein, *City Police* (New York: Farrar, Strauss and Giroux, 1973), p. 103.
9. *Chicago Tribune*, August 28, 1979, p. 1; August 29, 1979, p. 1.
10. Ellwyn R. Stoddard, "The Informal 'Code' of Police Deviancy: A Group Approach to 'Blue-Coat Crime,' " *Journal of Criminal Law, Criminology, and Police Science*, 59:2 (1968), pp. 201–213.
11. A discussion of the way the courts have come to handle the bribery/extortion distinction appears in Herbert J. Stern, "Prosecutions of Local Political Corruption Under the Hobbs Act: The Unnecessary Distinction Between Bribery and Extortion," *Seton Hall Law Review*, 3:1 (Fall 1971), pp. 1–17.
12. From *Police Corruption: A Sociological Perspective*, by L. W. Sherman, p. 11. (Copyright © 1974 by L. W. Sherman (New York: Doubleday, 1974). Reprinted by permission.)

13. *Ibid.*, pp. 9–10; see also David H. Bayley, *The Police and Political Development in India* (Princeton, N.J.: Princeton University Press, 1969).
14. This discussion is based upon Sherman, *Police Corruption*, pp. 10–12; Knapp Commission, pp. 61–69, 71–87; Rubinstein, pp. 390–423; and Key, *passim*.
15. Albert J. Reiss, *The Police and the Public* (New Haven, Conn.: Yale University Press, 1971), pp. 156, 160.
16. *Ibid.*, pp. 161–162.
17. *Ibid.*, p. 169. (From *The Police and the Public*, by A. J. Reiss. Copyright © 1971 by Yale University Press. This and all other quotations from this source are reprinted by permission.)
18. See, for example, the recollections of "Officer Smith," who was dismissed from a midwestern police department because of his involvement in active criminality, as reported in Stoddard, op. cit.; and the similar account of an ex-cop in Denver, reported in Mort Stern, "What Makes a Policeman Go Wrong?" *Journal of Criminal Law, Criminology, and Police Science*, 53:1 (March 1962), pp. 97–101.
19. Arthur Neiderhoffer, *Behind the Shield: The Police in Urban Society*, (Garden City, N.Y.: Doubleday, 1967), pp. 134–136. The large number of Irish officers bears out the age-old stereotype of the red-headed cop with a brogue. Irish-Americans have gone into police work in great numbers for several generations. Neiderhoffer quotes the "half-serious" observation of a former New York Police Commissioner that "if it weren't for the Irish, there would be no police. And if it weren't for the Irish, there would be no need for them." Neiderhoffer estimated, overall, that in the mid-1960s about 11,000 members (40%) of the New York police were Irish-American; this, in a city whose total population was at most about 10% Irish. *Ibid.*, pp. 135–136.
20. *Ibid.*, p. 37.
21. *Ibid.*, pp. 33–38. Working-class job categories as designated by Neiderhoffer included Clerical; Sales; Protective Service; Skilled, Semi-Skilled, and Unskilled Workers; Services; and Farm Workers.
22. *Ibid.*, p. 38.
23. *Ibid.*, pp. 103–151, and 231–242, for Neiderhoffer's complete attitudinal findings.
24. *Ibid.*, pp. 37–38. Neiderhoffer wrote his analysis before many women began to become police officers, but his generalizations seem likely to apply to working and middle-class women, at least somewhat, as well as to men.
25. See, for example, H. Carlson, R. E. Thayer, and A. C. Germann, "Social Attitudes and Personality Differences among Members of Two Kinds of Police Departments," *Journal of Criminal Law, Criminology and Police Science*, 62 (1971), pp. 564–567; J. P. Clark, "Isolation of the Police: A Comparison of the British and American Situations," *Journal of Criminal Law, Criminology, and Police Science*, 56 (1965), pp. 307–319; D. J. Dodd, "Police Mentality and Behavior," *Issues in Criminology*, 3:1 (1967), pp. 47–67; Joel Lefkowitz, "Attitudes of Police Toward Their Job," in J. R. Snibbe, and H. M. Snibbe, Eds., *The Urban Policeman in Transition* (Springfield, Ill.: Charles C Thomas, 1973), pp. 202–232; and R. C. Trojanowicz, "The Policeman's Occupational Personality," *Journal of Criminal Law, Criminology, and Police Science*, 62 (1971), pp. 551–559.
26. Thomas C. Gray, "Selecting for a Police Subculture," pp. 46–54 in Jerome H. Skolnick and Thomas C. Gray, Eds., *Police in America* (Boston: Little, Brown, 1975).
27. See, for example, Charles Bahn, "The Psychology of Police Corruption: Socialization of the Corrupt," *Police Journal*, 48 (January 1975), pp. 30–36; J. A. McNamara, *Role Learning for Police Recruits: Some Problems in the Process*, (Ann Arbor, Mich.: University Microfilms, 1967); James Q. Wilson, "Generational and Ethnic Differences among Career Police Officers," *American Journal of Sociology*, 69:5 (1964), pp. 522–528.
28. Joel Lefkowitz, "Psychological Attributes of Policemen: A Review of Research and Opinion," *Journal of Social Issues*, 31:1 (Winter 1975), p. 6; see also Richard R. Bennett and Theodore Greenstein, "The Police Personality: Test of the Predispositional Model," *Journal of Police Science and Administration*, 3 (1975); R. W. Balch, "The Police Personality: Fact or Fiction?", *Journal of Criminal Law, Criminology, and Police Science*, 63 (1972), pp. 106–119; M. Rokeach, M. G. Miller, and J. A. Snyder, "The Value Gap Between Police and Policed," *Journal of Social Issues*, 27:2 (1971), pp. 155–171.
29. Lefkowitz, "Psychological Attributes of Policemen," pp. 7–20.
30. *Ibid.*, p. 12.
31. Sherman, *Police Corruption*, pp. 12–14.
32. *Ibid.*, p. 12.

33. Peter Maas, *Serpico: The Cop Who Defied the System* (New York: Viking Press, 1973).
34. Robert Daley, *Prince of the City: The True Story of a Cop Who Knew Too Much* (Boston: Houghton Mifflin, 1978).
35. Maas, Chapters 10–13 and 15; Knapp Commission, Chapters 17–20.
36. Sherman lists a sixth dilemma or precondition—a pervasive status problem—which I would agree is closely linked to corruption. I have not described it here because its roots seem to be more systemic and personalistic than institutional, although departmental recruitment policies do indeed have their status implications. The status problem is not wholly absent from this analysis, however, for a pervasive feeling that police work is underpaid, misunderstood, and looked down upon by the general public is one aspect of the peer group socialization process to be taken up in the section on systemic perspectives. For data on how police compare to other occupational groups in terms of public perceptions, see J. B. Rotter and D. K. Stein, "Public Attitudes toward the Trustworthiness, Competence and Altruism of Twenty Selected Occupations," *Journal of Applied Social Psychology*, 1 (1971), pp. 334–343.
37. Reiss, pp. 121–122; see, in general, Chapter III. Quotation included from Harold L. Wilensky, "The Professionalization of Everyone?" *American Journal of Sociology*, 70:2 (September 1964), pp. 138–140.
38. Reiss, pp. 123–124.
39. *Ibid.*, p. 132.
40. Rubinstein, pp. 378–379.
41. *Ibid.*, pp. 379–380; Daley, pp. 201–204 and *passim*.
42. William F. Whyte, *Street Corner Society: The Social Structure of an Italian Slum* (Chicago: University of Chicago Press, 2nd ed. 1955), pp. 124–126.
43. See, on this point, Gay Talese, *Honor Thy Father* (New York: World Publishing Co., 1971), p. 72. Here, Talese describes young Bill Bonanno's feeling that his father, racketeer Joseph Bonanno, was not really a criminal but rather was merely catering to the tastes and demands of a hypocritical society. See also Jacob Chwast, "Value Conflicts in Law Enforcement," *Crime and Delinquency*, 11:2 (April 1965), pp. 151–161.
44. Gail Sheehy, *Hustling: Prostitution in Our Wide-Open Society* (New York: The Delacorte Press, 1973), esp. Chapter 5, "The Landlords of Hell's Bedroom," pp. 116–154.
45. The major exceptions to this generalization are many prostitutes, and drug addicts who are unable to quit their habits.
46. Rubinstein, p. 454.
47. Stoddard, op. cit.
48. Knapp Commission, pp. 65–66.
49. Dorothy Heid Bracey, "A Functional Approach to Police Corruption," Criminal Justice Center Monograph No. 1 (The John Jay Press, 1976), p. 5.
50. *Ibid.*, p. 8.
51. *Ibid.*, pp. 9, 11, 13, 17, 19, 20, 21, 23.
52. Daley, p. 292 (material in parentheses added).
53. Knapp Commission, Chapters 17–23; W. P. Brown, *A Police Administration Approach to the Corruption Problem* (New York: State University of New York, 1971); Lawrence Sherman, *Scandal and Reform: Controlling Police Corruption* (Berkeley: University of California Press, 1978).
54. Sherman, *Scandal and Reform* and "Police Corruption Control: Environmental Context Versus Organizational Policy," pp. 107–126 in David H. Bayley, Ed., *Police and Society* (Beverly Hills, Calif.: Sage Publications, 1977).
55. Even with an "unleashed" police force roaming the streets, not much of a fundamental nature would change. Crime would still be profitable, people would still want to spend money on illicit pleasures, and cities would still be difficult places to police. Corruption would if anything *increase* under these circumstances, as more coercive and arbitrary police behavior would increase both the suspect's incentives to offer a bribe and the officer's powers of extortion.
56. M. Stern, p. 101.

Watergate

Early in the morning of June 17, 1972, Frank Wills was working his regular shift as a security guard in Washington's Watergate complex.[1] At around 1 A.M., while patrolling an underground parking garage, Wills found a piece of tape over the lock of a stairwell door. He assumed that maintenance workers had taped the lock in the course of some routine job; after all, the tape had been placed horizontally across the lock and was thus visible even when the door was closed. Wills removed the tape, finished his rounds, and took a break.

At 1:50 A.M., Wills returned to the garage and noticed that someone had re-taped the lock. Now very suspicious, he called the Metropolitan Police. Three officers responded and began to search areas accessible from the stairway. On the sixth floor, they found another taped lock and a balcony door propped open. The police began a systematic search of the Democratic National Committee offices on that floor and quickly found the source of trouble—five men, dressed in business suits and wearing rubber surgical gloves, hiding behind a partition. At 2:30 A.M. they were placed under arrest. Police also seized their gear, which included 40 rolls of fresh film, a walkie-talkie, burglary tools, cameras, electronic bugging devices, and more than $1700 in cash, most of it in $100 bills with sequential serial numbers. Clearly, these were no ordinary burglars.

Richard Milhous Nixon spent June 17, 1972, in Florida, resting up from his recent journey to Moscow. The trip had been a success, as his earlier visit to China had been. It had even included a direct television address to the Soviet people. The president's good fortunes abroad were matched by favorable political trends at home. The Democrats seemed likely to nominate Senator George McGovern for president. Nixon was hardly displeased with this prospect, since he considered McGovern the weakest candidate the Democrats could field. His judgment was confirmed in November, when he was re-elected by the widest popular vote margin of all time and won every electoral vote save those of Massachusetts and the District of Columbia.

On August 10, 1974, Richard Nixon became the first American president to resign his office. Nixon's presidency lay in ruins. His standing in the polls was at an all-time low. Key figures had left his administration, many of them facing criminal indictment and trial. The House Judiciary Committee had solidly endorsed three articles of impeachment, and Nixon had lost round after round in the courts in his effort to withhold evidence from his accusers. When Gerald Ford took office that day, he told the American people that a "long national nightmare" had finally come to an end.

ANALYZING WATERGATE

The nightmare, of course, was the Watergate scandal—the most severe political corruption scandal the nation has ever endured. Teapot Dome was simple by comparison; most of its participants were in it for money. Watergate, by contrast, was many scandals. Watergate was burglaries and personal and official misconduct ranging from planning illegal domestic intelligence operations to cheating on income taxes and using public funds to remodel a private residence. Watergate was using the Internal Revenue Service to harass "enemies." It was "dirty tricks" on the campaign trail, illegal or unethical fund raising practices, and efforts to upset the checks and balances among the branches of government. There was even a sideshow: Vice-President Spiro T. Agnew, found to have engaged in bribery, extortion, and tax evasion, resigned in October 1973. Watergate included instances of all four categories of corruption we saw in Chapter 1.

Watergate was also a political turning point. It shook many people's faith in government and politics[2] and spawned a host of efforts at reform. President Ford's "full, free, and absolute pardon" of Nixon was evidence for some that there is one law for the wealthy and powerful and another for the rest of us, and it may have cost Ford the 1976 election. The rise of Jimmy Carter, increased resentment of "big government," and Proposition 13 may all be parts of the Watergate legacy. It is important that we sort out the major components of the scandal, examine possible reasons why they occurred, and look at Watergate and its aftermath in terms of the future of democratic politics.

In this chapter I attempt to perform this analysis by employing the approaches developed earlier in the book. This task poses a problem—just how much can a one-time scandal tell us about corruption? There have been many political machines, and police corruption has been unearthed in any number of cities. From these cases one can isolate common factors and assemble them into a general analysis. But there has been only one Watergate, and it was intimately linked to specific personalities, issues, and circumstances. If massive corruption returns to the executive branch, it will not be identical to the abuses of the early 1970s. Does a one-time episode, then, really offer insights into more general problems, or is it merely an aberration, interesting mostly because it is different? Indeed, can that one-time event really be "explained" at all in terms of lasting institutional and systemic factors? The fact that Watergate happened only once is a sticky problem, and because of it, I think, much "analysis" of Watergate amounts mostly to amateur psychoanalysis of Richard Nixon or to overly detailed descriptions of what John Ehrlichman really said about E. Howard Hunt to Charles Colson.

I think we not only *can* but *must* analyze and explain Watergate. Some aspects of the scandal may indeed have been unique, but others were not. The questions that analysis raises about the modern presidency, about the demands we make on the office, and about the uses and limitations of governmental power are basic ones. Watergate was not some historical aberration; it was a product of long-term trends in our system and institutions. The actions and personalities of key individuals took on importance precisely because they were expressed in the context of these trends and problems. Moreover, the interplay between individuals and situations, between mass and elite, that I discuss in this chapter suggests that the danger of similar episodes in the future remains great.

In this chapter I employ all three theoretical approaches in analyzing Watergate. The main thrust is systemic—that Watergate grew out of mutually reinforcing mass-elite political interactions in a time of polarization and stress. Institutional factors are important, too: the expansion of presidential staff and powers over the years and the environment of strong pressures and weak constraints that characterized the Nixon White House helped convert systemic stresses into criminal conduct. Finally, the personalistic perspective has a place in this analysis, because specific individuals—most notably Nixon himself— played pivotal roles as the scandal unfolded. Personalistic factors do not explain the basic misconduct, but they can help account for strategies of cover-up and response. In a sense, my strategy is to nest institutional and personalistic variables within a wider systemic analysis. No one approach fully explains Watergate, but together they can help us understand the scandal.

One final observation before we reach our actual analysis. To account for the events of Watergate is not to justify or excuse them. At times in this chapter I trace the origins of individual lawbreaking to the historical development of the executive branch and to political and social trends. I suggest that in Watergate certain segments of the public got the kinds of politics and administration they asked for. In that sense, Nixon did not "walk away from the job he was elected to do"; he did that job all too well. The important point, however, is that nobody compelled Nixon and his cronies to break the law. Indeed, an important part of democratic leadership is knowing when to *resist* the demands and excesses of one's constituents. Democracy in the Age of Nixon suffered a very close call. My goal here is not to excuse the wrongdoing but rather to make us a bit more watchful of it in the future.

CUTTING WATERGATE DOWN TO SIZE

For connoisseurs of political corruption, Watergate offered a little bit of everything.[3] Some elements of the scandal were clearly illegal, such as the break-ins at the Watergate and at Daniel Ellsberg's psychiatrist's office. Other elements, such as Nixon's claims of absolute executive privilege, were of dubious legality; Nixon eventually lost in the courts on this issue. Still other elements, such as the profanity and locker-room atmosphere of the Oval Office (which to one critic sounded like "the back room of a second-rate advertising agency in a suburb of Hell"),[4] were not illegal but were not exactly presidential either. Some misdeeds were done by the president himself. Other wrongful actions were taken by close aides and associates and still others were performed by peripheral figures. How can we sort all of this into a workable focus of analysis?

Paul J. Halpern, in the introduction to his excellent collection of essays, *Why Watergate?*, provides a workable definition and categories of analysis. Defining Watergate as "the events that eventually led to an investigation by a special Senate committee (the Ervin Committee), an impeachment inquiry by the House Judiciary Committee, and the resignation of a president,"[5] Halpern spells out three categories of activities—partisan, policy, and financial. *Partisan* actions included break-ins, harassment of "enemies," plans for domestic surveillance, and campaign dirty tricks. *Policy-related* activities included the secret bombing of Cambodia, the impounding of funds appropriated by Congress, and efforts to prevent enforcement of integration and anti-poverty legislation. *Financial* wrongdoing included Nixon's tax evasion, the sale of ambassadorships to campaign contributors, and the use of public funds to improve Nixon's private property in San Clemente.[6]

My primary emphasis will be the partisan and policy components of Watergate. Nixon's financial problems were indeed serious: revelations of his tax evasion probably hurt him in the eyes of the average citizen as much as any other aspect of the scandal. However, Nixon's personal finances were peripheral to the real damage of Watergate and can be understood rather easily—they amount to abuses of power for personal profit, much like those found in machine politics. Campaign finance abuses, which present more serious analytical problems, will be discussed in Chapter 6.

Partisan and policy activities were what made Watergate stand apart from previous scandals, such as Teapot Dome. They raise fundamental questions about the executive branch and its role in a democracy. They also pose the most demanding analytical challenges and the toughest tests of the perspectives outlined in this book. Halpern rightly regards the partisan actions as the "dominant theme of Watergate." Nixon's attempt to cover up these actions ultimately forced him to leave office. The policy actions are important too, for they amounted to an effort to remove the presidency from the web of checks and balances created by the Constitution. Financial activities are discussed occasionally, but they are not the major focus of this chapter.

THE PERSONALISTIC PERSPECTIVE: OBSERVATIONS ON THE PRESIDENTIAL PSYCHE

Specific individuals played a big role in Watergate. Unlike machines and police corruption, where we have evidence on large numbers of people acting in similar ways, the fact that Richard Nixon and not Hubert Humphrey was president made a great deal of difference. The specific individuals who surrounded him, from Haldeman and Ehrlichman down to Mardian and Ulasewicz, all played unique roles in the scandal. Personal background, values, ideologies, and perceptions presumably had something to do with the important decisions these people made. Hence, it makes sense to accord somewhat more weight to personalistic variables in explaining Watergate than we did in studying other kinds of corruption.

How should such an analysis proceed? We could look at the social characteristics of key actors—such as their ethnicity, family background, or education—but we would have little basis for saying these characteristics "caused" their actions. We could not make systematic comparisons to others of differing backgrounds in comparable situations. There would be problems, too, with examining individuals' "moral principles." If we discounted the participants' self-serving accounts of their actions, we would have little left to go on. People also have a way of applying their moral principles only to certain parts of their behavior: Richard Nixon's personal morality was highly conventional, but Watergate still took place.

Psychological concepts, however, may help us understand how key figures regarded themselves and their circumstances, and why they made the choices they did. There was probably more psychological and pseudopsychological commentary about Nixon than about any other president, even before Watergate. When Lyndon Johnson roared down the backroads of central Texas at 80 miles per hour tossing empty beer cans out of his Lincoln Continental, we regarded this as one Texan's way of blowing off steam. But when we learned that Nixon put catsup on his cottage cheese, some saw this as evidence of dark inner turmoil. Of course, not all of what we know about Nixon is that frivolous. As a boy the future president signed a note to his mother, "Your good dog, Richard."[7] He was strongly affected by the deaths of two of his brothers, his mother's hard work, and his father's temper. In his political career he seemed to move through crises in ritualistic ways. Studying the presidential psychology, then, makes sense: if psychological factors contributed to Watergate, should they not be most significant in the case of the scandal's central figure?

Presidential psychology cannot in itself explain the whole of Watergate, nor can it tell us why there were some kinds of wrongdoing and not others. It can, however, help us understand the president's responses once he got into trouble. Nixon's stubborn and ultimately disastrous cover-up was not unprecedented in his career, and it can be linked to important elements of his personality. Presidential psychoanalysis, however, must be done indirectly—by making inferences from observed behavior—and from a great distance. Hence, the analysis is partial at best and may be superficial. There is some evidence that Nixon may have undergone psychoanalysis at one point,[8] but we will probably never see an account of the experience. Erik Erikson and his students have shown that provocative psychoanalyses can be prepared from secondary evidence, and Mazlish has provided useful insights on Nixon,[9] but we have yet to analyze Nixon's mind directly.

Any psychological analysis of Richard Nixon must be general enough to include his successes as well as his failures. Here, after all, is a man who rose from near-poverty to the presidency. As Halpern has put it,

> What seems to be lacking most in the popular accounts of Richard Nixon's career is an understanding of how the very developments in personal and political style that he made over the years in response to the threat of personal anxiety and political failure (the very behavior patterns that we now condemn) have also been partly responsible for his political successes and his emotional and physical durability. . . . In short, what is missing is an appreciation of the irony in the Nixon history and an understanding of why he refused to abandon his decision-making style and Watergate policies despite their enormous political costs.[10]

The concepts underlying any study of the presidential psychology must be broad ones, then, and we must avoid selecting the evidence to fit the theory. Let us look at three perspectives on Nixon's psychological make-up. First, we will see a critique of the popular notion that Nixon is "paranoid." We will then turn to Garry Wills' description of Nixon's "crisis ritual," and finally to Barber's analysis of the presidential character. Barber's ideas—and, to a lesser extent, Wills'—can help us understand Nixon's response to his political troubles. These responses comprise, as I have suggested (and as Halpern's statement underlines), the central personalistic question of Watergate.

Nixon as "paranoid"

A popular view of the Nixon psyche is that the ex-president is "paranoid," a term often tossed around without much thought. Nixon, the argument runs, felt surrounded by enemies who were out to get him, and he thus lashed out repeatedly at them over the course of his career. Watergate was just the paranoid's ultimate way of striking back.[11]

Nixon did have deep-seated resentments. His campaigns, his enemies lists, and his taped conversations bear this out. This, however, hardly makes Nixon a "paranoid." Paranoia is a psychosis with specific clinical characteristics and correlates. It is not just a sense that the world is out to get us; if this were paranoia, most of us would be paranoid at least part of the time. Any firm conclusion that Nixon suffered from paranoia must await detailed evidence gathered in a clinical setting—evidence that we are unlikely ever to see.

Even if we *could* conclude that Nixon suffered from paranoia, it would not explain Watergate. The partisan component of the scandal did include lashing out at enemies, but there was more to Watergate than that. The policy aspects of Watergate—impounding funds, attempting to usurp the budgetary powers of Congress, resisting legal mandates to desegregate public schools—hardly seem attributable to paranoia. The policy aspects are better accounted for in terms of the president's political conservatism. His financial dealings can be explained even more simply: love for money may be crass, but it is not psychotic. We must remember too that Nixon, whatever his state of mind, did not personally commit all the crimes of Watergate. Many other people and several federal agencies took part as well. The presidency may be the nation's highest office, but it is difficult to imagine that Nixon's every quirk and whim was translated into action. Indeed, some of Nixon's deepest resentments grew out of his belief that many of the people under him were refusing to carry out his orders and policies. The problem of working relationships with subordinates cannot be explained away through psychological reductionism. It is a complex institutional question in its own right, and it is the focus of another section of this chapter.

Presidential responses to trouble

Not all psychological perspectives on Nixon and his downfall presume the presence of a psychosis. Garry Wills has identified in Nixon's behavior a pattern of ritualistic response to crisis, and James David Barber has extensively analyzed what he calls the "presidential character." Unlike commentators who assume that psychological factors are more or less independent causes of events, Wills and Barber return presidential psychology to the political sphere. Wills feels Nixon is best understood in the context of the values and dilemmas of his time. In fact, he suggests that in Nixon the American people got the kind of leadership they deserved.[12] Barber places great weight upon the "power situation" a president faces and upon the "national climate of expectations" at the time he or she serves.[13]

Barber and Wills correctly immerse the presidential psychology in real situations. By so doing, they suggest the psychological concepts need not explain whole situations but rather tell us why presidents reacted to situations as they did. Why, for example, did Nixon order a cover-up? Why not publicly repudiate misconduct, fire a few people, and endure a probably brief spell of public disapproval? Why, once the cover-up had become a clearly disastrous course of action, did Nixon stick with it? Why did he continue to defy the courts and Congress, only to be compelled to release even more damaging bits of information over an agonizing year and a half? Why did he keep his tape-recording system running, and why didn't he burn the tapes?

Crisis rituals. Garry Wills in 1973 likened Watergate to the six crises that gave Nixon's autobiography its title. Wills argued that Nixon thrives on crisis—that it is central to his conception of himself.

> Crisis is a spiritual category in Nixon's mind, a political "dark night of the soul" testing men, making them worthy. "The finest steel goes through the hottest fires." Thus crisis has a definite ritual shape, its stages well marked:
> (1) One must be attacked, and seem defeated . . .

(2) One must withdraw, and undergo purifying disciplines (mainly of lonely study and sleeplessness) . . .
(3) One must make the decision from which all later acts will follow . . .
(4) Once the decision is made, one can counterattack . . .
(5) The aftermath of crisis is very important to Nixon—the time when he must stick by the decision, not losing his nerve, not lapsing into carelessness after the straining soul's long night.[14]

Key elements of this "crisis ritual" are visible in the president's conduct during Watergate. Nixon certainly was attacked, and he frequently seemed to be losing ground, if not being defeated altogether. Several times during the crisis he withdrew to agonize over his fate, frequently in solitude at Camp David. From these ordeals he would emerge with a decision—to fire Haldeman and Ehrlichman, or to release the transcripts, but always to maintain the cover-up (though this of course was not publicly acknowledged), for the cover-up was the product of the first decisions of the crisis in June 1972. Once these decisions were announced, Nixon would swing to the offensive by launching an Operation Candor or by embarking upon a highly publicized journey to the Middle East. Finally, Nixon sought to hang on. Once the cover-up was launched, in June 1972, he stuck with it until its ruinous culmination in August 1974. At several points, he could have rescued himself with a public expression of remorse and some strategic firings; or he could have decided to destroy the tapes and other evidence in order to stymie his accusers. He did neither.

All of us have characteristic modes of action and reaction. Nixon's "crisis ritual" was not itself corrupt, nor did it, in itself, cause others to break the law. It did, however, obscure key aspects of reality. When one's responses to crises become as rigid as Nixon's, one may forget that not all crises are alike and make decisions disastrously ill-suited to the situation at hand. This is just what happened during Watergate, which, as Wills observed, differed from earlier crises.[15] Nixon could not decide things alone this time. Every new strategy made him more dependent upon the decisions of others, not all of whom he could control. He could never make *the* decision.

Much the same frustration emerged during the fourth step, the counterattack. Who, after all, was the enemy in Watergate? Nixon did attack his critics in the media and in politics; but some of the "enemies" were his own aides, employees, and governmental functionaries. As the cover-up unraveled, Nixon may even have seen himself as an enemy. There was no single figure—no Hiss, no Khruschev—to attack, and the counteroffensives quickly dissipated.

The unsuitability of the "crisis ritual" to Watergate is reflected in Nixon's repeated attempts to invoke it. He withdrew several times, made several agonizing decisions (though none that fundamentally altered the choice to mount a cover-up in the first place), and launched several counteroffensives. While he went over and over the ritual, trying to make it work, his presidency crumbled. In the end, the only part of the ritual he could hold onto was "holding on" itself, and this inflexibility cost him the White House.

Why would Richard Nixon do this? Other presidents have avoided this sort of rigidity and dealt with crises in more suitable ways. The answer, I think, lies in Nixon's general orientations toward himself and his work. James David Barber offers a way to understand these orientations in his study of the presidential character.

Nixon as active-negative. "Character," writes Barber, "is the way the President orients himself toward life—not for the moment, but enduringly."[16] If Nixon's pattern of reaction grew out of his character, an understanding of that character might yield an explanation of Nixon's responses to Watergate. Barber, in fact, was concerned early about "rigidification" in Nixon. In 1969, and again in 1972, Barber derived predictions from his analysis of Nixon's character that pointed to critical problems. A full discussion of Barber's analysis is beyond the scope of this chapter, but we can look at the major defining features of presidential character and see how they apply to Nixon and his actions.

Barber feels we can "foresee" a president's character and make useful predictions about his or her behavior by observing where he or she lies along two "baselines":

> The first baseline in defining Presidential types is *activity-passivity*. How much energy does the man invest in his presidency? Lyndon Johnson went at his day like a human cyclone, coming to rest long after the sun went down. Calvin Coolidge often slept eleven hours a night and still needed a nap in the middle of the day. In between the presidents array themselves on the high or low side of the activity line.
>
> The second baseline is *positive-negative* affect toward one's activity—that is, how he feels about what he does. Relatively speaking, does he seem to experience his political life as happy or sad, enjoyable or discouraging, positive or negative in its main effect.[17]

Barber then lays these baselines across each other and obtains four categories—active-positive, passive-positive, and so on—that he uses to study the careers of presidents since Theodore Roosevelt. These are not rigid categories of behavior, marked off sharply from one another, but rather sets of character dynamics that yield behavioral tendencies.

Richard Nixon was an active-negative president.[18] He poured immense amounts of emotion and energy into his political career. *Six Crises*, a revealing title in its own right, contains repeated accounts of political struggle that brought Nixon to the edge of physical and emotional collapse. All this effort brought little fulfillment: Nixon frequently felt alone and hated, saw himself as surrounded by enemies and as lacking the approval and glamour of the Kennedys. I do not suggest, nor does Barber, that an active-negative president is inherently corruptible. Instead, Nixon's active-negative personality contained tendencies that foreshadowed his response to political crises.

Active-negatives are locked in a struggle with both self and environment. If they master the self enough to channel their energies into politics, they can be formidable in their quest for power. An active-negative's combination of high effort and low satisfaction, however, can lead to problems. Barber feared that like Woodrow Wilson (a fellow active-negative whom Nixon greatly admired), Nixon would fall into a "rigid adherence to a failing line of policy."[19] Wilson had his long and losing crusade for the League of Nations; Nixon, it turned out, had his disastrous Watergate cover-up.

In 1977 Barber wrote a new chapter for the second edition of *The Presidential Character*, entitled "Nixon Came True."[20] Here, he reviews predictions he made about Nixon in 1969, as well as his 1972 analysis, and he finds them borne out by Watergate:

> Watergate was Nixon's rigidification . . . . That process was set off by "a serious threat to his power and his moral confidence." Nixon moved into his crisis pattern and tried repeatedly to escape by means of his usual get-on-with-it diversions. When that didn't work, he froze up and ruined himself, along the way sapping the spirit of a political generation.[21]

Presidents face "serious threats" all the time. But Barber and Wills point to what made Watergate special for Richard Nixon. In Watergate, his characteristic crisis responses, forged in the heat of a quarter-century of political conflict, were inappropriate. They did not—indeed, *could* not—work. As failure mounted upon failure, Nixon, who for a lifetime had poured immense effort into unrewarding pursuits, could only hold on for more. The result was disaster.

Assessing the personalistic approach

Wills and Barber help us understand Nixon's seemingly inexplicable adherence to the cover-up. This help in understanding is no small contribution. It was the cover-up, after all, that brought on a constitutional crisis and that eventually did Nixon in. This limited application of personalistic concepts, however, must be tied into the wider Watergate picture. The need for these linkages is illustrated by a few key questions that the individualistic approach cannot answer. First, every president has had frustrations, and many have raged against their foes; why did Nixon's administration produce *criminal* conduct? Second, why Watergate? Why did the widespread abuses of law and power in the Nixon administration take the specific form they did? Finally, why Nixon? If Nixon had such clear resentments and problems, how did he come to be president? These questions, though difficult, can be answered. I address them in the order stated, beginning with the institutional questions discussed in the section that follows.

THE INSTITUTIONAL PERSPECTIVE

Whatever Richard Nixon's state of mind was, the fact remains that many people indulged in misconduct. Whether or not we find personalistic perspectives convincing, we must look at the institutional dynamics of the executive branch to find out how so many shady doings occurred. These institutional factors account for the way orders, resentments, and whims were translated into actual misconduct, and they explain some of the specific forms and targets of wrongdoing, including many in the policy area.

I will begin the institutional analysis by looking at the evolution and the scale of the executive branch. I then discuss the environment of strong pressures and weak constraints in the Nixon White House and the ways they led to certain techniques and targets of abuse.

Building the modern presidency

If a stranger to American politics were to read Article II of the Constitution and then go out in search of the chief executive described therein, he or she would likely return totally baffled. When, the stranger might wonder, did we scrap the model of a limited presidency whose occupant received foreign ambassadors, reported from time to time on the state of the union, and otherwise worked as an equal partner with Congress and the courts? What manner of dire crisis produced today's superstar presidency, the "imperial" office so central to popular conceptions of politics?

These are naive questions, and deliberately so. The answer is that we never explicitly discarded Article II, but instead inherited a presidency vastly enlarged and strengthened by the actions of its incumbents. New presidential roles and powers have evolved over the years. Some of these powers were added in time of crisis. Abraham Lincoln's vigorous actions during the Civil War, for example, including his Emancipation Proclamation and suspension of habeas corpus rights, contributed to the presidential role as a crisis leader. Other new roles emerged as social and technological changes put new problems on the public agenda: nobody ever asked James K. Polk to act on petroleum shortages, for example. Some presidential duties and powers have arisen out of the growth of government—a president must be an administrator, at least indirectly, of 3 million civilian federal employees and of the maze of agencies and bureaus in which they work. Moreover, the rise of mass politics has made the president into a party leader and representative of popular constituencies. We could catalog the president's informally evolved powers in a number of ways,[22] but the basic point is clear: two centuries of politics and policy-making have added significant powers to the office. Though created in practice rather than by constitutional amendment, they are among the most significant tools at a president's disposal. Any chief executive who tried to play it "by the book," using only the powers and duties spelled out in Article II, would be a total failure.

The executive branch has grown with the president's powers. The Constitution does not mention the cabinet departments, but today they make up the bulk of the executive branch and are indispensable to government as we know it. The Executive Office staff has expanded similarly—from a handful of secretaries, aides, and advisers at the turn of the century to 6000 or more persons today, arranged in bureaus and councils, or appointed as advisers, counsels, and special assistants.[23] Within the Executive Office staff there is the White House staff, and it has grown rapidly as well.

Recent presidents have attempted to manage the executive branch in different ways. Roosevelt, Truman, and Kennedy immersed themselves directly in the administration of staff. They maximized, within practical limits, their contacts with advisers and staff and made themselves available for consultation. Truman, in particular, held time open for 15-minute appointments that could be arranged on short notice. Eisenhower and Nixon, by contrast, sought solitude and protection. Nixon delegated supervision of staff to H. R. Haldeman, who in turn rigidly controlled access to the president. Roosevelt, Richard Neustadt points out, maintained clear divisions between his institutional and personal staffs; Nixon, as will become clear later, did not.[24]

How is the growth of presidential powers and staff linked to Watergate? One popular notion is that growth of government is itself bad. But political events are never inevitable—much of the expansion has been caused and justified by the increased scale and complexity of society itself. We should also remember that although expansion took place during many administrations, Watergate took place in only one—Nixon's. The linkage of presidential powers to Watergate lies at a more subtle level, in the kinds of roles that were created in Nixon's White House and in strong pressures and weak constraints upon the people who held those roles. A look at some of these more detailed observations can show us how so much misconduct came to pass.

Life in the Nixon White House

Three factors are central to the institutional dynamics of Watergate. First is a *pattern of recruitment,* through which Nixon surrounded himself with people who shared many of his resentments, but who had no political base independent of that which Nixon gave them. This pattern of recruitment exacerbated two other institutional problems—*strong pressures* to "please the boss" by mixing institutional and personal duties, and *weak constraints* against wrongdoing. The pressures were intensified by stiff internal competition, by frustration over criticism and resistance from Congress, the bureaucracy, and members of the public, and by an inflated conception of Nixon's presidential mandate. Constraints were weakened by a fuzzy definition of roles, by personalization of authority and obligation, and by low internal dissent and debate. These institutional factors combined to make excessive, often illegal actions against partisan and policy-related targets a matter of course.

Patterns of recruitment. Richard Nixon tended to recruit aides and advisers who shared his view of the political world and probably many of his resentments as well. This is hardly unusual; we would not expect presidents to make wholesale appointments of people who oppose them. In Nixon's case, however, a second fact made for trouble. Many of Nixon's appointees were new to politics and public service and had no political base independent of that which Nixon gave them. Franklin Roosevelt had Louis Howe, a man steeped in political experience who felt no compunctions about telling the President of the United

States to go to hell. Nixon, by contrast, had his advertising-agency types whose political stature and clout depended upon the president's pleasure. Whether Nixon was proposing carefully considered policies or simply venting his resentments, these men were all too eager to please.

Strong pressures. The pressures bearing upon these politically rootless men were many and strong. One pressure was the blurring of the distinction between institutional and personal loyalties and duties. Another was strong internal competition to please the "old man," a competition perhaps exacerbated by the authoritarian management style of Haldeman. Other pressures included low access to and contact with the president himself, a collective sense of frustration with enemies real and imagined, and an exaggerated conception of the president's mandate. Let us briefly discuss these pressures.

Richard Neustadt, as noted previously, has observed that Franklin D. Roosevelt maintained a "sharp distinction between 'personal' and 'institutional' staff."[25] In Nixon's White House, by contrast, service to Nixon the president became identified with service and obligations to Nixon the person. Nixon's Watergate tactic of depicting public criticism and official requests for evidence as dire threats to the presidency was a symptom of this obfuscation, as was his disturbing tendency to speak of himself in the third person (instead of "I will not," it was often "the president will not"). The confusion ran deeper still, to the level of routine methods of dealing with problems and even to basic conceptions of what constituted a problem in the first place. John Dean reports that staffers were put to work investigating the creator of "Millhouse," a film unflattering to Nixon. Another investigation was directed against a nightclub comic who worked under the name "Richard M. Dixon."[26] These episodes were not only a waste of time and resources, they were an invasion of civil liberties. They were instances in which the official powers of the executive branch were used for Nixon the man, simply because he (and *not* the presidency) had been subjected to unflattering portrayals in public. This confusion of duties is probably an inherent danger in our scheme of vesting the role of chief executive and symbolic head of state in one person, but rarely has this confounding of the personal and the institutional been so complete.

One particular episode underscores the significance of this problem. Nixon had asked Dean, through Haldeman, to initiate Internal Revenue Service harassment against a magazine that had printed an article critical of Vice-President Agnew. Dean, who felt no such action could or should be taken, turned to Murray Chotiner for advice. Chotiner's reply illustrated the mixture of personal and institutional obligations in Nixon's administration: "John, the president is the head of the executive branch of this damn government. If he wants *his tax collectors* to check into the affairs of anyone, it's his prerogative. I don't see anything illegal about it" (emphasis added). Dean eventually initiated the IRS probe. "Thus," he later recalled, "within a month of coming to the White House, I had crossed an ethical line. I had no choice, as I saw it."[27]

Stiff internal competition to please "the boss," as well as Haldeman and Ehrlichman, was another institutional pressure upon the president's men. Positions on the White House staff are not rigidly defined by law but rather are established, abolished, or merged informally. The nature of one's duties and obligations and the limits of those duties are often learned only from experience, and, once learned, they might change again. There can be a strong degree of competition among staffers as to who will go furthest to please the boss, do favors for important individuals, and thus gain enhanced stature in the fluid, shifting world of internal politics. In the case of the Nixon administration, this competition was intensified by Haldeman's authoritarian style of management. Dean made his office of Counsel to the President into an informal law firm, doing favors for anyone who could return them. He soon found his status, as measured by perquisites of office (such as receiving a copy of the president's news summary and moving into a larger, redecorated office) rapidly on the rise.[28]

This internal competition, together with the crisis atmosphere of the Nixon White House, encouraged staff members to try to "out-tough" each other. Charles Colson gave us the most famous statement of this "toughness" when he boasted "I'd walk over my grandmother for Richard Nixon." In this atmosphere, if one man were reluctant to carry out dubious orders, somebody else probably would do it. So, rather than be "out-toughed" and thus lose face, the first man would often go ahead and do the dirty work. This competition extended to cooking up "tough" strategies of one's own. Colson devised a plan to firebomb the Brookings Institution so a White House henchman could enter the building in the midst of the confusion and steal sensitive papers from a vault. Dean saw the absurdity of this plan, and after some complex maneuvering he managed to get John Ehrlichman to veto it. Dean paid for his dissent: a few days later Egil Krogh told him "John, I guess there are some people around here who think you have some little old lady in you." Dean had little choice but to redeem his image of "toughness" through skullduggery of his own, so he instructed an aide to obtain Brookings' tax records and send them to Krogh.[29] Strong internal competition and efforts to "out-tough" one another thus increased the pressure toward misconduct.

Added pressure to bend or break the law grew out of a collective frustration with the slow pace of legislative and bureaucratic action. Many of the people who came to the Nixon White House brought with them a sense of mission, as we have seen. Converting that dedication into action and accomplishments is a most difficult task, however, particularly when a Republican president faces Democratic majorities in Congress and a bureaucracy that has served Democratic presidents for 28 of the preceding 36 years. Nixon and his aides were convinced that Democrats in Congress and the bureaucracy—particularly lingering Kennedy loyalists—were sabotaging Nixon policy initiatives. Daniel Ellsberg's release of the Pentagon Papers was only more evidence that the administration was surrounded by enemies.

All presidents and their aides become frustrated at one time or another with the difficulty of getting things done. But the extreme depth of frustration in the Nixon administration, and the way delays and disappointments were attributed to "enemies" instead of to the complexity of government, helped cause official misconduct. First, frustrations provided a childish justification for seeking revenge: "Our enemies are not playing fair, so we don't have to play fair either." Second, they pointed to particular targets for revenge. Sometimes the targets were legislators, bureaucrats, media figures, or public critics. Sometimes they were more shadowy groups, such as alleged "Kennedy loyalists" or "liberal leftists" in the bureaucracy. Finally, the frustrations and their attribution led to specific tactics. For partisan enemies, there were campaign dirty tricks, enemies lists, and the planting of rumors. For policy enemies, there were impoundment of congressionally appropriated funds, waging of war in Cambodia without approval, and selective non-enforcement of civil rights legislation. Sometimes, of course, policy and partisan tactics would overlap.

A final strong pressure toward wrongdoing was a collective interpretation of Nixon's mandate as being virtually limitless. Despite the fact that Nixon won in 1968 with a bare 43.4% of the popular vote, his first term resounded with majoritarian rhetoric. Kevin Phillips wrote of a "New Republican Majority," Scammon and Wattenberg saw Nixon's constituency as the "Real Majority," and Nixon himself created (and then heeded the inaudible voice of) a "Great Silent Majority." When the 1970 election cost the Republicans 12 House seats, gained them only two seats in the Senate, and cast a pall over Nixon's 1972 chances, he still claimed that "the real majority" had spoken in his support.

This sort of talk was not invented by Nixon; claiming the support of a majority is a fundamental tactic in our politics. But Nixon's men used this "mandate" as justification for acting on their resentments in illegal and unethical ways. If the majority rules, the argument ran, and if the president speaks for and governs in the name of that majority, then anyone who opposed the president is trying to frustrate the will of the majority. Such opposition is undemocratic; therefore, undemocratic strategies are fully justified in response. Never mind that democracy ideally includes the right to dissent; never mind that "the majority" was at times more imaginary than real and that its "will" was interpreted by the president. Real democratic majorities are shifting, temporary, and never of one mind on any issue, so to get around these untidy problems, why not act in the name of a *silent* majority that cannot speak for itself? The terms and claims of this "mandate" may sound democratic, but in logic and implementation they approach total license.

These institutional pressures—a blurring of personal and institutional roles, stiff internal competition to be "tough," frustrations with the vagaries of democratic decision-making, and an inflated conception of the mandate—all pushed Nixon aides and associates toward illegal and unethical activities. They did not, however, make wrongdoing inevitable. People *can* decide to abide by the law and bear the consequences. Some Nixon associates said no to wrongdoing; others did not. We may never know what made the difference in each case, but we can point to weakened constraints on behavior, which made it much easier to say yes than to say no.

Weak constraints on behavior. Sometimes people manage to stay out of trouble in spite of themselves. When our scruples let us down, we may encounter institutional constraints on our behavior. These can be in the form of incentives (a person who refuses to break the rules may be praised, or even given a raise). More frequently they are negative sanctions (an employee who breaks the rules may be demoted or fired). Constraints may also be active, such as the continuous investigation of conduct, or passive, such as the mere promulgation of rules. In the Nixon White House, institutional constraints were remarkably weak. They were weakened by at least three major factors—fuzzy definitions of roles, personalization of authority and obligations, and low internal dissent, facilitated in the last case by infrequent contact with the president. As a result, there was little to stop a person from converting the pressures already discussed into action.

As noted previously, executive branch roles are often defined loosely, their limits easily altered and expanded as time goes by. Thus, just as there may be no rigid specification of what one should do in a given role, there may be few clear guidelines specifying what *not* to do. Indeed, abiding by one's formal job description was seen in the Nixon White House as a delaying tactic used by "enemies" in the bureaucracy. Moreover, the constraints of civil and criminal law were given little notice. Presidential business transcended normal laws, a notion made explicit in claims of virtually limitless executive privilege and national security powers. Many staffers also held jobs that had no direct analogue in earlier administrations and thus little in the way of precedent to define their roles. Other staffers might have held several posts over the years, their sole common denominator being loyalty to Richard Nixon.

Authority and obligation in the Nixon administration were highly personalized. Dean's dealings with Haldeman, for example, were not structured by an institutionalized relationship of Counsel to the President to presidential Chief of Staff. Instead, it was Dean, personally obligated to Haldeman. Personalized authority can weaken a subordinate's ability to discount a superior's whims, moods, resentments, and, in Haldeman's case, his authoritarian style of management. Personalities like Haldeman's can be buffered by well defined roles and responsibilities, but in the fluid, personalized networks of the Nixon White House, subordinates would go to great lengths to avoid his displeasure— even if it meant doing things that were unethical or illegal.

The factor that did the most to undermine constraints on behavior was the low level of internal dissent. Some presidents, such as Truman, put up with a good deal of argument and disagreement. Franklin D. Roosevelt seemed to relish it. In the Nixon administration, however, consensus and obedience were the rule. Disagreements and debates frequently were regarded as problems in themselves rather than as valuable parts of the problem solving process. Would-be dissenters had to consider that they would probably have to go it alone, perhaps at great personal cost. As a result, few *did* dissent. The president's men continued to concoct and act out schemes that in a more open institution would quickly have been dismissed as ludicrous or dangerous.[30]

The dissent problem was compounded by poor access to the president. Haldeman regulated the flow of people and information into the Oval Office. Competing views on policy and politics were not routinely transmitted to the president. In place of the more open debate and discussions of some other administrations, Nixon's tapes revealed to us an isolated president spinning out "scenarios" in the company of only his closest associates. Particularly important in the study of Watergate is the question of dissent over illegal or improper behavior. If someone wanted to blow the whistle on an illicit scheme, what could he do? He would end up, at best, dealing with Haldeman or Ehrlichman, who, as Watergate unfolded, were more and more deeply involved in wrongdoing themselves. This is not to say that if a whistle blower *could* have gotten through to Nixon, all would have been put to rights. It is merely to note that a system in which subordinates rarely get direct access to the man at the top lacks a key potential constraint on behavior—the threat of executive intervention.

The institutional perspective thus begins with patterns of recruitment of aides and associates and points out factors creating *strong pressures* toward excessive or illegal action and *weak constraints* against it. In no way do I suggest that the way Nixon ran his White House made Watergate inevitable. The institutional focus simply illustrates how misconduct can become institutionalized in a large and complex organization. Of course, that organization did not function in isolation. How these people came to power and what we asked them to do are important questions for systemic analysis.

THE SYSTEMIC PERSPECTIVE

Seymour Martin Lipset and Earl Raab, in the midst of the crisis, wrote that America had long been approaching "An Appointment with Watergate":

> As the witnesses testified before the Ervin Committee one could hear the rustling of a two-hundred-year-old American ghost. The Watergate affair, standing as it does for the whole bag of "White House horrors," was not just the creation of evil men; it was the sympathetic rumbling of a deep strain in American society, of which Richard Nixon has come to seem the almost perfect embodiment.[31]

The origins of Watergate, Lipset and Raab suggest, are not to be found solely in Nixon's head or in the institutional security blanket he wrapped around himself. Instead, they reside in our system and in the ways we use it. In this section I argue that this systemic notion is indeed persuasive. Personalistic factors may account for crucial responses once the scandal broke, and institutional dynamics were important in converting resentments into actual wrongdoing. The systemic perspective, however, best accounts for the way Nixon and company reached positions of power, and it offers an understanding of their relationships with their mass constituency. It points to the political crisis atmosphere of the late 1960s and early 1970s and to the ways ordinary institutions and processes brought forth extraordinary and illicit official conduct. A major implication of this perspective is that Watergate was not merely the political mugging of an innocent citizenry by evil men who somehow sneaked into power. Watergate was the doing of people who held power because a plurality of voting citizens gave it to them. This plurality ceded power to the president and his men with the expectation that they would do certain things with it; and in Watergate, at least some of us got what we wanted. This is not to absolve the Watergate malefactors of responsibility; it is to imply that whether or not such scandals occur in the future is partly up to us.

A systemic approach must ultimately come to terms with two major questions left unanswered by the individualistic and institutional analyses. First, why Nixon? How was it that this particular president, with his resentments and his approach to managing the government, came to power at the crucial time he did? Since Nixon was chosen (indirectly) by a mass electorate, this question directs our attention to his relationship with his constituency. What did mass and elite expect of each other? How did they perceive and communicate with each other? The second major question is this: if extreme official actions grew out of this mass-elite interaction and out of the political crisis of the times, why did they take the form of Watergate? Why the particular targets and tactics that were used, instead of, say, an extraordinary effort at reconciliation politics? The systemic analysis that follows is an attempt to answer these questions.

In a sense, the systemic view subsumes the individualistic and institutional factors already discussed. Nixon's resentments and characteristic responses to crisis were integral to his relationships with the mass constituency and to their demands of him. The institutional dynamics of the Nixon White House provided mechanisms for converting demands and resentments into action. By placing these aspects of Watergate in their wider systemic setting, we can incorporate them into the analysis without assuming that any one thing explains the whole scandal.

The systemic model

Nixon's presidency and the scandal that destroyed it grew out of the political discord of the late 1960s. But Watergate also illuminates problems in our democracy that are as old as our nation itself. Simply stated, the systemic argument is this: In the mid- and late 1960s, the nation was confronted with a number of especially difficult problems, such as ghetto and campus unrest and a war we could not win. Government responded to extraordinary problems in traditional but ineffective ways. To "win" the war, for example, it held to conventional strategy and simply committed more troops and resources to the battle. These responses were not popular; some regarded them as excessive, others as insufficient; few were satisfied. Some constituencies, in particular, became quite resentful, feeling that their own needs and values were being ignored while others who seemed to be the troublemakers were being catered to (recall, for example, the George Wallace constituency). A candidate for the presidency who shared many of those resentments in a very personal way sought to assemble these constituencies of resentment into a winning coalition. The candidate's and his constituents' resentments reinforced each other to the point that, when the candidate was elected president, he and many of his followers considered his win a mandate to take extraordinary actions against extraordinary problems—to deal with them by any means necessary. These extraordinary actions took place against two types of targets. The first type of target was "troublemaking" groups and political "enemies" of the president—the partisan targets of Watergate. The second type of target included those institutions and decision-makers whom Nixon and his men judged ineffective or downright hostile—the policy targets of the scandal. This systemic perspective is illustrated schematically in Figure 5-1.

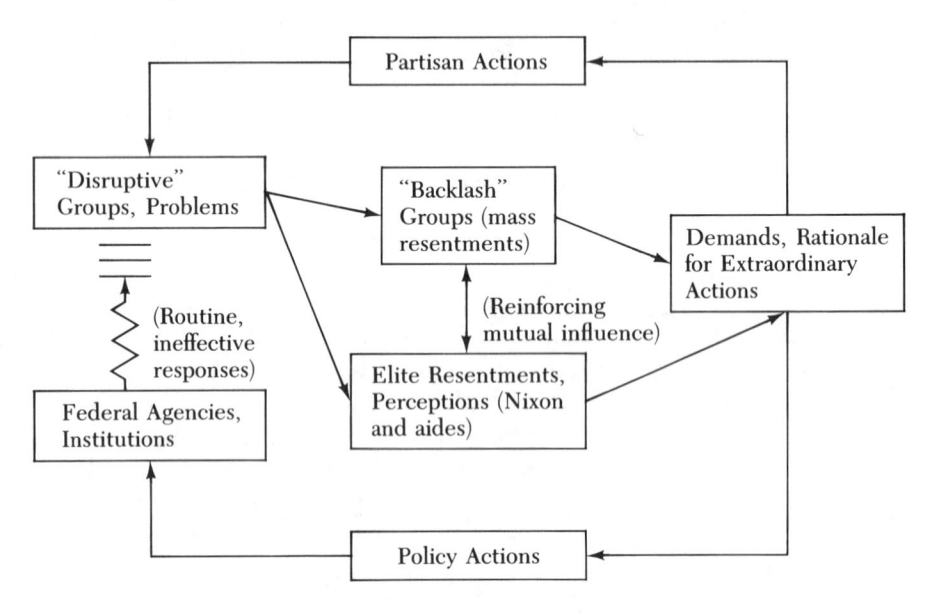

FIGURE 5-1. Systemic Model of Watergate

The systemic approach represented in Figure 5-1 places specific types of wrongdoing in their wider political context and illustrates the partisan/policy duality of the scandal. Further, it holds out a role for mass demands in helping create the scandal, an aspect of the model that raises difficult questions about power and leadership in a democracy. Finally, it suggests that the normal institutions and linkages of our political system, when subjected to extraordinary stresses and demands, can produce extraordinary results. This last, in my view, is the most disturbing long-term implication of Watergate. These problems receive more attention later; for now, let us explore the terms and linkages of the model.

Disruptive problems, routine responses. The social and political unrest of the 1960s has been well chronicled elsewhere. Discontent over the Vietnam war, ghetto insurrections and campus riots, culture conflict over sex and drugs, growing fear of crime—all of this and more made the 1960s a time of polarization, conflict, and resentment.

Government responses to these problems were not as effective as many of the resentful constituencies had wanted. The War on Poverty did not make poverty go away. People who wanted "law and order" still had to put up with street crime and with campus and ghetto militants. War policies satisifed neither hawks nor doves. A nation whose policy-makers had once boasted of "fine tuning the economy" later encountered the nagging problem of "stagflation." Many people were unhappy, and politics-as-usual did not seem to help.

A politics of mass resentment. This combination of disruptive problems and ineffective governmental responses encouraged "backlash politics." Much of the discontent between 1964 and 1974 came from groups such as the poor and minorities who felt that redress of long-time grievances was coming much too slowly, if at all. Especially after George Wallace's 1964 foray into several northern Democratic presidential primaries, however, much of it also came from "backlash constituencies" who felt too much was changing, too fast. Some felt their values were being scorned. Others felt they were being asked to pay the bill for someone else's party. Still others used a resentment of change to clothe old-style racial and class prejudices in contemporary rhetoric. Some people were fearful of threats to their safety or to their social status. Resentments and conflicts between groups are not new to American politics, but more than at any other time since the Depression, resentful citizens were ready to discard politics-as-usual in favor of the politics of retribution.

Elite response. Often, when a large number of people (and potential voters) express strong sentiments that parties and elites do not successfully address, some other elite comes along to pick up the pieces. Such was the case in the 1960s. By 1968, George Wallace and his American Independent Party, with their attacks against "hippies, militants, and pointy-headed bureaucrats," were able to play a prominent role in the presidential race. Wallace for a time threatened Hubert Humphrey in the polls, and there was some concern that for the first time in the century a presidential election would go to the House of Representatives.

Richard Nixon, however, mobilized these constituencies of resentment better than any other national political figure. Wallace, with his accent, his regional base, and his open support for segregation, was at best a long shot for the presidency, whereas Nixon was a bona fide national candidate. He had been vice-president, had represented the entire nation on journeys abroad, and had spent the two years leading up to the 1968 election cultivating a "New Nixon" image—statesmanlike, mature, calm, and reflective. Where Wallace would rail at "the bureaucrats" and seek to block integration by standing in the schoolhouse doorway, Nixon would speak loftily of "the forgotten man," and then as president he would quietly try to prevent the enforcement of integration laws. Both Nixon and Wallace were trying to parlay "backlash" resentments into a national plurality. But Nixon, as Lipset and Raab have observed, was better able to voice these resentments in the "cosmopolitan" style we expect of national leaders.[32]

Just how central this combination of "local" resentments and "cosmopolitan" style was to Nixon's campaign can be seen in an example noted by Garry Wills.[33] Nixon gave a radio speech on May 16, 1968, entitled "A New Alignment for American Unity." In it, he pledged to "forge a unity of goals, recognized by men who also recognize and value their own diversity." It was a speech phrased in lofty, statesmanlike rhetoric. Nixon proposed to unify "the traditional Republican . . . the new liberal . . . the new South . . . the black militant . . . [and] the silent center, the millions of people in the middle of the American political spectrum who do not demonstrate, who do not picket or protest loudly." This, Wills is quick to observe, is a curious coalition indeed: "Nothing positive united Nixon's five groups. Their common note is resentment of government. . . ." This mixture of the politics of resentment with a cosmopolitan style was perfect for 1968: it mobilized backlash constituencies yet offered a presidential image. The style was diplomatic, but the purpose was solely to ride the wave of backlash sentiments into the White House.

Nixon and the backlash constituencies were engaged in a kind of mutual stimulation. The presence of so much bitterness in 1968 made it advantageous for him to campaign as he did. And because he had long been skilled in the articulation of resentments, he was able to shape the diverse discontents of that year into just enough of a coalition to win. Candidate and constituency fed on each other; the resentments and convictions of each reinforced the other's. Agreement between mass and elite is central to the idea of democratic politics, but in a time of polarization and stress, such mutual manipulation led to extraordinary mass demands and elite responses. We installed the politics of retribution in the White House in 1968, and in so doing, we took a crucial step down the road to Watergate.

Extreme demands and responses. This mutual stimulation produced both the demands and the rationale for extreme responses. Though nobody voted for Nixon in hopes that he would bug the DNC, many people did vote for him hoping he would "do something" about hippies, Blacks, liberals, "subversives,"[34] and a frustrating war. "Doing something" could mean many things, but for many Nixon backers (and probably for Nixon himself) it meant being bold and forthright where others had been "permissive" or "gutless." Nixon was seeking a license to engage in the politics of retaliation, and his constituencies were eager to grant it. The targets of retaliation—"disruptive" people and groups and public officials who feared or even sympathized with them—were not, in the Nixonian view, playing the game by the rules. Therefore, retaliation against them need not follow the rules either.

These generalizations, of course, do not apply equally to all of Nixon's backers or aides or even to all of Nixon's own sentiments and motives. Most people who backed Nixon in 1968 were not right-wing zealots but rather people who sincerely felt they were making the best choice for their nation. The point is that resentment, a sense of injury and injustice, and a desire for retaliation were central themes in Nixon's quest for presidential power. Once Nixon reached the White House, they became central themes in policy-making. Here, they joined with the inflated conception of presidential mandate discussed in the section on institutional factors. A license had been granted to "do something" extraordinary, and the president and his men went right to work.

A dual assault. "Doing something" extreme meant many things. It meant unleashing Spiro Agnew and his leaden rhetoric. It meant a bitter and divisive campaign strategy for the midterm elections of 1970, with the president taunting his critics and making shrill "get tough" speeches on crime and campus unrest. Later, it meant efforts to dismantle the anti-poverty programs enacted in the 1960s. It also meant a dual assault on the two major sources of frustration and resentment for the "backlash constituencies"—"disruptive" groups and events, and federal officials, agencies, and programs that could not or would not "do something" about them. These assaults comprised, respectively, the partisan and policy components of Watergate.

We have come full circle, then, from the problems and crises of the 1960s, to the resentments of Nixon and his constituencies, and finally to the extraordinary and often illegal responses they produced. I have defined the terms and linkages of the systemic analysis; it is time now to assess the value of the analysis itself.

Evaluating the systemic approach

Better than either the individualistic or institutional views, the systemic perspective answers two critical questions—"why Nixon?" and "why Watergate?" The first question is illuminated by looking at Nixon's careful combination of resentments and discontent with a cosmopolitan, "presidential" style. This combination enabled Nixon to ride a wave of discontent into power and compelled him to make good on pledges to "do something." The systemic perspective also helps us understand why we got Watergate instead of some other response to the stresses of the time. Nixon and company did not lash out at random. They understood that disruptive events and ineffective responses lay at the heart of their own and their constituents' discontents, and they developed their partisan and policy offensives with those targets in mind. In a perverse sense, they were acting out their mandate. We should recall that as the scandal unfolded many people were not at all bothered by some of the things they learned.

Another advantage of the systemic analysis is that it subsumes individualistic and institutional observations made earlier in this chapter. The question of why official actions crossed into the realm of illegality can be answered by the identification of strong pressures and weak constraints in the institutional section. The ruinous cover-up can be better understood in personalistic terms. The systemic view is not intended to explain the minutiae of Watergate; instead, it pulls the many levels of the scandal together into a comprehensible whole. Finally, a systemic explanation suggests that Watergate was no historical accident, no manifestation of unique flaws in the Nixon psyche. It places Watergate fully in the mainstream of our politics and history and compels us to ask whether or not similar abuses of power can happen again. This question will be discussed later; for now, suffice it to say that I am pessimistic.

One criticism of the systemic model might be that it makes Watergate appear inevitable. It might look inevitable because we are taking a set of (so far) unique events and linking them to the events and tensions of an entire political era. It might appear that once the polarization of the 1960s took hold, we began an unavoidable downward slide.

This is not so, of course. Real choices by real people enter into the systemic analysis at several key points. Nixon's campaign strategy and the decisions to indulge in extreme tactics were such choices. Even the mass resentments were partly a matter of perception and volition. Some blue-collar workers resented aid to minorities and hence supported Nixon or Wallace, but many others did not. The systemic view does not let Nixon and company off the hook by suggesting that people *had* to act as they did. The model simply points to some reasons why they chose those actions.

Another criticism is more basic: how can the systemic view explain one-time events in terms of factors and relationships that are always present in our politics? There are *always* problems and ineffective responses. There are always unsatisfied people and elites who cater to them. There is always at least the temptation to take extreme steps in the name of some goal. Presidents and their aides are always criticized, and they always find the slow workings of government frustrating. The systemic model, it could be said, merely depicts politics-as-usual; how can it account for Watergate? The answer is that Watergate did indeed grow out of politics-as-usual. It grew out of actions, sentiments, and relationships that differed only in degree, and not in kind, from what we see every day. Most of the preconditions for another such scandal are with us today. Watergate could easily happen again.

By way of analogy, consider a mathematical equation, one as simple, perhaps, as the formula for finding the area of a polygon. If we enter moderate values into the equation, we receive moderate-sized results. If we insert extreme values, large or small, we obtain extreme results, even though the terms of the equation and their relationships remain the same. So it is with the political relationships spelled out in the systemic model. Problems are nothing new, but the problems of the years leading up to Nixon's election were more serious than most. A nation that had slept through the Eisenhower years suddenly was witnessing assassinations, campus and urban riots, and a divisive war. Resentments are nothing new either, but by 1968 more people were angrier than at any other time in the recent past. Finally, candidates who cater to their constituencies are not new; indeed, they are an essential part of democratic politics. Richard Nixon, however, was unusually adept at parlaying resentment into political power. The politics of the 1960s placed extreme strains on conventional institutions and linkages. As with the equation in our analogy, what we got were extreme results.[35]

The case for a "politics of patience"

If all of this is true, then Watergate poses problems for democratic politics more serious than the Nixon government's specific misdeeds. They have to do with our demands and expectations of the political system and the people we choose to run it. If in Watergate at least some of us got what we wanted, does this not suggest that we should be careful of what we ask?

Patience and tolerance are essential to democratic politics. Formal provisions for the vote and civil liberties do not guarantee a democratic system. The framers of our government also felt that to prevent tyranny, power must be fragmented, dispersed through a system of checks and balances, and made difficult to amass and hold on a permanent basis. If the same people and factions won all the time, there would be little reason for the losers to support the system, whatever its formal guarantees. But if today's losers can believe they have a chance to win the next time, then they have reason to support the system, to abide by its rules, and to believe in its guarantees. Tensions can be eased even more if there are not just two factions—today's winners and losers—but many, with shifting and overlapping memberships and lines of division. Where this is the case, it is even less likely that any group will always win.

Patience enters in when it becomes necessary to come to terms with political defeat and to remember that losing a few disputes does not justify disregarding the rules of fair play. It was this sort of patience that was lacking in the kind of politics that brought Nixon to power. Nixon's was a politics of revenge, an effort to wipe out past defeats with a victory *now* that would alter the political balance for a long time to come. It was also a politics of polarization, an effort to wipe out multiple and overlapping factions and to align a great "silent majority" against everyone else.

If these values and strategies had been imposed upon an unwilling citizenry by force or deception, then ridding ourselves of Nixon might have solved the basic problems of Watergate. But those values were not forced on us. They were chosen through the electoral process. Not every Nixon vote was a vote for revenge, but many of them were. The implications are disturbing, for, to a large extent, the politics of patience must begin with and be sustained by us.

I do not imply that all was perfect with our politics until Nixon appeared on the scene. It was not. Another assumption of democratic politics—that multiple factions will contend with roughly comparable political resources—did not hold true in the 1960s and does not hold true today. Nor do I suggest that we should refrain from making demands upon our institutions and officials. The point is that what we ask for, how we ask for it, and how we regard the rights and freedoms of those who differ with us will have much to do with whether or not Watergate-type abuses happen again.

More Watergates?

On this score I am pessimistic. One of Watergate's legacies has been political cynicism. Trust in politicians, parties, and institutions was seriously damaged by Watergate (see Chapter 7). Though fundamental allegiance to our political system escaped more or less intact,[36] people now are more likely to believe the worst about their leaders and politics in general. The Proposition 13 mentality is based in part upon the notion that public officials cannot be trusted to spend tax money wisely. I find it disturbing that the predominant mass response to this perceived problem was not to take a more active role in monitoring what governments do but rather to say "leave me (and my money) alone." Birch Bayh, when he ran for president in 1976, claimed that being a politician was an honorable career; his candidacy got nowhere. Single-issue politics—the strategy of drawing a single line of division and demanding victory now—may be the coming style. The greatest irony of Watergate is that it may have undermined the very tolerance and trust necessary to inhibit similar scandals in the future.

Many people who were appalled by Watergate still found solace in the notion that in the end "the system worked." I am not so encouraged, if only because I am convinced that the workings of "the system" helped *cause* the scandal. Even if the system did rid us of Richard Nixon, it "worked" slowly and reluctantly. Key discoveries, such as the uncovering of the White House tapes, were made almost by accident. Nixon's vacillations and his paralysis in the face of trouble did at least as much to bring him down as "the system" did. A more ruthless president, one able to destroy evidence of wrongdoing quickly and decisively, would probably have survived Watergate and served out the full term.

Our chances of avoiding future Watergates also depend, in part, upon the variables identified by the institutional and systemic perspectives. These factors seem to have changed in degree, but not in kind. The institutional and systemic preconditions for Watergate still exist. In the institutional case, executive branch roles and relationships are still loosely defined, and individuals still work in an environment of strong pressures and weak constraints. Jimmy Carter's experiment in restoring cabinet government was pronounced dead at Camp David in mid-1979 and had been in poor health for some time before that. If the wrongdoing of the Nixon White House has not yet reappeared, it is probably only because the memory of the Nixon calamity remains relatively fresh, and not because of any fundamental institutional change.

The systemic dynamics of Watergate continue to exist as well. There is somewhat less polarization now than there was in 1968, but the basic linkages remain much the same, and the situation could change. If continued inflation or energy shortages produce widespread fears of declining status and well-being, severe conflict could arise again as people fight over what is left. It is not difficult to imagine a politics of retaliation emerging from energy and economic crises.

The personalistic approach made a more limited contribution to our understanding of Watergate, helping explain how Nixon reacted once he and his administration ran into trouble. Still, presidential personality must figure in our prognosis. Here Barber reminds us that, although Nixon is gone, his personality could well return. "[Nixon] will be back, in his essentials," Barber writes, "the next time the public elects an active-negative President."[37] It will make much difference who we choose as president. Ironically, it may be that the rough and tumble of mass politics demands and rewards some of the very traits we wish to avoid in our leaders. Benjamin Franklin was pessimistic on this point at the Constitutional Convention:

> And of what kind are the men that will strive for this profitable preeminence, through all the bustle of cabal, the heat of contention, the infinite mutual abuse of parties, tearing to pieces the best of characters? It will not be the wise and moderate, the lovers of peace and good order, the men fittest for the trust. It will be the bold and the violent, the men of strong passions and indefatigable activity in their selfish pursuits. These will thrust themselves into your government, and be your rulers.[38]

If Franklin is even half right, we had better pay attention to the recruitment of national elites on a continuing basis—not just on election day. By then it may be too late.

BEYOND WATERGATE: CONSEQUENCES AND REFORMS

Winners and losers in Watergate

Watergate is the most difficult of our three types of corruption in terms of assessing winners and losers. The scandal was large and diverse, and many of the things that were won or lost (strategic advantage in a campaign, trust in elected officials) were shared widely or were intangible. The financial component of Watergate is fairly simple in its pattern of costs and benefits. Nixon, through his tax manipulations and in the remodeling of his San Clemente house, reaped monetary and material benefits at the expense of taxpayers and public agencies. The partisan and policy dimensions of the scandal, however, present a more complex picture, a tentative accounting of which appears in Table 5-1.

Despite all the difficulties of assessment and comparison, patterns are visible here resembling those found in Chapters 3 and 4. Generally speaking, *benefits*, many of which were material, flowed to those who had money or special influence and connections. Nixon and company presided over governmental bottlenecks in many areas, such as milk price supports, and they exacted a hefty price from many of those who received such benefits. Another bottleneck involved the sale of ambassadorships to large campaign contributors. *Losses* were both tangible (higher milk prices) and intangible (loss of trust). These losses were borne mostly by people and groups who could not or did not seek influence through money or special connections. Watergate activities, like machine politics and police corruption, were regressive: they benefited the political haves at the expense of the have-nots.

TABLE 5-1. Winners and losers in Watergate (gains and losses in parentheses)

	Major winners	Minor winners	Minor losers	Major losers
P A R T I S A N	Nixon and political associates *(political advantage through "dirty tricks," etc.)*	Nixon aides *(internal advancement, status)*	Workers and voters for victims of "dirty tricks"	Victims of "dirty tricks" (e.g., Muskie) *(loss of political advantage)*
	CREEP and campaign *(weaker opposition)*	"Backlash constituencies" *(largely symbolic revenge against "disruptive" groups)*	Targets of IRS and other harassment	Citizenry *(trust in public officials, institutions)*
			Persons on "enemies list" *(intangible political costs, personal harassment in all three cases)*	
P O L I C Y	Major corporate and special-interest contributors (e.g., milk lobby, ITT, etc.) *(money)*	Nixon aides *(stronger influence over public agencies, officials)*	Consumers (e.g., higher milk prices)	Beneficiaries of impounded programs *(policy benefits)*
	CREEP and campaign *(money)*	Major individual contributors *(sale of ambassadorships, other favors)*	Congress *(temporarily weakened powers of purse)*	Citizenry *(weakened balance among branches)*
		"Backlash constituencies" *(largely symbolic benefits on race, cultural issues)*		Victims of secret war initiatives (e.g., bombings in Laos, Cambodia)
				Minority groups *(non-enforcement of laws)*

Options for reform

Systemic reforms. Most post-Watergate reforms have rested on an implicit systemic view. Many of them emphasize campaign finance problems, suggesting that lax regulations not only allowed Nixon to cut specific deals for money, as in the milk price case, but also made it possible for Haldeman to keep more than $300,000 in his safe for dirty tricks and funded large budgets for such shady dealings as Project Gemstone. Cut back on the amount that could be gotten from each contributor, the argument ran, and "fat cats" would be unable to buy elections. Limit total contributions and there would be none left for the G. Gordon Liddys. We have restricted the size of single contributions to presidential candidates and have set fund-raising ceilings. Federal funds to match small contributions are available to presidential candidates who meet certain criteria of widespread support. Financial disclosure laws were enacted and procedures for soliciting and receiving contributions regulated. These laws have been criticized on a number of grounds; in 1976 Congress rewrote parts of the federal elections law to meet the objections of the Supreme Court. These laws and other campaign finance recommendations are the subject of extended discussion in Chapter 6, where they serve as a case study in the problems of reform. Hence, I will say little about them here except that they often create problems of their own and probably cannot in themselves prevent another Watergate.

The basic linkages and relationships of the systemic model are untouched by reform. It is far from clear that we can alter these relationships: one can hardly outlaw resentment. Nor could we try to prevent elites and their constituencies from seeking to win elections on the basis of shared grievances. Indeed, it is far from clear that we *should* attempt to alter systemic linkages. One fairly sure way to prevent mass and elite from whipping each other into a political frenzy would be to weaken or cut mass-elite linkages such as electoral systems and rights of expression. The framers of the constitution, acting out of similar concerns, provided buffers between mass and elite such as the Electoral College. Mass-elite linkages are, however, essential to democratic politics, and to weaken them seriously would also be to weaken lines of accountability and perhaps invite even greater abuses of power.

We could also alter the systemic model by going to the other extreme—cutting the president's powers. But this has its problems too. Checks and balances would be upset, and the leadership functions that have been added to the office over the years would have to be reconstructed elsewhere. Moreover, if the evolution of the modern executive holds any lesson for us, it is that expansion of presidential powers has never depended upon or been conclusively limited by formal mandates. Reduction of powers might also eventually lead to larger abuses. If Nixon's frustrations over not being able to get things done contributed to Watergate, then a reduced presidency might be even more frustrating, and its occupants might take even more extreme steps to get things accomplished.

Stronger political parties might be able to moderate interactions between elites and mass constituencies, but parties are embedded in a complex social and political context. We cannot simply strengthen the parties without facing up to the many wider trends that weaken them.

Institutional reforms. Here, perhaps, more can be done; yet reform efforts have focused relatively little upon the institutional roots of Watergate. Can we lower pressures upon people in the executive branch or increase constraints on their behavior? This is more easily said than done, but perhaps a White House organization scheme that immerses presidents in decision-making rather than isolating them would be an important step in the right direction. Making the president accessible to others—especially to officials with dissenting points of view—could encourage genuine debate over important issues. Presidents could even strive to institutionalize dissent by seeking out individuals with a variety of views and setting them to work on problems in a competitive way. The appointment of politically savvy individuals with legitimate political bases of their own might break through the dependency syndrome we witnessed in the Nixon White House. These arrangements might lessen some of the pressures upon staffers to go to extreme lengths in service of the president. Such changes would be difficult to establish and maintain, however, as presidents organize their staffs to suit their own working styles. Moreover, as the presidential honeymoon ends and an administration becomes immersed in controversies, all presidents—being human—tend to forget their pledges to run an open presidency and begin to insist on loyalty instead.

Strengthening constraints would be difficult too. Legislative limits on each executive branch role would be cumbersome and perhaps unconstitutional. And, if history is any guide, a president thus constrained might simply appoint new counsels, advisers, and commissions. Dissent within the executive branch might strengthen constraints somewhat, but the freedom to dissent cannot be created by law or executive order. In many cases, people will still find it convenient to get along by going along. Perhaps the most effective constraints are those that presidents communicate to the people around them through their working style and approach to organizing their administrations. These informal constraints, of course, depend a great deal upon what kind of person occupies the Oval Office.

Personalistic reforms? The personalistic perspective on Watergate is intriguing, but it suggests little in the way of specific reforms. The kind of person we elect makes a great deal of difference, but we can hardly administer psychological examinations to potential candidates. All we can really do is examine a person's past behavior and then—in the midst of the hoopla of an election campaign—reach some assessment of fitness for office. We can attempt to organize such observations, perhaps by applying categories such as Barber's to observed behavior. But even if we agree on what sorts of categories to use—no simple question—the connection between personality and conduct is never as clear before the fact as after. Finally, even if we propose reliable standards of psychological assessment that the average voter can understand, the voter will still—quite rightly—balance psychological judgments against many other issues. "Other things" will never be equal enough to allow a choice on psychological grounds alone.

Watergate and the study of corruption

In the analysis of Watergate presented in this chapter I have tried to weave a unique set of personalities and events into the broader scheme of American politics and into the general study of corruption. Watergate can tell us much about corruption, particularly because its seemingly unique events can be traced back to more persistent institutional and systemic problems. If Watergate can be understood in a systemic way, then so can police corruption, machine politics, and other kinds of corrupt activities. We should not be content to explain these more common cases of corruption in terms of single personalities, political quirks, or failures of morality, and thus fail to come to terms with the more fundamental questions that corruption raises about politics and our understanding of it. One of these questions is that of reform. It is that general question, and the specific consideration of post-Watergate campaign finance reforms, that I take up in Chapter 6.

SUMMARY

Watergate can be broken down into three major types of misconduct—partisan, policy, and financial. Because the first two were the most serious and unprecedented aspects of the scandal, they are the focus of the analysis. The personalistic perspective, emphasizing presidential personality, provides a useful understanding of Nixon's responses to the crisis and thus of the cover-up and the administration's defense strategies. It does not tell us how Nixon came to power, or how possibilities for wrongdoing were converted into actual behavior. This latter question is best analyzed in institutional terms. Here, we examine strong pressures to take part in illegal or unethical activities and weak constraints on behavior. Still, there is the question of how such men came to power and of what sorts of constituencies and expectations guided their decisions. These are the concerns of the systemic analysis, which focuses on the ways Nixon and his backlash constituencies turned politics-as-usual into the politics of retribution. The systemic view raises serious questions about democracy in an age of resentment.

The prognosis on our chances of avoiding similar scandals in the future is a pessimistic one. The systemic and institutional factors that contributed to abuses of executive power are still very much with us. The personalistic component—a president with a certain psychological make-up, whether we understand it in terms of Barber's "active-negative character" or otherwise—could be restored as well. Though the details of future scandals may differ sharply from those of Watergate, the potential for significant abuses of executive power remain great. There is no sure prescription for preventing such abuses. Some proposals, in fact, might be worse than the evils they were intended to inhibit. Most post-Watergate reforms are based on an implicit systemic analysis of the scandal.

Notes

1. This account of the Watergate break-in is based upon J. Anthony Lukas, *Nightmare: The Underside of the Nixon Years* (New York: Bantam Books Edition, 1977), pp. 278–283.
2. Roger G. Dunham and Armand L. Mauss, "Waves from Watergate: Evidence Concerning the Impact of the Watergate Scandal upon Political Legitimacy and Social Control," *Pacific Sociological Review*, 19:4 (October 1976), pp. 469–490.
3. Readers interested in the legal case against Richard Nixon might wish to consult the following: Richard Ben-Veniste and George Frampton, Jr., *Stonewall: The Legal Case Against the Watergate Conspirators* (New York: Simon and Schuster, 1977); William A. Dobrovir, Joseph D. Gebhardt, Samuel J. Buffone, and Andra N. Oakes, *The Offenses of Richard M. Nixon: A Guide to His Impeachable Offenses* (New York: Quadrangle, 1974); American Civil Liberties Union, *Why President Richard Nixon Should be Impeached* (Washington: Public Affairs Press,

1973); and Leon Jaworski, *The Right and the Power: The Prosecution of Watergate* (New York: The Reader's Digest Press, 1976), esp. Chapter 11.
4. Joseph Alsop, quoted in James David Barber, *The Presidential Character: Predicting Performance in the White House* (2nd ed.), (Englewood Cliffs, N.J.: Prentice-Hall, 1977), p. 473. (Copyright © 1977 by James David Barber. Published by Prentice-Hall, Inc., Englewood Cliffs, New Jersey 07632. This and all other quotations from this source are reprinted by permission.)
5. Paul J. Halpern (Ed.), *Why Watergate?* (Pacific Palisades, Calif.: Palisades Publishers, 1975), "Introduction," p. 1. (All quotations from this work are reproduced with permission of the publisher.)
6. *Ibid.*, pp. 2–3. In each category Halpern lists additional cases of misconduct, which I have omitted here for brevity.
7. Bela Kornitzer, *The Real Nixon: An Intimate Biography* (Chicago: Rand McNally, 1960), p. 57.
8. Arthur Woodstone, *Nixon's Head* (New York: St. Martin's Press, 1972).
9. Erik H. Erikson, *Young Man Luther: A Study in Psychoanalysis and History* (New York: W. W. Norton, 1958). On the specific case of Richard Nixon, see Bruce Mazlish, *In Search of Nixon: A Psychohistorical Inquiry* (New York: Basic Books, 1972).
10. Paul J. Halpern, "Preface to the Psychological Study of Richard Nixon," in Halpern, *Why Watergate?* p. 202.
11. Max Ways has made a somewhat analogous but better reasoned argument that Nixon was "consumed by self-pity." See Ways, "The Tragic Flaw in the Nixon White House: Self-Pity," pp. 169–179 in Halpern, *Why Watergate?*
12. Garry Wills, *Nixon Agonistes: The Crisis of the Self-Made Man* (Boston: Houghton Mifflin, Signet Edition, 1971), p. ix and *passim*.
13. Barber, pp. 8–9.
14. Garry Wills, "The Outsider on the Inside: Richard Nixon's Seventh Crisis," in Halpern, *Why Watergate?* pp. 191–192. (Wills' article originally appeared under the title "Richard Nixon's Seventh Crisis" in the *New York Times Magazine*, July 8, 1973. Copyright © 1973 by the New York Times Company. Reprinted by permission. Barber also has spelled out a Nixon "crisis ritual" of four phases: "Fastening," "Tensing," "Release," and "Letdown." See Barber, pp. 386–394.
15. Wills, in Halpern, p. 191.
16. Barber, p. 8. (original emphasis deleted). Barber's *The Presidential Character* has occasioned much publicity and comment. For some critical reactions, see James H. Qualls, "Barber's Typological Analysis of Political Leaders," *American Political Science Review*, 71:1 (March 1977), pp. 182–211 (see also Barber's "Comment," pp. 212–225 in the same issue of the *Review*); and Alexander George, "Assessing Presidential Character," *World Politics*, 26:2 (January 1974), pp. 234–282.
17. Barber, *The Presidential Character*, p. 11.
18. *Ibid.*, Part Five, Chapters 10–12.
19. *Ibid.*, p. 347.
20. *Ibid.*, Chapter 14, pp. 457–484. Portions of this chapter also appear in Barber, "The Nixon Brush With Tyranny," *Political Science Quarterly*, 92:4 (Winter 1977), pp. 581–605.
21. Barber, *The Presidential Character*, p. 470.
22. For an account of this expansion of powers with particular emphasis on Nixon, see Arthur M. Schlesinger, *The Imperial Presidency* (Boston: Houghton Mifflin, 1973). See also Edward S. Corwin, *The President: Office and Powers* (New York: New York University Press, 4th rev. ed., 1957); and James MacGregor Burns, *Presidential Government: The Crucible of Leadership* (Boston: Houghton Mifflin, 1965), esp. Part One, Chapters I–III.
23. Thomas E. Cronin, "The Swelling of the Presidency," in Halpern, *Why Watergate?* p. 93.
24. Richard E. Neustadt, "The Constraining of the President," in Halpern, *Why Watergate?* pp. 122–126.
25. Neustadt, in Halpern, p. 124.
26. John W. Dean, *Blind Ambition: The White House Years* (New York: Simon and Schuster, 1976), p. 40.
27. *Ibid.*, pp. 32–36.
28. *Ibid.*, pp. 39–40.
29. *Ibid.*, pp. 45–48. Henry Kissinger and others at the White House suspected that Daniel Ellsberg and Morton Halperin had stored secret documents at Brookings "that would extend the Pentagon Papers into the Nixon years." Dean, p. 45.

30. An extended treatment of the correlates and consequences of low-dissent decision-making can be found in Irving L. Janis, *Victims of Groupthink: A Psychological Study of Foreign-Policy Decisions and Fiascoes* (Boston: Houghton Mifflin, 1972).
31. Seymour Martin Lipset and Earl Raab, "An Appointment with Watergate," in Halpern, *Why Watergate?* p. 17.
32. *Ibid.*, pp. 24–26.
33. This discussion of Nixon's "presidential" rhetorical style is based on Wills, *Nixon Agonistes*, pp. 72–76.
34. Recall, in this regard, Nixon's continual scapegoating of liberal Attorney General Ramsey Clark. After saddling Clark with crime, riots, and allegations of "permissiveness," Nixon always drew applause with a strident promise to "appoint a *new* attorney general." Such talk excited many Nixon backers, who presumably forgot that every incoming president appoints a new attorney general.
35. We have seen this pattern before. Recall, for example, the "Red Scare" and Palmer Raids of the post-WWI era.
36. Dunham and Mauss, "Waves from Watergate," pp. 485–486.
37. Barber, *Presidential Character,* p. 458.
38. Quoted in Halpern, "Introduction," *loc.cit.*, pp. 11–12.

The Dilemmas of Reform

Reform has been an issue in American politics ever since the colonists first began to create their institutions of government. The impulse to return to a social or political Eden by changing our laws and institutions is one of the basic themes of American politics. As Richard Hofstadter has observed:

> A great part of both the strength and weakness of our national existence lies in the fact that Americans do not abide very quietly the evils of life. We are forever restlessly pitting ourselves against them, demanding changes, improvements, remedies, but not often with sufficient sense of the limits that the human condition will in the end insistently impose on us.[1]

Many reforms are aimed at problems having little to do with corruption. Others are attempts to win, or to maintain, political control. Reform does not always improve our politics or yield redemption from past sins and evils. This chapter is entitled "Dilemmas of Reform" because in it I argue that reform is extraordinarily difficult. Still, reform is frequently our response to corruption; it has at times been quite successful; and it frequently produces important political changes, intended or otherwise. So reform is of great interest, and no study of corruption can omit a consideration of it.

The sort of extensive review of reform in America that Hofstadter offers is well beyond the scope of this chapter. Instead, I discuss theories about and difficulties and rewards of reform. My stance is largely a critical one: I argue that some reforms have done more harm than good and that many others are largely irrelevant to the corruption that brought them about. Still other reforms serve the political and economic "haves" while handicapping the rest of us. Yet reform has at times been successful, and where it has, it has been based on careful analysis of corruption and political systems.

The first part of this chapter spells out the general approaches to reform suggested by our three theories of corruption. Then comes a discussion of the difficulties most frequently encountered by reform efforts, ranging from lack of information to a misunderstanding of government's role in society. The chapter ends with a case study of campaign finance reforms, which I contend reflect many of the lasting problems of reform.

GENERAL APPROACHES TO REFORM

Reforms are as varied as corruption itself, but most anti-corruption measures grow out of a particular view of corruption, be it personalistic, institutional, or systemic. Our three theoretical perspectives thus provide a way to categorize reforms.

Personalistic reforms

One approach to reform rests on the notion that we have entrusted public roles and powers to people who cannot or will not use them honestly. This view has generated many reforms, beginning with the oldest of them all—throwing the scoundrels out. Uncounted anti-corruption crusades have proceded on the supposition that changing faces in government would reduce or end corruption. Sometimes this strategy succeeds, at least for a while; often it does not. The old scoundrels may win power again, or their "honest" replacements may become scoundrels in their own right. Or, we may find that the scoundrels were not who we thought they were. Sometimes power resides with low-profile figures who hold no public office but who control the people in office.

Other personalistic reforms seek to change behavior. Some of these reforms are *positive*, in that they are intended to encourage "good behavior" (the definition of which can be a highly debatable issue). Positive reforms include selective hiring, firing, and promotions to sort out more honest or less corruptible individuals. Another positive reform is moral education: those who see corruption as a consequence of weak ethical and moral commitments have proposed periodic workshops and renewed training that would be reinforced by reminders from top leadership that honesty is of the essence in public service.[2] Moral education, it is suggested, helps officials form clear judgments of right and wrong behavior and enables them to resist the temptations of their jobs.

Negative policies rest ultimately on the deterrence value of disclosure and punishment. Typical strategies include close supervision of workers (and often supervision of supervisors), monitoring of work, and auditing of the finances and information flow of public agencies (an institutional reform as well as a way to deter individual wrongdoing). Financial disclosure requirements for officials and candidates are also based on negative personalistic assumptions.

Both positive and negative personalistic reform strategies probably prevent some kinds of corruption. Urban reformers won enactment of several such reforms, such as civil service, and there is probably less blatant thievery in local government now than in earlier days. Still, though the personalistic view of corruption is probably the most popular, it is also the least valid. The reforms it suggests have serious shortcomings, the gravest of which is the assumption that personal factors are the primary causes of corruption. Public decision-makers work within a complex institutional and societal setting and must contend with strong pressures from that environment. The fact that kicking the scoundrels out has so often failed to stop corruption suggests that these pressures are critical influences on official conduct. The bottleneck phenomenon remains a part of decision-making no matter how often we shuffle personnel.

Thus, deterrence strategies encounter some basic problems. Foremost of these is the discovery of corruption in the first place: unlike robbery, for example, corruption is a crime in which all direct parties normally have a strong interest in secrecy. Most corruption never comes to light or is revealed too late to do anything about it. Just as generals supposedly prepare to fight wars of the past, we can enact deterrence legislation against past corrupt practices, and it may be of some value. But we will be hard put to anticipate new corrupt practices before they occur; deterrence may be of little use against innovative corruption. Even when we have unearthed a corrupt practice and devised a law against it, we have not won the battle. Anti-corruption laws ideally should impose costs greater than the expected benefits of corruption, and they should be enforced vigorously enough that deterrence is not undercut by a low probability of getting caught. Achieving this ideal is not easy. The money at stake in major bribery and extortion cases often far exceeds the maximum fines that can be imposed, and enforcement is often so uncertain (especially if there have not been recent revelations of scandal) that persons contemplating corrupt transactions may entirely discount the penalties of the law.

Even this cost-benefit approach overstates the deterrence value of negative sanctions. It assumes that decisions to engage in corruption are orderly calculations in which the would-be malefactor recognizes the same costs and benefits as do those enacting the law. Clearly, this will rarely be the case. It also assumes that costs and benefits are estimated independently for each possible case of corruption. This, too, is a shaky assumption, since a few successful transactions may lead one to further discount probable costs: "They didn't catch me the first few times, so why would they catch me now?" In other cases, such as the Watergate cover-up, early misdeeds are like a bad investment. Just as a bad investment may require one to pour in more and more money, lest the original investment be lost, the early corrupt acts of Watergate had to be covered up with more and more deceptions. This strategy, which Nixon and company pursued to a disastrous culmination, illustrates the way corrupt acts do not always occur independently of each other.

Positive incentives to encourage and reward honest behavior have their problems too. These reforms rest on much the same set of doubtful assumptions about cost-benefit calculation as do negative sanctions. Even if we accept the cost-benefit approach, it would seem that for there to exist any incentive the rewards of honesty would have to at least equal the rewards of dishonesty (both sets of rewards being discounted by the perceived probability of receiving them). This weighting can be difficult to bring about. State-operated lotteries, for example, are touted as ways to compete with illegal gambling yet end up being less rewarding than the illicit game, as noted earlier. Or consider the bureaucrat who must choose between a small "merit raise" and a lucrative kickback scheme: from a cold-blooded cost-benefit standpoint, this is no choice at all.

Positive incentives raise another problem: who decides what constitutes desirable behavior? Public decision-making is a high-stakes game, and honest decision-making is still decision-making. The news media and other political observers can generally identify the sorts of official conduct we do not want, such as the use of public funds for private purposes. But what *do* we want public officials to do? This is a much trickier question, one that is tied intimately to the issue of who gets what out of politics, and one that critics of official conduct frequently do not consider. Our prescriptive standards thus tend to be almost mythical in character (witness frequent reform proposals for "non-political administration"). The urban reform movement provides ample evidence that the power to wrap highly political decisions in the protective cloak of "non-political administration" is a considerable power indeed. At the very least, we should remember that when we set up standards of official conduct we also make important political and policy choices.

Institutional reforms

Personalistic reforms are often "institutional" in that they are enacted through, and enforced by, public agencies. Further, reforms directed at the workings of institutions have personalistic implications. In practice, most reform proposals involve something of both approaches.

My specific concern in this section is the changing of institutions' structures and functions to fight corruption. Americans may be skeptical about the perfectibility of humanity, but we have a long history of tinkering with our laws and institutions and of discarding them outright in favor of new ones. Institutional reforms are of two general types—those directed at improving the housekeeping functions of an agency and those intended to correct biases or flaws in its basic structure. Examples of housekeeping reforms include codification of operating procedures, improvement of internal auditing and cash-flow controls, and stricter regulation of access to strategic information. Structural changes include such reforms as the council-manager plan and "lateral entry" recruitment of police commanders.

Overall, institutional reforms have probably been more effective than personalistic strategies because they are based on a more complete understanding of how corruption takes place. They can significantly affect who gets access to decision-makers, what sorts of deliberations will take place, and what kinds of decisions are eventually reached. Of course, I would hardly claim complete success for these reforms; they have not always produced better policy, politics, and civic life. Institutional reform has yielded a mixture of benefits and costs.

Institutional reforms can probably best attack such corruption as embezzlement, graft, and the illicit use of privileged information. These kinds of misconduct rely on secrecy and the use of one's institutional position and privileges for personal benefit. Institutional housekeeping reforms can make the maintenance of secrecy more difficult. They can modify and monitor the interrelationships of an agency's parts and can at least inhibit corruption. Imaginative malefactors may find ways to circumvent reforms, but others will be discouraged and will either drop their schemes or shift them elsewhere. The more tightly an agency monitors its housekeeping, the more likely employees and clients will complain about the constraints of bureaucratization. In some instances new rules will even occasion new corruption. Overall, however, institutional reforms of this sort do have a record of partial success.

The more sweeping type of institutional reform—reordering entire structures and their relationships with the polity—has been plagued by more problems than housekeeping reform. One reason is that we replace old imperfect institutions with new imperfect institutions. At best, the new structures have flaws and unrecognized biases of their own. At worst—as in the case of the commission form of local government, devised in the wake of disaster—new structures are poorly conceived or adaptable only to a limited range of situations.

A more basic problem with structural reform is that, as noted earlier, governmental structures and rules are almost never neutral in their impact. The creation of new institutions always confers advantages on some people and disadvantages on others. Electing city-council members at large, rather than from wards, may (or may not) inhibit the growth of machines; but it also may work against residentially segregated minority groups. It is true that institutional changes can increase popular confidence in government, at least for a time, and this is an important benefit. But decisions about institutional reform are still decisions about what kind of politics and policy we want, whether we realize it or not. People who *do* realize this have at times used reform as camouflage for their own political agenda.

Systemic reforms

Systemic reform appears rather infrequently in our history, if only because we have tended not to think of corruption in systemic terms. Hence, much of the discussion that follows is hypothetical in nature. There could be many types of systemic reforms, but their common denominator is a focus on government's relationship to society.

The most comprehensive systemic approach can be termed "market-oriented" reform. It attempts to do away with the governmental bottleneck altogether by removing certain goods and services from public control. Consider, as an extreme example of market-oriented reform, the repeal of Prohibition in the early 1930s. Prohibition produced widespread bribery of enforcement agents as well as other sorts of lawbreaking. Lifting Prohibition removed both the incentive to offer bribes and government agents' power to extort payments. Less extreme examples of market-oriented reform might involve inspection powers. If inspectors in a given industry are parties to bribery and extortion, eliminating inspections is one way to end the corruption. A variant on this theme is to maintain inspections but to shift responsibility for them to other agencies. Another market-oriented reform is to maintain government regulation of an activity, such as gambling, but to provide legitimate alternatives, such as state lotteries.[3]

Another major type of systemic reform accepts the bottleneck but seeks to reduce some of the pressures within it. These policies fall into three very rough categories—reforms aimed at the ways people seek to influence decisions, those aimed at the ways decisions are made, and those affecting the kinds and amounts of goods that are allocated. For want of better terms, these can be called "demand-side," "policy-process," and "supply-side" reforms.

"Demand-side" reforms. Many kinds of corruption involve transactions between private clients and public officials. If clients can be made to disdain corrupt exchanges, fewer illicit relationships might develop. This, of course, is easier said than done; influencing government decisions can be a high-stakes game.

One way to regulate demand is to spell out explicitly what clients may and may not do to advance their interests. Campaign-finance laws, for example, place limits on contributors' efforts to get certain candidates elected. It is also generally illegal for citizens to offer gratuities (not to mention outright bribes) to police officers and other officials. Other reforms are more subtle, aimed at changing the image of government and its officials, for example, or discouraging traditional practices that are widely accepted in unofficial settings. In the first case, recall Scott's observations (Chapter 2) on social distance between clients and decision-makers. When a low-status client approaches a high-status, well educated public employee, he or she often sees the official's power as personal and arbitrarily applied. The client may feel the public employee has to be flattered, ingratiated, and possibly bribed. In turn, the public employee may take advantage of the client's trepidations through extortion. In such a situation government could launch a campaign to reduce this social distance by informing citizens of their rights and responsibilities and by portraying officials as approachable human beings using public power in a just and uniform fashion. The limitations of this strategy are obvious: such campaigns may not only be contrary to long-established social stratification and patron/client norms but may also be pure fiction and thus have little credibility among public employees and clients alike.

For this reason demand-side reforms are more often focused upon *specific* kinds of behavior and norms, such as the traditional gift-giving practices found in some nations or the obligations of kinship. It is hard to acclimate people to the notion that gift-giving is not appropriate in dealing with a public employee or that the obligations of kinship end where the public sector begins, although these strategies have at least been attempted, particularly in Africa and Asia. They are directed at the "demand side" of the systemic conception of corruption.

"Policy-process" reforms. These initiatives are similar to many institutional reforms in that they seek to regulate the procedures by which decisions are made. The particular reforms I have in mind here, however, reflect a systemic conception of decision-makers' roles. Reformers could, for example, try to inculcate certain role conceptions in the civil service. This is in a sense the obverse of the notion discussed previously. Decision-makers could be urged to regard their power as institutional, not personal, and to resist norms and pressures (such as kinship or offers of money) that run contrary to prescribed procedures. Again, however, the shortcomings are clear. At best, these role conceptions would take many years to take hold, if they could be effectively taught at all. They might well conflict with deep-seated aspects of political culture or seem utterly irrelevant in a poor nation with a large public sector. More likely, "new role conceptions" would amount to mere verbiage, and many would find it not at all difficult to choose between being a good civil servant or a wealthy one. Many newer nations in particular have established or inherited all the trappings of classic Weberian bureaucracy but have found "appropriate" role conceptions very difficult to create.

A more specific proposal is higher pay for public employees. Higher pay might reduce the attractions of illicit money, lend added status and prestige to public service, and perhaps even increase allegiance to legitimate institutions and norms. Higher pay scales could also make it easier for public agencies to attract and retain skilled and intelligent workers. This proposal is systemic in the sense that it recognizes that public decision-makers work in a real world of competing pressures and incentives. The problem with this proposal—apart from the political and fiscal difficulties it would entail—is that it assumes civil servants take "dirty money" because of financial need. There is no reason to believe that corrupt individuals want only a finite amount of money and would simply substitute "clean" earnings for "dirty." We could argue just as plausibly (and with an equal lack of direct evidence) that the limited pay raises most agencies could offer might merely whet one's appetite for more income of all sorts.

A more general systemic strategy might address the basic problems of policy-making itself by streamlining the process. Routine decision-making processes constitute a bottleneck because they are expensive, time-consuming, and uncertain in their outcomes. People who seek benefits from an agency may become frustrated with legitimate policy processes and seek alternative paths of influence. Officials can take advantage of this frustration by exploiting their many opportunities to use power arbitrarily. Either way, corruption can result; why not simply make the policy process less expensive, time-consuming, and uncertain?

This approach would probably be popular, because we frequently blame all manner of evil on "bureaucratic red tape." It may also have some merit as a reform. But it is a strategy that must be employed cautiously because it has so many implications. Let us recall, to begin with, that in many instances the policy process is not *supposed* to be convenient for clients. Complaints about "red tape" are often rather indiscriminate; little distinction is made between, say, a widow applying for Social Security benefits and contractors seeking to build a bridge for a state government. The widow is seeking benefits to which she is entitled by law, and she is thus entitled to have her claim processed quickly and courteously. The contractors, on the other hand, are involved in a much more complex process in which decisions must be made about the site, the cost and speed of construction, inspections and technical standards of work, and, of course, who will be awarded the job. Decisions here are not spelled out in the law, nor are bridge contracts distributed as legal entitlements; many goals and interests besides those of the contractors must be considered. A streamlined Social Security process is probably a desirable thing and might help prevent the bribery and extortion that have developed in the social-service agencies of some other nations. But streamlining the awarding of bridge contracts would be far less desirable, for quick decisions are not always good decisions.

Reducing the uncertainty of the policy process is clearly undesirable in most cases because it would leave few, if any, decisions to make. That which creates uncertainty for the client creates necessary discretion for decision-makers. Together with the value of the benefits sought, uncertainty can enable public officials to extract necessary concessions and compliance with standards from clients.

Reducing the expense of the policy process for clients is almost as problematical. Bribery may at times be less expensive than normally sanctioned paths to influence: instead of hiring attorneys and consultants, why not buy a bureaucrat? Perhaps this cost differential could be reduced by lowering filing fees, for example, or by requiring less elaborate proposals or applications for some benefits. But this would not necessarily halt corruption. If clients believe they can "buy" benefits outright (thereby reducing uncertainty to near zero), they may well go ahead with illicit deals without much regard to expense. In other cases, "paying up" may have no influence upon eventual decisions but rather may represent the basic "ante" needed to get into the game in the first place. American entrepreneurs have encountered this situation in many dealings abroad; bribe money buys access but not final decisions. Here too, clients will probably decide whether to pay without weighing the costs of corruption against the nominal expense of legally sanctioned processes because the real cost of legitimate strategies is in effect total loss of any chance at winning benefits.

Much of the expense of public decision-making is in fact eminently defensible. Technology and social change raise increasingly complex issues; even routine questions, such as where to locate a new road, can raise tricky technical and political issues that require extensive study. We could cut the cost of building nuclear reactors by not requiring the submission of detailed plans and site surveys, but how safe would we feel after they were built?

I do not totally dismiss the notion of fighting corruption by streamlining the policy process. I would, however, recommend the strategy with great caution, and even then only for the implementation of routine, long-standing policies such as issuing liquor licenses or adjusting tax assessments. In policy formation, in decision-making on issues that are new, highly complex, or technical, or in areas where substantial variations are apt to occur from case to case (such as in the licensing of nuclear power plants), streamlining can do much more harm than good.

"Supply-side" reforms. As a final systemic strategy, we could reexamine the stakes of decision-making. Increasing the number of certain kinds of benefits might reduce corruption by increasing chances of satisfaction through routine processes. Taking other benefits out of the governmental arena (the sort of "market-oriented" reform discussed previously) might remove the need to influence public officials altogether. This sort of reform strategy, however, would throw away so many other important policy choices that it would make the entire approach unworkable. This is an issue of more than theoretical interest; proposals to dispense with various laws and regulations are at times based on promises of reduced corruption. But corruption must be looked at in as wide a context as possible. When viewed in a wider context, costs will often seem small compared to the substantive consequences of the law or regulation itself. In many cases we may decide to keep the policy no matter what corruption surrounds it. Whether we decide to live with that wrongdoing or to fight it, we will then be regarding corruption for what it really is—one of many problems involved in putting public power to use, and not a dilemma so serious that it warrants abandoning worthwhile policies altogether.

No hope for reform?

Although this discussion of personalistic, institutional, and systemic reforms has not held out much encouragement for would-be reformers, I do not mean to suggest that all reform is futile. Reforms of administrative procedures in local government undoubtedly have reduced corruption, and civil service reforms at all levels of government can contribute to less corrupt administration as well. I also do not wish to imply that reforms cannot change politics and policymaking, for they can and do. The problem is that because reforms are implemented in a complex political setting that is only partially understood, their effects may differ greatly from what reform advocates may have had in mind. Charles Jones has observed in the case of Congress that "reform, as a type of policy, is a multifaceted concept. What is intended as change may not in fact be realized. Or what is realized in the short run may be quite different from what develops in the long run."[4] At the very least, reforms can affect which people and issues gain access to the policy process, which deliberations take place, and which decisions result. We should also acknowledge that the success or failure of reform—by whatever standards we choose to judge it—depends upon systemic factors too. Where reforms are backed up by a moralistic political culture (as in Minnesota or Wisconsin), we might expect them to be more effective than in a more individualistic setting such as Pennsylvania or New Jersey. Presumably, other system variables discussed in Chapter 2 will also influence the impact of reform.

What I have tried to do, perhaps by somewhat overstating the shortcomings of reform, is to drive home the point that good intentions alone are not enough to eradicate corruption. Corruption develops and persists because of dynamics fundamental to political systems. Unless reforms are based on an awareness of that fact (and sometimes even if they are), they will not produce desired results and may even do more harm than good.

The next two sections of this chapter expand on these themes. First I discuss the basic dimensions of corruption that make reform so difficult. Then I examine recent attempts to reform campaign financing to see how those problems manifest themselves in actual cases.

WHY IS REFORM SO DIFFICULT?

All reform efforts encounter five problems more or less inherent in corruption:

1. a lack of information on corruption,
2. sporadic and transitory public concern,
3. the sheer complexity of politics,
4. "ripple effects," or problematical extended consequences of reform, and
5. the systematic roots of corruption.

Lack of information: Or, you can't hit what you can't see

No one knows how much corruption there is. We simply have no way of finding out who is engaged in what sorts of wrongdoing at any one time, or what kinds and amounts of malfeasance took place at any time in the past. We do know, for example, that between 1970 and 1979 federal prosecutors indicted 784 federal officials, of whom 621 were convicted. Among state officials there were 359 indictments and 251 convictions; and at the local level, there were 1265 federal indictments and 906 convictions.[5] These data, however, are from only one part of the judicial system, and no one would argue that all corruption is eventually discovered. Reformers thus face a "data problem" much like the one I have encountered in writing this book. We can only make educated guesses about the etiology, incidence, and internal dynamics of corruption.

One reason this data problem persists is that parties to corrupt transactions normally have a strong interest in keeping them secret. At least some victims of muggings or burglaries will report the crimes to police, but in cases of corruption there is frequently no direct victim. Indeed, many kinds of corruption—such as police "pad" schemes or kickback relationships—take place on a continuing basis, and the longer they can be kept secret the more rewarding they will be. Even where corruption becomes known to persons not directly involved, they may decide to ignore it, as we saw in the case of the police.

Another reason corruption is difficult to detect is that many anti-corruption safeguards can themselves be corrupted. Just as an embezzler keeps two sets of books, air force personnel falsified records of aircraft missions in order to cover up secret bombings in Indochina. The data gathering and monitoring systems employed by government agencies to keep track of money, personnel, and equipment can at times be used to cover up the very abuses they were intended to reveal.

Finally, corruption can be flexible, even innovative. Even if we carefully search out the kinds of corruption with which we are familiar, new varieties may emerge elsewhere. Corruption may grow out of idiosyncratic relationships, and those involved may have an interest in adapting to changing situations. Technological change spurs "corrupt innovation," too—local governments may be able to reduce the sort of "honest graft" Plunkitt enjoyed, but can they prevent computer crime in the 1980s?

Because reformers do not know how much corruption there is, they may simply misunderstand the basic problem; certainly they cannot know what new forms will emerge in the future. It should not surprise us, then, that reforms intended to prevent an often invisible phenomenon frequently meet with only mixed success.

Sporadic public concern: The apathy–scandal–apathy cycle

Sometimes we are told that an aroused and concerned public that demands honorable behavior from its public officials could serve as a major force for reform. This may or may not be true; the strength of public opinion as a check against corruption probably depends on the level of government and size of the community, on which regions of the country are involved, and on which functional areas of policy-making are affected. Whatever its *potential* power, however, in practice public concern about corruption tends to be episodic, unfocused, and limited to superficial conceptions of the problem. This is not always the case; public concern during Watergate became quite focused as the scandal developed. A diffuse and superficial public awareness, however, can hinder reform efforts. Even the best reasoned proposals for change require sustained public support if they are to be enacted and successfully implemented.

Concern about corruption swings between periods of scandal and stretches of apathy partly because of the way the costs and benefits of corruption are distributed. While the benefits of corruption often accrue to those who have money, position, or special access, the costs tend to fall upon those who do not have these political assets, who most need the services of public agencies, and who depend most upon formal, legally sanctioned processes for access to decision-makers. Moreover, the rewards of corruption tend to be tangible, concentrated, and obtainable in the short run—as in the case of bribe money—but the costs are often long-term and intangible (such as lost political options). Or, if the costs are tangible, they are so widely shared that they are relatively small for any one person (as in the case of dairy price increases that arguably resulted from Nixon's deal with the milk producers). Thus, few citizens have a *compelling* direct interest in fighting corruption. Episodes of scandal may touch off mass concern, and Peters and Welch have shown that congressional candidates accused of corruption are significantly penalized at the polls.[6] Such allegations, however, rarely lead directly to defeat. In the face of life's other troubles, concern about corruption is often short-lived.

Even when scandal does erupt, public concern is often very diffuse. In Pennsylvania, for example, anger over official misconduct runs deep. It helped Richard Thornburgh, a former federal prosecutor, win the 1978 gubernatorial election. But this anger, for most people, lacks focus: many complain that "politicians are picking our pockets," and they feel that corruption is linked in unspecified ways to high taxes and poorly maintained roads, but popular awareness does not go much beyond that. Media coverage of corruption is almost equally unfocused, with little distinction made between an official's padding an expense account and the widespread abuse of a county jobs program. With this sort of information to go on, it is not surprising that public concern about corruption eventually tails off into cynicism, and then into apathy, instead of leading to a deeper understanding of the roots and results of corruption.

Popular solutions for corruption thus tend to be of the "throw the scoundrels out" variety. At best, enthusiasm for institutional reform is limited to quick fixes, such as "sunshine" legislation. Proponents of carefully reasoned reforms thus have trouble finding public support during periods of apathy, and they have trouble harnessing it in times of scandal. The anger that erupts in the wake of a scandal may lead to the hasty adoption of poorly conceived measures whose failure will only deepen public distrust. Thoughtful advocates of reform may conclude, in fact, that the only thing worse than a public that does not get excited about corruption is one that suddenly *does*.

The complexity of politics: Close encounters with real life

Corruption frequently turns out to be much more complex than reformers imagine. Consider the case of campaign finance. If the problem were simply that "fat cats" were buying candidates and elections, then reforms would be easy to devise (though not necessarily easy to enact). We would simply limit the size of contributions and prevent giving in the name of others. We could then congratulate ourselves on having reformed campaign finance.

In real life, things are not so simple. The more we have tried to reform campaign finance, the more complexities we have encountered. I say more about this later, but for now, consider the following complications:

- Many campaign finance abuses consist not so much of "fat cats" buying elections but rather of politicians extorting from businesses and individuals.
- "Fat cats" are not the only sources of political money; there are many sorts of contributors, and their spending, motives, and timing differ significantly.
- What should be counted as a contribution? Only money, or also contributions in kind? Does spending against candidate A constitute a contribution to candidate B? Does spending to advance a point of view on a current issue constitute a contribution to candidates who take that same position?

- If we provide public financing for campaigns, who should qualify for aid, and on what basis? If we set qualifying standards low, do we flood the field with frivolous candidates? If we set them high, do we prevent new parties and points of view from getting a fair hearing?

Other complications involve the role of political parties, the advantages of incumbency, and desirable levels of spending. What may seem to be a clear-cut problem turns out to be an extraordinarily complex political process. Even carefully devised legislation is apt to substitute new problems for old ones.

"Ripple effects": Sometimes the cure is worse than the disease

If reforms are devised based on poor information about corruption, are rushed into law by waves of diffuse public reaction, and are unequal to the full complexity of politics, it should not surprise us that they can create unanticipated problems. Reforms are also at times inspired by a strikingly non-political view of politics: "efficiency" is celebrated, power is regarded as inherently dirty, and running a government is seen as little different from running a hardware store. But "efficiency" has little meaning in many policy areas (what is an "efficient" way to resolve tenant-landlord disputes?), and much decision-making can hardly *not* be "political." Reforms spawned by these non-political perspectives can create problems of their own by imposing a strait jacket upon political processes. Decision-makers lose needed leeway for bargaining and compromise; segments of the community that have traditionally used political clout (as opposed to economic power or professional expertise) to advance their interests find influence more difficult to sustain. Agencies are hard put to respond to new needs and issues (or changes in old ones) that do not fall within their formal mandates. Reform crusades can raise expectations of increased services at reduced cost, yet these results often do not come to pass; public disillusionment can result. Reform is by no means doomed to failure, but at times it causes problems of its own.

The systemic roots of corruption

Reform advocates sometimes forget that governments function within a social setting and that much governmental corruption involves the active participation of citizens. Failure to take account of these systemic interactions can lead to reforms that miss the mark. What appears to be moral weakness on the part of police officers, for example, may actually be a conflict-reducing response to being caught between the letter of the law and the public's actual tastes. Other causes of corruption may be beyond the reformer's reach: kinship obligations, for example, will not be erased by any amount of legislation.

Another systemic factor that reform usually cannot change is the governmental bottleneck itself. Governments distribute important goods, sanctions, and decisions. Pressures for corruption can and do grow out of that process. We may have to accept those pressures as integral to the governmental process and

The Dilemmas of Reform 153

live with some of the corruption that results. This sort of realism runs contrary to the optimistic non-political outlook of many reformers, but it may be an essential first step in deciding what—if anything—to do about political corruption.

DILEMMAS OF REFORM: FROM THEORY TO PRACTICE

Much of the foregoing discussion has been on an admittedly general level, for I have tried to point out problems common to many types of reform. How do these problems emerge in actual practice? The rest of this chapter examines campaign finance legislation as a case study of the difficulties of reform. Campaign finance laws were the most prominent item on the reform agenda of the 1970s; their successes and problems should tell us much about reform in our political system.

Campaign finance legislation: A case study of reform

One aspect of Watergate that particularly appalled many people was the sheer amount of money Nixon and company had at their disposal. The Committee to Re-elect the President raised $63.2 million for a race against weak opposition.[7] H. R. Haldeman kept more than $350,000 in cash in an office safe, much of it apparently left over from the 1968 campaign.[8] "Dirty tricks" and lawbreaking were well financed. Many observers felt that this glut of money played a central role in the scandal—if not directly causing wrongdoing, then making it much easier to carry out illicit schemes. Whatever part the money played, Watergate fueled an already growing movement to revise the way we fund election campaigns.

Concern about campaign finance did not begin with the Nixon years.[9] Though nationwide mass campaigns were unknown in the early years of our history, running for office could still be an expensive undertaking. "People-to-people" electioneering often involved the liberal distribution of strong spirits, as George Thayer reports:

> One master of this form of campaigning was none other than George Washington. When he ran for the Virginia House of Burgesses from Fairfax County in 1757, he provided his friends with the "customary means of winning votes": namely, 28 gallons of rum, 50 gallons of rum punch, 34 gallons of wine, 46 gallons of beer, and 2 gallons of cider royal. Even in those days this was considered a large campaign expenditure, because there were only 391 voters in his district, for an average outlay of more than a quart and a half per person.[10]

In the early 19th century, the franchise was extended, more voters were allowed to vote directly for presidential electors, and the first American political party system began to take hold. These developments made mass campaigns both more possible and more necessary. By Andrew Jackson's time, widespread distribution of printed material, "macing" of public employees, interest-group donations, and paid "floaters" who voted several times all contributed to an increasingly vigorous scramble for campaign funding. Thayer reports, for example, that the 1828 Kentucky gubernatorial race featured individual contributions as large as $10,000. In the 1838 New York mayoral election, the Whigs paid "floaters" $22 for their first vote and $18 for each additional vote. A year later, a Whig official raised $8000 from various New York businesspeople in the form of cash wrapped in a bandana.[11]

A complete review of campaign finance practices is beyond the scope of this chapter, although highlights would include the rise of urban machines, Mark Hanna's bankrolling of William McKinley, and the role of railroads and oil companies in the politics of several states. Growing concern about such events led in 1925 to the enactment of the federal Corrupt Practices Act. Passage of this law, like that of recent legislation, came in the wake of executive branch scandal, although (again, like the later laws) it could hardly have prevented many of the events that hastened its enactment. The 1925 act limited spending by House candidates to $5000 and limited Senate candidates to $25,000. It required disclosure of expenditures and contributions made with the candidate's "knowledge and consent," and it reaffirmed an earlier prohibition of contributions by corporations and nationally chartered banks. Thayer notes, however, that the legislation was "riddled with loopholes":

> The $5,000 and $25,000 expenditure limitations, for instance, could be evaded simply by claiming that certain expenses were made without the candidate's "knowledge and consent." Furthermore, no audits were required. The reports, filed in Washington, were generally unavailable to the public and were on file for only two years. The law also exempted certain costs such as stationery, postage, printing and telephone bills from the official tally. . . . No primary election receipts and expenditures had to be reported at all. Thus, in states where a primary victory was tantamount to election, the law was next to useless. Finally, the ban on bank and corporate contributions was evaded either by having the money donated in the name of a corporate officer or by setting up "educational" or "nonpartisan" organizations through which the money could be channeled.[12]

The 1925 law also restricted a political committee's contributions to a presidential candidate to $5000, but it said nothing about how many committees could be established. Candidates could establish "committees" comprised of everyone from chiropractors to Croatians and graciously accept $5000 from each. Despite and indeed *because* of its flaws—which made the law a source of very little discomfort to anyone playing politics for keeps—the Corrupt Practices Act remained the basic law governing federal election campaigns until 1972.

In the mid-1960s proposals began to emerge for reforming campaign finance. The idea of a federal tax "check-off" for one dollar contributions to a public election fund was debated in Congress as early as 1966. In 1970 Congress passed the Political Broadcast Act, which, had it not been vetoed by President Nixon, would have regulated media spending. The Federal Election Campaign Act of 1971, a comprehensive law superseding the 1925 legislation, was signed by Nixon on February 7, 1972. The old law was to expire on March 10, 1972, and the new one would not take effect until April 7. There thus ensued a month-long interregnum during which the nation essentially had no federal campaign finance law. The Nixon campaign used this period, during which no disclosure of contributors' names was required, for its most intensive fund raising.[13]

Watergate revelations led to the Federal Election Campaign Act Amendments of 1974, which were a significant turning point in campaign finance law. The 1974 amendments instituted public funding of presidential campaigns and comprehensive limits upon expenditures and contributions, and they established the Federal Election Commission (FEC) to enforce the law. The amendments were challenged in court on First Amendment and other grounds, and in *Buckley* v. *Valeo* in early 1976 the U.S. Supreme Court struck down several of the law's central provisions. Though the court ruled that limitations on contributions were constitutional, it held that limitations on spending could apply only to candidates accepting federal funding. Congress enacted the Federal Election Campaign Act Amendments of 1976 to meet the court's objections and in the process completed the body of law under which federal election campaigns are now conducted.

Here are some of the major provisions of the current law[14]:

- No individual may contribute more than a total of $25,000 to federal election candidates in a calendar year. Gifts are limited to $1000 per candidate in each primary and to $1000 for a candidate's general election campaign. No one may contribute more than $20,000 a year to a political party committee. Foreign nationals may not contribute at all; businesses and unions may contribute only funds collected on a voluntary basis. Cash contributions may not exceed $100.
- Spending limits apply only to presidential candidates accepting public funds. To qualify for funding, a candidate must raise $5000 in contributions of $250 or less in each of 20 states. Qualifiers receive funds matching all private contributions of $250 or less, or the first $250 of larger gifts, during prenomination campaigns. Nominees accepting public funds for general election campaigns may use public funds only. Candidates of major parties (those winning more than 25% of the most recent presidential vote) receive funds in an amount determined for that year by the FEC. Nominees of minor parties (those winning 5% to 25% of the most recent presidential vote) qualify for smaller amounts based on their share of the vote. New parties may receive funds after the election if they win 5% of the vote or more. Public funds are raised through the one dollar tax check-off.
- All contributions in excess of $50 must be reported to the FEC. Individuals spending more than $100 on behalf of a candidate must also report.
- A six-member FEC, appointed by the president and confirmed by the Senate, oversees enforcement and investigates possible violations. No more than three members may belong to the same party. FEC regulations are subject to congressional disapproval.

Clearly, these are sweeping revisions in the ways we finance federal election campaigns. Together with changes in party rules and delegate selection, they constitute what Gerald Pomper has termed a "basic transformation of American politics." Pomper is not exaggerating; he has argued persuasively that a correct understanding of these changes was crucial in Jimmy Carter's rise to the presidency.[15] The stakes of reform can be quite high, and its consequences can ripple outward through the entire political system.

Good intentions, bad legislation: An evaluation of campaign finance reforms

Campaign finance reformers were motivated by legitimate concerns about money, power, and justice in American politics, but the laws they produced are flawed. My critique centers around four problems, each of which corresponds to one of the dilemmas of reform discussed earlier in this chapter—a poor conception of the problem, growing partly out of the difficulty of getting information on corruption; implementation problems, related to the sheer complexity of electoral politics; short-term biases, or "ripple effects"; and long-term problems, illustrating the need for a systemic perspective.

Misunderstanding the problem. There is no denying that campaign finance raises serious questions about political justice, but current reforms suffer from a poor understanding of what those questions are. Although the generalization does not apply universally, reform has in general been directed at what could be called the "fat cat myth." The myth holds that the problem with campaign finance has been that large individual and interest group contributors have become so dominant a force that they have been able to "buy" elections and favorable decisions. Fred Wertheimer of Common Cause in 1976 painted that sort of picture of pre-reform politics:

> We had reached the point in this country where the presidency was on the auction block, where the question of who became an ambassador was a question not of merit but of money, where political decisions were based as much on the capacity to use campaign contributions to buy influence as on anything else. We were faced with a fundamental threat to our form of government.[16]

Recent reforms are consistent with this "fat cat myth." Contribution limits strike directly at large givers, and limitations on spending—a major feature of the 1974 legislation, sharply curtailed by *Buckley v. Valeo*—would have hit "fat cats" indirectly by limiting the amount of money a candidate could put to use. Disclosure is intended to reveal links to large contributors, and public funding drives private money out of general presidential campaigns altogether. If "fat cats" did dominate federal politics, these reforms would probably curtail their direct influence.

We cannot fault reform advocates completely for proceeding on the basis of the fat cat myth, for Watergate did feature a number of large contributors in shady roles. Moreover, available information on campaign finance practices was not nearly as extensive then as it is today. There have indeed been "fat cats" in American politics; for that matter, there still are. It is also true that political donors tend to come disproportionately from the more affluent and educated strata of society: Adamany and Agree report that 24.1% of those in the $20,000-and-over income category contributed to campaigns in 1968, and 32.0% did so in 1972. Among those making less than $5000, the percentages were 3.0% and 3.7%.[17]

Classic "fat cats," however, hardly make up the whole picture. There are many kinds of contributors, giving varying amounts for differing motives with widely varying frequency. Even if we categorize donors by the very rough standards of large, small, frequent, or infrequent, we begin to appreciate the complexities of political finance, as Table 6-1 shows.

Even the rough categories in Table 6-1 show some of the diversity of political contributions. If we were to add motives for giving to the breakdown, or if we used more precise categories (a gift of $1000 is beyond the reach of most people but small potatoes for others), the complexity would increase. Motives are especially important because they range from civic duty (the tax check-off), to personal friendship, to a desire for access or an explicit quid pro quo. Motives vary even among those whose gifts are large and frequent. Welch argues that "economic interest groups contribute in order to obtain access to elected officials [while] ideological groups give in order to influence election outcomes."[18] It might seem that large and frequent givers would still have a built-in edge; some campaigns are financed through a few large contributions. Yet others—notably those of Goldwater, Wallace, and McGovern—have been financed through many small gifts from ideologue/emotional givers. U.S. House and Senate candidates in 1976 and 1978, taken as groups for each year, obtained less than half of their funds from interest groups or in the form of individual gifts larger than $500.[19] A final problem with the myth is that the link between giving money and getting influence is not always as direct as it might seem, as I discuss later.

Defenders of the current laws might reply that by targeting "fat cats," the laws have at least restored a balance between them and other contributors. But this argument ignores the diverse motives, resources, and behavior of the "other" contributors. Reaching a balance among these groups, even if we can agree on what balance is desirable, is not as simple as assigning handicaps to golfers. The argument also underestimates the cleverness of classic "fat cats":

TABLE 6-1. Political contributions classified by size and frequency of gifts

Size	*Frequency*	
	Often	**Seldom**
Large	"Fat cats"	Self-financed candidates
	Special-interest groups	Explicit quid pro quo, bribes
		Affluent ideologues/emotional givers
Small	Partisan givers	Occasional small giver
	"Maced" public employees	Non-affluent ideologues/emotional givers
	Tax check-off	

barred from giving to publicly funded presidential general election campaigns, many large contributors have simply shifted their money to congressional races. Finally, even if it is true that "fat cats" hold disproportionate amounts of power in our society, it is doubtful that their power rests primarily on their ability to finance campaigns. Meanwhile, a law targeted at large, frequent contributors could limit the political options of other people who could hardly be accused of dominating politics with their money. These limitations on choices and expression come in for more discussion later.

Anti-political values? Another misconception implicit in some reform efforts is the assumption that raising and spending political money is inherently dirty business and that campaign spending increases simply because ruthless candidates and their contributors will do anything to get what they want. As a result of this assumption, the basic thrust of recent legislation has been to limit the presence of money in politics sharply, if not to eliminate it.

Politics and campaigns, however, are essential to democracy. Our campaigns do tend to be undignified spectacles marked by an absence of genuine debate on issues, yet even in their present state, they convey information, mobilize citizens to participate in the electoral process, and encourage a give-and-take between mass and elite. Making a contribution, or deciding *not* to make one, is a form of political expression. In particular, it is an expression that conveys, however imperfectly, the *intensity* of one's feelings, something votes cannot do.[20] I readily concede that people with much money to spare can convey that intensity more effectively than can the rest of us. But I would still suggest that contributing to campaigns is a good and valuable means of political expression, one we should not "reform" without careful thought.

Campaigns do cost money. Even the various proposals for "improved" campaigning, such as granting free television time to candidates for presentations on key issues, would cost money. Moreover, the cost of campaigning has risen: candidates winning House seats for the first time in 1974 spent an average of $106,000 on their campaigns; for first-time winners in 1978, the average was $229,000.[21] Rising expenditures, however, do not in themselves show that overambitious candidates and contributors have turned politics into an auction. Spending rises because of inflation and because of increases in the size of the electorate, both through population growth and extensions of the franchise. New technology—the advent of television in the 1950s or today's opinion polling and computerized direct mail—also adds to costs. Campaigns are hastily assembled efforts in which candidates do not have time to find out which techniques work and which do not. So they do as much of everything as they can[22]: if you *can* buy TV time, you *do*. This, of course, drives campaign costs upward.

I do not mean to suggest that we conduct and finance our election campaigns in the best of all possible ways. But to assume that campaigns are unsavory doings funded by dirty money spent in distasteful ways is to miss the positive role campaigns play in democratic politics. It is indeed a very questionable starting point from which to begin reforming campaign finance.

The sufficiency issue. If we regard campaigns, contributions, and spending as potentially good things, then we might ask whether there is too much money in our campaigns—or too little. We might also inquire about the distribution of funding: was the real problem in 1972 that Nixon had more than $60 million to spend or was it that his opponents had so much less? Presumably there is some threshold amount of spending necessary for a fully competitive campaign, an amount that increases with the size and population of the jurisdiction in question. What constitutes "competitive" depends also on the amount of money available to one's opponents. It is hard to see how we open up our politics by driving expenditures down toward—or below—that competitive threshold. Deciding how much spending is appropriate is not easy, but it is only logical that competition would be enhanced by bringing more candidates *up* to that threshold, or even well beyond.[23] Perhaps the most vivid example of the sufficiency problem is found in "safe districts" in the House. In these districts, multi-term incumbents become so secure that few contributors will take a chance on a challenger who will almost certainly lose. Effective competition is starved out by lack of funds.

The sufficiency problem is a sticky one. Congress and the courts have endorsed the idea of using public money to finance campaigns. Yet simply channeling public money to challengers in "safe" districts will not necessarily square things, for Jacobson has shown that incumbents tend to spend only what they must. Faced with a poorly funded challenger, they spend very little; if a well heeled opponent emerges, incumbents normally can raise additional money with ease.[24] So substantial are the advantages of incumbency that even well financed challengers are likely to lose unless they can spend significantly more than the incumbent. Public funds may end the "starvation" of challengers, but unless they are virtually unlimited, they will not make challengers truly competitive.

Another problem is determining who gets public money. Despite the current law's third-party provisions, significant funding during a campaign is available only to presidential candidates and nominees of the two major parties. If we are to have public funding, it should be made more widely available. But how wide is wide enough, or too wide? We gain little by funding frivolous campaigns, yet many third-party and independent candidates are worthy of support. Drawing an eligibility line around public funding is a problem not effectively addressed by the law because its architects were worried about too much money, and not too little.

Money's clout. A final conceptual problem is the assumption that contributions automatically buy influence. Money is an exceptionally versatile political resource, and contributors and candidates can become quite cozy. It does not follow, however, that campaign money automatically buys political clout.[25] Recall, first, that by no means are all important decisions made by elected officials. If anything, there is a tendency at several levels of government for elected officials to set the general outlines of policy and to leave the details—

often highly significant—to bureaucratic agencies. There, decision-making is often removed from campaign contributions by a considerable distance. Recall too that elected officials work within an environment of multiple, conflicting political pressures. A contributor is only one of many people seeking influence— an *important* one, perhaps, but nonetheless only one. The official's actions will not merely reflect contributors' pressure, for as a human being he or she approaches decisions with pre-existing values, beliefs, and convictions. How the official perceives the contributor will influence the outcome too. Moreover, it is possible that the contributor's message is unclear or that opportunities to do something for the contributor may never arise. Finally, although money is necessary to win elections, it is no guarantee of victory. A winning candidate is indebted to many people for many things—endorsements, backing of all kinds from party and organizations, and of course votes—and not just to contributors for money.

Thus, campaign contributions do not necessarily buy influence. Even where it seems to have occurred, the case may not be so clear-cut: consider an imaginary representative from a steel-making district who receives sizable contributions from industry and union Political Action Committees (PACs). If the representative votes consistently for bills benefiting the steel industry, has she been "bought"? Or is she voting pretty much as she would have anyway, given the central role of steel in her district's economy? In fact, the representative probably needs industry and labor much less than they need her. More than 90% of the House incumbents who seek re-election win in most years, and as Jacobson has pointed out, incumbents tend to spend on campaigns only as they must. The representative can probably win re-election without PAC support. She need not even be very concerned about PAC-funded challengers, for why would a PAC risk losing access by backing a long shot opponent? The 1976 congressional elections bear this out: $3.50 in PAC money went to incumbents for every dollar contributed to challengers,[26] a fact consistent with Welch's view that economic interest groups seek access, not specific election outcomes. Access is not the same as influence, and it does not guarantee favorable votes. Thus, few representatives—and even fewer safe-seat, high-seniority incumbents who hold pivotal committee assignments—owe their seats to an interest group. If such incumbents run into political trouble, it is probably because they have failed to represent their districts' interests, not because they have offended major contributors.

Problems of implementation. Three major problems stand in the way of making reforms work—how to identify campaigns and contributions, a data glut, and enforcement difficulties. These implementation problems exist not because reformers drafted sloppy legislation but rather because of the sheer complexity of electoral politics.

Identification and definitions. Exactly what constitutes a contribution or a campaign? These are usually easy to identify, but in some cases they are not, and recent reforms have made such questions both more important and more difficult to answer.

Most contributions are direct gifts (or occasionally, loans) to a candidate's campaign committee. Many, however, are not: Some people spend money on their own in support of a candidate. Others buy advertisements criticizing a candidate's opponent. Still others advertise on issues closely identified with certain candidates. These variations raise problems. If Mobil Oil advertises heavily in favor of oil-price decontrol in a state where senatorial candidate A strongly favors decontrol and candidate B opposes it, is Mobil making a contribution to A? There are other complications: how should we count contributions in kind? What about the wealthy, self-financed candidate? Should his or her own money, or that of family members, be counted in the same way as contributions from others?

Deciding what constitutes a campaign can be just as difficult. Some candidacies are clearly frivolous. Reform legislation has also given us the "non-campaign," in which a candidate who has done badly withdraws from "active candidacy," but continues to solicit contributions and matching funds to avoid debt. In the past, these candidates would have dropped out altogether, but because of the new laws public funds continue to flow to essentially dead campaigns (while active independents and third-party hopefuls receive nothing). John Anderson's 1980 race presents a variation on this theme. By shedding his Republican label to run as an independent, he lost his claim to matching funds during the pre-nomination campaign. Further, he was entitled to no general-election funding unless he won more than 5% of the vote, in which case he would be paid *after* the election. This aspect of the law clearly discourages candidates from exercising a legitimate strategic option, and it could deprive voters of an alternative as well. On the other hand, is an independent effort truly a campaign if it is assured of appearing on the ballot in only a handful of states? Anderson was able to get onto the ballot in all fifty states, but if we provide funds for other independents, should we set some minimum number of states—perhaps distributed among several regions—as a criterion for funding? There are no perfect answers for these questions, for they raise complex issues of political expression and strategic advantage. They are examples of the complexities anyone will encounter in reforming the political money process.

The data glut. There was a time when we knew very little about political finance—when fund-raisers and contributors could operate more or less in secrecy. Recent legislation has changed all that. Frequent disclosure of contributions and expenditures is now required by federal law and by many states as well. Federal reports once went to the Secretary of the Senate or to the Clerk of the House, where they were kept more or less inaccessible for a short time and then discarded. Now they go to the Federal Election Commission and are readily available for study. Never before have we had so much information about money in politics.

The irony is that now we have too much data. Hundreds of candidates each submit many disclosure statements a year, as frequently as a few days apart just before an election. Most reports disclose thousands of contributions and expenditures. Add to this the huge amounts of similar data disclosed under various state laws, and we begin to get a picture of the overwhelming amount of information turned up by the new laws. "Overwhelming" is the right word, for there is so much information that no one—especially during a campaign—can digest and comprehend it. Common Cause labored heroically to report on political finance in the 1972 House and Senate elections; the result was a ten-volume opus that did not appear until 1974.[27]

This "data glut" is more than a matter of inconvenience. One of the key arguments for disclosure is that candidates who disclose shady dealings will be punished at the polls. If voters are ever to exercise this sanction, however, readily-understood information on finances must be made widely available very quickly. Given the crushing amounts of data turned in to the FEC, this is unlikely to happen. In the heat of a campaign, the news media cannot digest and publish the data. Neither can poorly-funded candidates. A well-funded candidate could assign a researcher to check out the opposition's reports, but to use the data in a campaign invites a similar probe of one's own finances.[28] Finally, other electoral factors, such as party label and stands on the issues, will rarely be equal enough to allow most voters to choose on the basis of disclosure data.

Enforcement problems. As with many other laws, there are difficulties in enforcing campaign finance reforms. As suggested previously, sorting out the data submitted to the FEC is such a long and difficult process that violations of the law might be missed or discovered only long after an election. A related problem is the complexity of filing reports: intentional violations of the law might be difficult to distinguish from honest mistakes. Or, contribution limits might be circumvented by methods familiar under the old laws. When a PAC or individual contributor has reached the limit, additional contributions could be made through employees or friends who are reimbursed later. The middlemen would be acting legally, yet the real source of the money could still be made clear to the recipient.

A final, more basic enforcement problem has been pointed out by Adamany and Agree, who note that most of the law's penalties are aimed at campaign committees. This makes some sense, since committees do the bulk of fund raising and spending. But Adamany and Agree remind us that the primary beneficiaries in campaign finance—legal or otherwise—are not committees but rather contributors and candidates. The law may well overlook those with the greatest incentive to indulge in dirty dealing.[29]

Short-term results: Biases and dysfunctions. The problems discussed above grow for the most part out of the sheer complexity of political finance. Yet difficulties with reforms can also cause problems in our politics. This section spells out some of these "ripple effects."

Reform and political expression. Campaign contributions are a form of political expression. Campaign finance laws regulate that expression through both direct limitations and disclosure requirements. Limitations allow one to contribute only so much and to give it only through established procedures. Disclosure constrains expression indirectly: if one's contributions are made public, one may suffer reprisals from elected officials or from the public. Indeed, cases may arise in which would-be contributors can do little but sit on their money. Consider the hypothetical case of a PAC, closely identified with a major business firm, which has some money to spend on House races. The races are too close to call. The PAC and its parent firm have no specific interest in which candidates win, but they want access to the eventual winners. Before disclosure, the PAC might simply have given to both major candidates in close races, perhaps tilting a bit toward the one who seemed more sympathetic on key issues. With disclosure, however, the logic changes: one does not want to be on record as having contributed to the winner's opponent because the winner might get revenge by denying access or support on key votes. Even winners who themselves got money might take revenge, so the best strategy may be to give to no one. Races this close may not occur that often, but this can be a problem too: the combination of disclosure and likely wins for incumbents tends to freeze out contributions on behalf of challengers. Disclosure can make things even easier than normal for incumbents. It is no accident that under current laws, which include disclosure requirements, PAC money flows decisively to congressional incumbents.

How much, if any, restriction on political expression through contributions is justifiable? Answers range from a flat assertion that no form of expression should ever be restricted, to the position that most political money is fine but that extreme uses must be curtailed, to the argument that expression through contributions is qualitatively different from conventional speech, posing antidemocratic dangers that justify regulation. Obviously, it is a difficult question involving disagreement on basic principles. We must also separate legitimate dangers from scare stories: few would approve of a single "fat cat's" buying an important election, but how often does this happen? A final difficulty involves the goals of reform. Ironing out political inequalities is a laudable goal, but much of that inequality grows out of the structure of the economy and society at large; it is simply beyond the reach of campaign reforms. What assurance do we have, then, that in exchange for limitations on political expression we will get better public policy, however we may define "better"? Put another way, we frequently abridge personal freedom in the name of public purposes, but at what point do the costs of curbs on expression outweigh gains realized through reform?

My opinion is that the costs of restricting expression through campaign contributions are fairly high, though not as high as some critics might contend.[30] More important, however, *the benefits are exceedingly small*. Very little equalization is accomplished: the $25,000 contributions limit constrains only a very few. A genuine equalization of contributions would require limits set so low—

at, say, $100 or $250—that it would make political giving meaningless as a form of expression and thoroughly impoverish political campaigns. Yet even limits set this low could not "drive money out of politics"; they would probably just divert money into other arenas—some possibly much more corrupt than campaign finance.

There is also the question, posed earlier, of how real the dangers of current campaign finance are. Political contributors' views are probably not representative of the citizenry as a whole, but neither are those of farmers, students, or trade unionists. Distinctive views should not be cause for limiting political expression. In reality, the genuine "horror stories" of political finance are few, most involving candidates such as Senators Helms of North Carolina,[31] Heinz of Pennsylvania, and Metzenbaum of Ohio. Even here, evidence of clear bias is lacking; Heinz is a moderate Republican, Metzenbaum a moderate to liberal Democrat. Both ran in large states where campaigns are expensive. The same observation about bias can be made about "fat cats": many are very conservative,[32] but there are also moderate to liberal "fat cats" such as Stewart Mott.

Two-party bias. Federal campaign finance laws clearly create problems for independent and new-party candidates. Despite the law's provision for pro-rated funds for minor-party nominees, the barriers that stand before such candidates are imposing. In effect, a third-party or major independent candidate must somehow mount a campaign under the same contribution limits as the major parties and poll at least five percent of the total vote to qualify for public funds *after* the election. And unless the party exceeds the five percent threshold by a considerable margin, its subsidies will be tiny compared to those of the major parties. In an era when many scholars and members of the public are dissatisfied with the workings of our party system,[33] campaign finance laws have preserved the status quo. New parties face almost insuperable handicaps; old parties are propped up by public money. Speculation on the possible death of our two major parties can be laid to rest: they will always be with us, if in no other form than as labels, so long as they represent passable routes toward public campaign funds. If the current laws had been in effect in his era, Abraham Lincoln probably would have had to run for president as a Whig.

One-party bias? Some critics have even alleged a "bias within a bias," contending that reforms favor Democrats over Republicans. Eugene McCarthy, an independent presidential candidate in 1976, raised that notion when he was asked after the election whether his comments on two-party bias still stood:

> I think I was wrong in part: the Federal Election Campaign Act favored *one* of the major parties, not both of them. It established the first state political party in the history of this country, which is the Democratic party. . . . President Sadat of Egypt announced the other day he was going to establish a three-party system. He said the Egyptians were mature enough to handle three parties. Apparently we are not.[34]

The one-party bias argument begins with the fact that the Republican party is considerably smaller than the Democratic party. To be competitive, Republican candidates must frequently win over many more independent voters than their Democratic opponents, a task requiring well funded, highly visible campaigning. To the extent that campaign finance reforms make this sort of campaigning more difficult, Republicans could be handicapped. A similar argument is that an affluent GOP "core" could, in the absence of limits, contribute enough to make GOP candidates competitive. Of course, the bond between Republicans and large contributors may not be that secure: in 1964, for example, "big money" went to Johnson while Goldwater raised large numbers of small contributions.[35] Still, if the assumption about an affluent GOP "core" is true for even some Republican candidates, here too they might be handicapped.

Gary Jacobson has examined the one-party bias issue in detail, estimating statistically the probable effects of reform on congressional campaigns. Spending limits and public funding have not been enacted for congressional races, but bills proposing them have been debated in both houses, and partisan bias has become an issue. Jacobson found that campaign spending is more crucial to Republicans and therefore that spending limits favor Democrats. This bias is at least partially independent of incumbency, an asset enjoyed by more Democrats than Republicans. In Senate races without incumbents, Jacobson notes, "subsidies with limits favor Democrats, matching funds without spending limits favor Republicans."[36] McCarthy's argument that reforms have enshrined the Democrats as a "state party" is exaggerated, but Jacobson's findings suggest that reforms do accord at least some advantage to many Democrats. Perhaps it is most accurate to say that current reforms preserve the "1½-party system" under which they were drafted.

Incumbent bias. If, in the aftermath of Watergate, someone had proposed to reform our politics by making it easier for public officials to win re-election, the person's sanity would have been questioned. Yet in many ways campaign finance reforms enhance incumbents' already sizable electoral advantages. The most important incumbent advantage is name recognition. Exposure in past campaigns and incumbents' powers to do favors and make news make them well known, even to voters with little interest in politics. Challengers, by contrast, almost always begin their campaigns mired in obscurity. Incumbents have an easier time raising money. If they are Senators or Representatives, they enjoy the franking privilege (free use of the mails), access to broadcast taping studios, and staff support for research and casework. The list of goodies does not end there; Lewis Perdue has estimated that a House incumbent enjoys as much as $1 million worth of perquisites during each two-year term.[37]

Contribution limits make it necessary for challengers to develop a broad base of support from scratch, while incumbents' support bases are already in place. Large numbers of contributors are difficult for an unknown to find. In the past, seed money from a few large givers could have gotten things started, but this option is now closed off. Disclosure may also deter gifts to challengers, as noted earlier. Challengers must usually spend more than incumbents to have any chance of victory because of incumbents' built-in advantages. Spending limits—even if imposed in exchange for public funding—could make it impossible for a challenger to spend more than an incumbent. For a challenger, equal money does not mean an equal shot at victory; instead, it may well hasten defeat. These observations apply unevenly to federal elections, for only presidential races are conducted under the full list of reforms. Congressional elections are, however, subject to disclosure requirements and contribution limits, which do aid incumbents. Congressional incumbents will probably not remedy this situation if, as Mayhew tells us, they place re-election first among their priorities.[38]

Reform advocates contend that competition has actually been equalized. They note that in 1976 and 1980, many incumbents lost in elections conducted under reform legislation. We must remember, however, that the incumbent president who lost in 1976 was a non-elected successor to an unpopular administration and that some of the House incumbents who lost had only a tenuous hold on seats won in the post-Watergate election of 1974. And for those incumbents who lost in 1980, events in the economy and in world affairs, together with—for Democrats—President Carter's presence at the head of the ticket, were probably more decisive factors than any inherent effect of reforms on political competition. The claim that reforms have evened electoral competition rests on a misconception of the campaign-spending process. If incumbents, backed by a few "fat cats," had routinely spent many times as much as their challengers, then contribution limits might have evened things a bit. Expenditure limits and public funds could have balanced the competition even more. Yet, as already discussed, Jacobson has shown that incumbents spend only as they must. Only when faced by a well heeled challenger do they respond with extensive spending, and they do this with relative ease. Given the advantages of incumbency, the incumbent/challenger contest remains uneven at almost any level of spending. Legislation that hampers a challenger's fund-raising capability only makes the contest *more* uneven. Jacobson concludes that because reforms intensify current trends, they favor incumbents in normal times. Only when short-term factors strongly favor one party, as in 1974 (and possibly 1980), are challengers aided. In those cases, reforms tend to aid only challengers from the advantaged party.[39]

I have argued in this section that campaign finance reforms—which were proposed as ways to open up our politics and elections—instead limit political expression without providing compensatory benefits; prop up the current "1½-party system" in an era when many are dissatisfied with its performance; and tend to enhance incumbents' already sizable advantage over challengers. Not only have reforms accomplished almost the opposite of what was intended, at least in the short run; they raise long-term problems as well, which are the focus of the concluding section of this chapter.

Long-term consequences. Because I can only speculate about the long-term systemic results of campaign-finance reform, I will keep these observations brief and focus on two areas—the continued decline of our political parties, and the range of choices open to the electorate.

Political parties play a sort of magic, even contradictory, role in many analyses of our political system. Stronger parties are proposed as a remedy for drift and stagnation, on the one hand, *and* for unrepresentative policy-making on the other. But strong parties do not in themselves guarantee more justice or fewer Watergates. Nor can we step in and simply "strengthen the parties" without changing many other things in society, for parties are part of a complex web of economic, social, and political linkages. Still, political parties can, as Ladd points out, compete, represent, and organize—all important tasks in a mass democracy.[40]

Campaign finance reforms may prop up the labels and competitive imbalances of our current party system. But together with other recent developments, such as the proliferation of primaries and the rise of mass-media campaigning, reform laws may seriously weaken the party organizations themselves and create significant long-term problems in the process. If reforms are biased against Republicans (or, what may be partially the same thing—if they are biased in favor of incumbents), they reduce Republicans' ability to compete. A party that cannot compete can hardly represent or organize. If Democrats are advantaged over Republicans *and* protected from new-party challengers, then reforms reduce Democrats' need to compete and to represent. It may also reduce their ability to organize as well, since a "party of almost everybody" would reflect all the strains and divisions of society itself. Neither party would be much of an institutionalizing force in mass politics. In time, neither might amount to much more than a label, awarded as grand prize of the primary-election horse race, which guarantees access to public funds. If parties are reduced to such a state, it would not be surprising if voter turnout, citizens' interest in and knowledge of politics, and their satisfaction with the system were to decline as well.

A second troubling possibility involves the range of choices available to voters. Third parties and independent campaigns do not often win elections, but they do place new issues on the political agenda: witness the impact of George Wallace's presidential campaigns. They also provide an "exit option" for groups not satisfied with their current treatment. Campaign finance reforms weaken both of these functions by according favored status to the two major parties and by making it more difficult for new groups to raise enough money to wage credible campaigns. The result, over time, may be a narrowing of our political agenda and of our range of choices. The rise in 1976 of "outsider" Jimmy Carter, whose strategies were uniquely suited to post-reform politics, might seem to contradict this forecast. Recall, however, that Carter was an "outsider" only in terms of region and absence of a national constituency—not in terms of his views. Carter brought very little that was truly new to the contest, while in the same year Eugene McCarthy, who did attempt to offer distinctive views on issues, was severely constrained by reform legislation. If two-party bias does significantly narrow our range of choices, then perhaps the reduction of parties to mere labels would be a blessing in disguise. Insurgents could at least *call* themselves "Democrats" or "Republicans" and step up for a spin at the public-funding jackpot. Still, this hardly seems a promising strategy for grappling with the challenges of years to come.

Conclusions

Campaign finance reforms are, I think, bad laws based on good intentions. Two redeeming aspects, however, deserve notice here. First, the reforms have focused our attention on the general issue of money in politics. They have also probably prevented some of the abuses associated with political money: slush funds and large deliveries of small, unmarked bills are probably more difficult to conceal now than in the past. Reformers' research and the law's disclosure requirements have given us vast amounts of information on where the political dollar comes from and where it goes. Second, my critique is intended not to show that campaign finance reformers were fools but rather that the primary reform effort in the 1970s reflects dilemmas common to many attempts at reform. Earlier, I suggested that reform efforts are plagued by a lack of information on the basic problems. They are hampered by sporadic and transitory public concern, the sheer complexity of politics, lack of thought about extended consequences, and an incomplete understanding of government's systemic role. All of these problems are present in the effort to reform campaign finance. These reforms are unique in one respect, though: the wealth of data they have yielded has at least given us a clearer picture of the political money system, and it may help us cast aside such misconceptions as the "fat cat myth." If so, we may be in a position to reform the reforms, correcting at least a few of the problems discussed in my critique.

Where, then, have we gotten? I have argued in this book that corruption is not always bad but that often it is regressive and undemocratic in its consequences. Yet I have also gone to great lengths to criticize efforts at reform. What, if anything, should we do about this double dilemma? An answer to this requires the discussion of some complex questions about corruption and democracy, and these are the focus of Chapter 7.

SUMMARY

Reform efforts are based at least implicitly on some conception of corruption, be it personalistic, institutional, or systemic. The approaches to reform that result may be considerably less distinctive in practice than in theory, but in general, personalistic reforms are aimed at the behavior of people who hold public roles; institutional reforms change the setting within which these people work; and systemic reforms modify government's relationship to the society it serves. Most reform strategies are institutional or personalistic in nature, or both.

Reforms are not always successful. At times, they are irrelevant to the corruption they were enacted to prevent. Sometimes reforms are harmful in their own right. Reform is difficult because of a lack of information on and understanding of corruption; sporadic and superficial public concern; the sheer complexity of politics; "ripple effects" that emerge only after reforms are instituted; and because of government's role in the political system.

Campaign finance reforms—judged here to be bad legislation based on good intentions—show how these problems emerge in practice. The reforms were based on a poor understanding of what political money problems actually existed. They contain a number of implementation problems, short-term biases, and long-term problems. They show that reform is not a task to be taken lightly nor begun without careful consideration of the basic corruption problem and the political results that are desired.

Notes

1. Richard Hofstadter, *The Age of Reform* (New York: Vintage Books, 1955), p. 16. (Copyright © 1955 by Alfred A. Knopf, Inc. Reprinted by permission.) See also William J. Crotty, *Political Reform and the American Experiment* (New York: Thomas Y. Crowell, 1977).
2. George C. S. Benson, Steven A. Maaranen, and Alan Heslop, *Political Corruption in America* (Lexington, Mass.: Lexington Books, D. C. Heath, 1978), pp. 160 and 247.
3. Even the "honest outlet" for gambling and other behavior may not be all that honest. Allegations surfaced in April 1980 that Pennsylvania's "Daily Number" lottery game had been fixed. The story was that the three machines used to generate the number, which juggled ten numbered balls in a draft of air and then selected one supposedly at random when a small chute was opened, had been rigged to select fours and sixes. On the day in question, the number selected was 666, and play on that and other combinations of fours and sixes was much higher than normal. In May 1981, two persons were convicted of fixing the drawing.
4. Charles O. Jones, "How Reform Changes Congress," in Susan Welch and John G. Peters (Eds.), *Legislative Reform and Public Policy* (New York: Praeger, 1977), p. 12.
5. Public Integrity Section, Criminal Division, U.S. Department of Justice, "Federal Prosecutions of Corrupt Public Officials 1970–1979" (Washington, D.C.: mimeo, February 27, 1980), Table 1. Data covered the period from January 1, 1970 to December 31, 1979. As of the latter date, 21 federal, 29 state, and 63 local officials were still awaiting trial. Persons who did not hold public office were also involved in these cases; 1,106 of them were indicted, 858 were convicted, and 306 were awaiting trial. The total number of persons convicted plus those awaiting trial can be greater than the number of persons indicted if persons indicted several times have been convicted of some offenses and still await trial on other indictments.
6. John G. Peters and Susan Welch, "The Effects of Charges of Corruption on Voting Behavior in Congressional Elections," *American Political Science Review*, 74:3 (September 1980), pp. 697–708.
7. David W. Adamany and George E. Agree, *Political Money: A Strategy for Campaign Financing in America* (Baltimore: Johns Hopkins University Press, 1975), p. 31.
8. J. Anthony Lukas, *Nightmare: The Underside of the Nixon Years* (New York: Viking Press, Bantam Books Edition, 1977), pp. 196–197.
9. A number of early and contemporary works on political finance are listed in the Selected Bibliography at the end of this book.
10. George Thayer, *Who Shakes the Money Tree? American Campaign Financing Practices from 1789 to the Present* (New York: Simon and Schuster, 1973), p. 25. (Copyright © 1973 by Simon & Schuster, Inc. This and all other quotations from this work reprinted by permission.)

11. *Ibid.*, pp. 27–29.
12. *Ibid.*, pp. 62–63; quoted section is from p. 63.
13. Lukas, pp. 187 and 189.
14. This summary of current federal election finance laws draws from American Enterprise Institute, "Regulation of Political Campaigns—How Successful?" (Washington, D.C.: American Enterprise Institute, 1977), pp. 55–60; and from personal communications with the Public Information office of the FEC.
15. Gerald M. Pomper, "The Nominating Contests and Conventions," in Pomper, et al., *The Election of 1976* (New York: David McKay, 1977), p. 3, and Chapter 1.
16. American Enterprise Institute, "Regulation of Political Campaigns—How Successful?" p. 5.
17. Adamany and Agree, pp. 29–31, and esp. Table 3.1, p. 30.
18. W. P. Welch, "Patterns of Contributions: Economic Interest and Ideological Groups," in Herbert E. Alexander (Ed.), *Political Finance* (Beverly Hills, Calif.: Sage Publications, 1979), p. 199. Material in brackets added.
19. Congressional Quarterly, *Elections '80* (Washington, D.C.: Congressional Quarterly, Inc., 1980), pp. 133–135.
20. Ralph K. Winter, in association with John R. Bolton, "Campaign Financing and Political Freedom" (Washington, D.C.: American Enterprise Institute, 1973), p. 5.
21. Congressional Quarterly, *Elections '80* (Washington, D.C.: Congressional Quarterly, Inc., 1980), p. 135.
22. Adamany and Agree, p. 76.
23. The Supreme Court's *Buckley v. Valeo* ruling, in which expenditure limits were struck down for candidates not receiving public funds, was a step in the right direction on this issue. So too would be a number of "second generation" reform proposals currently being discussed in Pennsylvania, among other states, which would be based at least partially on the "leveling up" principle.
24. Gary C. Jacobson, "Public Funds for Congressional Campaigns: Who Would Benefit?" in H. E. Alexander, *Political Finance*, pp. 99–127; and "The Effects of Campaign Spending in Congressional Elections," *American Political Science Review*, 72:2 (June 1978), pp. 469–491.
25. I am indebted to Charles O. Jones and W. P. Welch for their comments on this issue.
26. Roland D. McDevitt, "The Changing Dynamics of Fund Raising in House Campaigns," in H. E. Alexander (Ed.), *Political Finance*, p. 152.
27. Common Cause, *1972 Federal Campaign Finances* (10 vols.) (Washington, D.C.: Common Cause, 1974).
28. The "data glut" is discussed in greater detail by Adamany and Agree, pp. 113–114.
29. *Ibid.*, p. 102.
30. Winter, "Campaign Financing and Political Freedom," *passim*.
31. Senator Heinz' 1976 expenditure of $3 million on his Senate campaign was at the time the most ever spent in such a race. In 1978, however, North Carolina Senator Jesse Helms spent more than $7.4 million on his successful campaign, and John Tower of Texas spent more than $4.3 million on his. Total figures for senatorial races may be a bit misleading, since the states vary so greatly in size and population. More meaningful, perhaps, are figures for House races, in which districts are at least roughly comparable in population. In 1978, five incumbents spent less than $5000 in winning re-election. Democrat William H. Natcher of Kentucky spent only $20. Nine House candidates (only two of them incumbents) spent $500,000 or more, by contrast; they were led by Carter Burden of New York, who spent more than $1.1 million. Burden, like five other members of the "half-million club," was an unsuccessful candidate. In 1974, by contrast, the largest expenditure on a House campaign was $537,474, the total spent by the Democrat and Republican *combined* in the Tenth District of Illinois. Congressional Quarterly, *Elections '80*, pp. 133–135.
32. Kirkpatrick Sale, "The World Behind Watergate," *New York Review of Books*, May 3, 1973, pp. 9–11.
33. The term "one-and-a-half party system" was first used by Nelson Polsby, "Strategic Considerations," in Milton Cummings (Ed.), *The National Election of 1964* (Washington, D.C.: Brookings Institution, 1966), p. 107. Everett Carll Ladd gives us a concise analysis of the current state of that system in *Where Have All the Voters Gone? The Fracturing of America's Political Parties* (New York: W. W. Norton, 1978). These and other comments on the party system were written before the Reagan win in 1980, whose full impact has yet to be seen.
34. American Enterprise Institute, "Regulation of Political Campaigns—How Successful?" p. 2.

35. Adamany and Agree, pp. 30–31; Thayer, pp. 80–90.
36. Jacobson, in Alexander, p. 119.
37. Lewis Perdue, "The Million-Dollar Advantage of Incumbency," *Washington Monthly*, 9:1 (March 1977), pp. 50–52 and 54.
38. David R. Mayhew, *Congress: The Electoral Connection* (New Haven, Conn.: Yale University Press, 1974), esp. part 1.
39. Jacobson, in Alexander, pp. 123–124.
40. Ladd, *Where Have All the Voters Gone?* pp. xvii–xxiv.

Corruption and Democracy

7

Two major questions remain in this analysis of political corruption. First is a matter of overall assessment: what are the costs and benefits of corruption? Second, what should we do about it? This final chapter examines both questions, drawing from the theory and case studies presented thus far.

In regard to the first question, I argue that though some corruption is broadly beneficial, and though much is insignificant, the costs of corruption usually outweigh its benefits. There are several types of costs, but the most serious ones are intangible—a loss of trust in democracy, in leaders and institutions, and in each other. These costs of corruption are paid by those who can least afford them. In regard to the second question, my proposed responses to corruption are less prescriptions for reform—for as I discussed in Chapter 6, reforms face formidable problems—than they are observations about citizenship in a democracy and about preserving the essential values that corruption can so thoroughly undermine. These suggestions will never eradicate corruption, but they might help us avoid some of its worst costs.

COSTS AND BENEFITS OF CORRUPTION

We often think of corruption as a disease spreading relentlessly through a body politic, undercutting its strength and integrity and robbing its citizens in the process. This view is understandable, for corruption by definition involves wrongdoing by people holding positions of public trust; but reality, as usual, is more complex. As Colin Leys has put it, "It is natural but wrong to assume that the results of corruption are always both bad and important."[1] Some corruption is undeniably very costly; yet at least some corruption is broadly beneficial, and the greatest part of corruption in most systems is simply insignificant.

Corruption can be good for you

If we regard corruption as a form of influence, then an important part of weighing its costs and benefits is to ask, "Who is using this influence to get what, from whom, and for whom?" If we look at instances of corruption on that basis, it is not difficult to see that at least some corruption benefits large numbers of people.

Consider, as a first example, the urban machines. In the short run, at least, they delivered significant services and benefits—tangible and symbolic—to large numbers of the urban poor. These benefits were not extensive, did not flow to all the poor on the basis of need, and were (as I argued in Chapter 3) outweighed in the long run by lost political opportunities. Yet they *were* benefits, widely distributed. They would not have been available had not a machine based partly on corruption been strong enough to provide them. Machine benefits also flowed to businesses, which got city contracts and franchises, and to citizens, who used the bridges and streetcars the business-machine "connection" produced. We could even suggest that machines, through their balancing act between social classes, were able to bridge over a number of potentially bitter social divisions. I do not imply that everyone in the city benefited equally (or even at all) or that benefits came without cost. I merely suggest that benefits were significant and widespread and that we cannot understand how machine corruption flourished without remembering that fact.

Other hypothetical examples further illuminate the benefits of corruption. What if a governor, knowing that a corporation is looking for a site on which to build a new factory, commits the state to building highways that open up a site for the plant on land that happens to be owned by the governor? This is a definite conflict of interest and is probably corrupt as we have defined corruption. But if the factory is built on the newly opened land, many people may get jobs they would not otherwise have gotten. As another hypothetical instance, what if the purchasing agent for a school district buys supplies from a firm owned by a relative in violation of departmental regulations, and gets a substantial price break? What if the firm that spreads around the most money just before the city council awards a paving contract also happens to be the best qualified and goes on to do a quick, high-quality job? Or, consider two cases suggested by Colin Leys:

> The Uganda Minister of Information was much criticized for giving a lucrative and unusual monopoly of television set sales to an American contractor, in return for building a transmission station at cut rates: even had corruption been involved the policy did produce a television station much more quickly and cheaply than the policy adopted in neighboring Kenya. To take another example, one may ask whether the Russian consumer would be better off without the operations of the illegal contact men who derive illegal incomes in return for their aid in overcoming

bottlenecks in the supply of materials for production. Even in the case of petty bribery or extortion it is relevant to ask, what is the alternative?[2]

I do not suggest that these events bear no costs, or even that those costs are outweighed by the benefits in all cases. Yet the benefits are there. Corruption can speed things up, produce favorable decisions, buy policy benefits, and enlist support for institutions, leaders, and policies. Depending on who you are and what your interests are, all of these things can be good for you. The argument here is not that there exists a category of "clean corruption" that is free of all costs. Rather, it is that all corruption benefits *someone* so long as all parties deliver their parts of the deal. And in a significant number of cases the list of beneficiaries becomes quite long, at times subsuming large segments of society.

Propping up the system

Just as corruption is not always bad, it does not necessarily undermine systems and institutions. We sometimes speak of governments as "shot through with corruption," implying that they are about to collapse. But corruption can strengthen governments and enable institutions to survive long after they have become formally inadequate and obsolete. Corruption can do this, first, by producing informal adaptations and innovations. Scott tells us that the quasi-feudal institutions of Stuart England were able to accommodate, through the sale of royal offices, a rising class of people that commanded wealth but not hereditary status.[3] Local governmental institutions in America during the heyday of machines were utterly unequal to the problems of urbanization and industrialization, but machines managed to hold things together informally. Where important problems or clients have no place in the formal policy process, corruption can buy a place, adapt procedures, and produce gratifying results. Corruption can, within the shell of the formal structure, even foster the growth of informal "para-systems" that perform the real job of deciding who gets what. Stanislav Andreski has used the memorable term "Kleptocracy" to describe such corrupt "para-systems" in Africa.[4]

In addition to accommodating potentially troublesome groups and demands, corruption can preserve obsolescent institutions by creating widened public support for them. Simply put, if through corruption a government "delivers" for people, it will be in the people's interest to support the government. If government can deliver for enough people, it may acquire an instrumental legitimacy it would otherwise lack. Kwame Nkrumah's Convention People's Party in Ghana, for example, ruled for nearly a decade in this fashion. Its ability to deliver, combined with Nkrumah's personal prestige, made it the only game around for those seeking government benefits.

Corruption's role in propping up established leaders, institutions, and parties is neither good nor bad in itself. In some cases, institutions supported through corruption are relatively open to influence from many segments of society, and the corruption involved channels at least some benefits to large segments of the population. More frequently, corruption postpones needed changes and prevents democratic political currents from transforming a system. Which of these scenarios takes place depends on what kinds of groups win or lose through corrupt influence and on what kinds of politics and economic arrangements are being preserved. The point is that corruption does not necessarily undermine the established order; it may do just the opposite. This fact is another facet of the overall conservatism of corruption that has been mentioned in earlier chapters and that comes in for further discussion later.

Insignificant corruption

Corruption may in some cases be broadly beneficial, but in many more instances it is simply insignificant. Some corruption probably does occur when officials go on junkets or submit expense accounts, for example, but just how serious a problem is this? The added cost of government directly attributable to such corruption is not great, and no one in society suffers much. A motorist who pays a traffic officer $20 to avoid a speeding ticket also engages in corruption; yet again it is difficult to ascertain serious direct costs from this transaction.[5] In fact, in an informal sense, the motorist is still paying a fine.

Insignificant cases might have a long-term cost, however, if they pave the way for more serious wrongdoing. New York City's Knapp Commission concluded in its report that one way to fight serious corruption ("meat eating") is to begin by wiping out petty wrongdoing ("grass eating").[6] This supposition has a strong common-sense appeal, but it may not be accurate. Many people who engage in small-time corruption never progress beyond that level; others, such as some urban police, start out in serious corruption. At issue here is a personalistic view of corruption in which initially honest people are steadily tempted into more serious wrongdoing once they "step over the line." This "original sin" conception of the problem may fit some people and cases, but others it does not. In many instances (most notably policing) it is far from clear where "the line" exists. Even if we were to combat petty corruption vigorously, the systemic and institutional incentives for major wrongdoing would remain powerful. The notion that petty corruption necessarily begets more serious problems remains unproven. Much corruption is insignificant, both in the short *and* the long term. If clean government is our goal, we should carefully sort out major cases from minor and concentrate our efforts on the truly damaging instances of corruption.

ASSESSING THE DAMAGE

Undeniably, some cases of corruption involve major costs, tangible and intangible. We would be foolish to ignore the fact that corruption takes benefits away from those who otherwise would have received them (and often from those who need them most), leads to expenditures of public resources that otherwise might not have been made, and affects the ways we go about conducting politics and public business. Yet here too the picture is more complex than it seems at first glance. Although the tangible, short-term costs of corruption are real, they may be less serious than we assume. The most serious costs of corruption, I would suggest, are intangible and realized only over the long term.

Dollars and cents and services lost

For the same reasons that no one knows how much corruption there is, no one can tell us how much corruption costs. We might in a particular case estimate the value of goods and services stolen or estimate the amounts of bribery or extortion money involved. Sometimes these figures are quite large. But we will never know how much corruption adds to the cost of public services or know the total value of services illegally diverted from rightful recipients to corrupt beneficiaries because we simply do not know how much corruption goes on. These short-term, tangible costs of corruption are considerable, especially compared to our salaries or tax bills. Yet there are some reasons to think that the overall material costs of corruption are not as large as we frequently assume.

Many people in my region of western Pennsylvania, for example, attribute the area's notoriously bad roads to corruption in state and local agencies. The roads are indeed bad. Particularly in the early spring, most of them are reminiscent of a close-up view of the craters of the moon. And there is corruption in highway agencies. The State Department of Transportation, the Turnpike Commission, and many units of county and local government have been hit by indictments, convictions, and investigations.

Is it reasonable, then, to attribute the bad roads problem solely to corruption? Of course not. Even if all of these agencies were magically cleaned up overnight, western Pennsylvania would still be a hilly region with poorly draining soil, repeated freeze-thaw cycles, and a bridge and highway system built many years ago. All of these factors make for bad roads. Even where corruption is revealed, it cannot explain all costs. When the headlines read, "Bribery Revealed in $20 Million Bridge Project," it is tempting to assume that corruption has cost us $20 million. Usually, however, it has not; probably corruption's cost has been a small slice out of the $20 million that would have been spent anyway. Patronage in the highway work force is another object of much complaint. The popular image of road workers is one of dim-witted political hacks so unafraid of hard work that they lie down beside it and sleep. This image is untrue: although patronage definitely exists in road crews, few patronage workers devoted much working time to politics,[7] and it remains to be shown that these people are markedly less skilled or more lazy than non-patronage workers or than private-sector workers in similar occupations. Indeed, to attract the highly motivated, non-political highway crews many people would like to see, the state would probably have to substantially *increase* its highway spending.

My purpose here is not to deny that corruption has definite short-term, tangible costs. Rather, my intention is to question how great those costs are. We should perhaps be skeptical of claims that official wrongdoing costs us substantial amounts in added taxes and lost services. Certainly costs exist; but compared to the total scope of government services and activities, the costs of corruption might actually be rather small.

The real damage: Long-term and intangible

Corruption does its most serious damage to the intangibles of democracy—to the values of trust, forbearance, and justice so essential to making our system work. A system with no corruption will not be perfectly democratic, of course, but significant corruption puts these essential democratic values under severe strain. Three long-term costs rate as the most serious—a loss of trust in government and in each other; a possible trend toward "me-first" politics; and the fact that in the long run corruption is a regressive form of influence, benefiting the haves at the expense of the have-nots.

A crisis of trust? Even the most carefully devised schemes of representative democracy ultimately rest on political trust. Government has immense power over our lives, yet no citizen can possibly completely comprehend how those powers are being used or account for how every dollar is spent. Representatives may pledge to obey "the will of the people," but that will is fragmented and changeable, providing little guidance for action on many important issues. We can monitor some of what government does, but at some point we simply must be able to trust our representatives and public employees to do an honest, competent job. We must also be able to trust each other, to believe that others are playing the game by the rules and that the system is not somehow rigged against us. Democracy, as we have approximated it, is a fragile thing even when trust is strong. If trust is lost, it is hard to imagine how a system like ours could survive.

One of the great dangers of corruption is that it can weaken this trust in government and in each other. If revelations of corruption lead people to feel that their representatives wish only to get rich at public expense, that their taxes are being wasted or simply stolen, and that their competitors in the political arena simply buy what they want through bribery, it is plausible to suggest that their belief in and support of leaders and institutions may be seriously damaged. Even when the vast majority of government officials and decisions are honest, mere belief by citizens that corruption is rife can damage political trust. What *the public* regards as corruption—and not the analyst's technical definition of the problem—is the issue here. This public conception of the problem includes most (but by no means all) of what the analyst sees as corrupt *in addition to* suspicions and allegations of corruption, even if unproven. Paradoxically, vigorous efforts to *fight* corruption can produce a public perception that corruption is worse than ever. Would-be enemies of official misconduct, then, must choose their cases and techniques with the utmost care. They must be aware that—particularly in cases of only moderate corruption—the fanfare surrounding their efforts against corruption may damage public political trust more than did the corrupt acts themselves.

There is considerable evidence that many citizens question the honesty of their public servants. William Watts and Lloyd Free report that in their 1976 national opinion survey, when citizens were asked which problems concerned them most, "corruption or law-breaking on the part of government officials" tied with violence and the rising cost of living as the second most serious public problem, ranking just below "crime in this country."[8] This concern has been growing over a long period of time: Table 7-1[9] reports survey results in which people were asked how many officials are "a little crooked."

Clearly, the trend through 1976 was toward increased cynicism about the honesty of public officials. The biggest increase—from 45% answering "quite a lot" in 1974 to 61% in 1976—should be viewed with some caution because a different survey group gathered the 1976 data and because the item for that year specified "government *in Washington*." This wording focuses respondents' attention on the then-recent Watergate scandals, and Margolis and Haque have argued that such references can also introduce significant biases into survey items.[10] There is also some evidence that people tend to believe there is more corruption at the federal level than at the state level, and more at the state level than at the local level.[11] Moreover, there may be significant differences, among respondents and over time, in what people mean by "crooked." In one year, it may refer predominantly to theft; in another, to lying. Even so, it seems that in the mid-1970s people were much more likely to question the honesty of public officials than they were roughly 20 years before.

Does this distrust of public officials spill over into a national mood of distrust and pessimism regarding our social and political system? Here, the evidence is more tentative. Ladd reminds us that it is difficult to generalize about "crises of confidence" from questions on specific issues and that the "national mood" is shifting and ambiguous at best. Still, survey data suggest that there may be good reason to be concerned about the effects of corruption on public trust. Table 7-2 presents data on popular perceptions of the nation's past, present,

TABLE 7-1. National survey responses to questions on how many public officials are "a little crooked," 1958–1976 (percents)[9]

	Sept.–Nov., 1958	Sept.–Nov., 1964	Nov.–Dec., 1968	Nov.–Dec., 1970	Sept.–Nov., 1972	Fall, 1974	July, 1976
Quite a lot	23	29	25	31	34	45	61
Not many	43	49	52	49	46	42	24
Hardly any	26	18	19	16	16	10	6
Don't know	8	4	4	4	4	3	9

Items: 1958–1974, University of Michigan Survey Research Center. "Do you think that quite a few people running the government are a little crooked, not very many are, or do you think hardly any of them are crooked at all?" 1976 Hart Survey: identical item except for wording, "people running the government in Washington. . . ." (From "The Polls: Corruption in Government," by H. Erskine. In *Public Opinion Quarterly*, 1973–74, 37(4), 630–31. Copyright 1973 by The Trustees of Columbia University. Reprinted by permission.)

TABLE 7-2. Responses to "ladder" questions, 1959–1976 (percents)[12]

	1959	1964	1971	1972	1974	1976
Past	6.5	6.1	6.2	5.6	6.3	6.0
Present	6.7	6.5	5.4	5.5	4.8	5.5
Future	7.4	7.7	6.2	6.2	5.8	6.1

From "The Polls: The Question of Confidence," by E. C. Ladd, Jr. In *Public Opinion Quarterly*, 1976–77, 40(4), 549–50. Copyright 1973 by The Trustees of Columbia University. Reprinted by permission.

and future situations from surveys during the years 1959 to 1976. Respondents were shown a picture of a ten-step ladder, the top representing the best possible situation for the nation and the bottom representing the worst. They were then asked to indicate which step they felt the nation was on at the time of the survey, which step it had been on five years earlier, and which step they felt it would be on five years later. In Table 7-2, higher figures indicate better situations, lower figures represent worse situations.

The survey data indicate a general reduction in satisfaction with the present and optimism about the future. The least favorable rating for present and future, together with a modest increase in "nostalgia" for the past, occurred in the Watergate year of 1974. We can hardly attribute the entire 1959–1974 decline to political corruption, since during that era the nation experienced the Vietnam War, domestic violence, and economic difficulties. Watergate's damage does not seem to have been permanent, either, as there was modest improvement in present and future rankings in 1976. Still, it seems that Watergate did the national mood no good. Over the long run, perceptions that public officials are "a little crooked"—and pessimism about the nation's present and future situations—tended to increase together.

More detailed data support this view. Table 7-3 shows the result of Yankelovich surveys that asked people to comment on whether "people who work hard and live by the rules" are getting a "fair break." Again, we cannot attribute all of the sentiments summarized in Table 7-3 to political corruption. It is nonetheless striking, however, that skepticism about one's chances for a "fair break" in our system (at least as measured by this item) peaked around the time Watergate reached its climax.

These items were intended to measure a more or less diffuse "national mood." What about the specific issues of ties to and support for leaders and institutions? Here a number of studies about the impact of Watergate reveal a consistent pattern: the nation's worst political scandal produced sharply reduced trust in and approval of President Nixon, the presidency in general, and even of wider circles of leaders and institutions, at least temporarily. This loss of faith did not, however, seem to extend to our basic social and political system. In 1973 F. Christopher Arterton surveyed the political attitudes of school children using questions originally asked in 1962. He found a distinct shift toward "wholly negative" attitudes toward the presidency along with a "moderate deterioration in attitudes toward other parts of the political system." Arterton correctly

TABLE 7-3. Responses to Yankelovich "fair break" survey (percents)[13]

ITEM: "People who work hard and live by the rules are not getting a fair break these days." (Respondents were asked whether statement describes the way they feel.)

	March 1974	Sept. 1974	Jan. 1975	May 1975	June–Sept. 1976
Fully describes	44	58	53	51	44
Partially describes	38	31	31	29	37
Doesn't describe	18	11	17	20	18

From "The Polls: The Question of Confidence," by E. C. Ladd, Jr. In *Public Opinion Quarterly*, 1976–77, *40*(4), 548. Copyright 1973 by The Trustees of Columbia University. Reprinted by permission.

regarded the latter as potentially much more serious.[14] Several other studies of children's and young people's reactions to Watergate turned up broadly similar results.[15] Dunham and Mauss analyzed national survey data on adults, gathered in 1973 and 1974, and found sharp reductions in the "strength of bonds" to the executive branch and to "all governmental leaders" but only insignificant declines in bonds to "the social system."[16] Breakdowns of data on respondents' income, age, education, and existence of an arrest record (which Dunham and Mauss used as a measure of deviance) suggested that "the pain of the Watergate scandal was felt most by that segment of the public sometimes called 'middle-America.'"[17] This particular locus of disillusionment is of special concern, for it was precisely that "middle-American" constituency that had been closely bound to Nixon and his policies and that has generally supported our system quite strongly.

Clearly, a doomsday verdict is not warranted here: Watergate and corruption in general have not demolished political trust in America. Watts and Free found that although their "composite score" of confidence in the executive branch (a 100-point scale derived from national survey data) declined from 67 in 1972 to 45 in 1974, it rebounded to 55 in 1976.[18] Confidence in specific individuals and offices suffered markedly—but only temporarily—because of Watergate. Faith in the more basic, if more abstractly conceived, aspects of our politics escaped the worst impact of scandal.

Yet the data do suggest that corruption poses a definite threat to political trust. Perhaps Watergate's damage to faith in "the system" was limited because the scandal seemed to revolve around specific personalities and because it was so unprecedented in most people's experience. If this explanation is true, then repeated episodes of serious corruption involving many agencies could, over time, damage even the most basic aspects of trust in our system. The survey data provide no guidance on this point, and fortunately we have not been so wracked by major scandal that we have already answered this question through hard experience. But it seems at least plausible that there might be some tipping point at which our citizenry, having witnessed much pervasive corruption and feeling that it has been victimized in the process, indeed loses this basic trust.

Such a loss of faith could increase law-breaking and the use of corruption by citizens for their own purposes. It could also cause a breakdown of such system-supporting behaviors as payment of taxes, which are based on voluntary compliance. As noted previously, the doomsday scenario is hardly warranted at present; but the amounts of corruption we see in the near future could have much to do with whether or not it eventually comes true.

Me-first politics. If large numbers of citizens believe that government's policy processes are rigged through corruption, they may well conclude that they have no incentive to play the game by the rules or to enter into compromises in hopes of winning more benefits later. Instead, they may resort to "me-first" tactics in which the ends of politics come to justify extreme means. Earlier, I suggested that single-issue politics and demands of the Proposition 13 variety may be tied to such sentiments. Certainly corruption is not the only influence that contributes to me-first politics, but if people believe that their taxes are being stolen and that the game of decision-making is rigged, then they may conclude that it is not how you play the game but whether you win or lose. Even if they merely suspect that many other people feel this way, me-first political initiatives would seem to follow.

Poll data on this notion are few and inconclusive, but consider the results of another Yankelovich item in which people were asked whether the statement, "People have become too selfish and self-centered" describes the way they feel (Table 7-4).

Again, some caveats are in order. This item does not tell us whether or not the respondents respond to "me-first" appeals, for it asks them to describe the motivations of *others*. Still, the perception that "me-first" was becoming the dominant attitude of American society seems to have peaked with the climax of Watergate. Perhaps this and the other survey results taken together tell us that serious episodes of corruption at least temporarily heighten alienation from the trusting and compromising values so essential in a complex representative democracy. It is not clear that Americans have suffered a fatal crisis of confidence in their institutions or political systems, but corruption does seem to pose def-

TABLE 7-4. Responses to Yankelovich "selfishness" survey (percents)[19]

ITEM: "People have become too selfish and self-centered. They put their own pleasures ahead of the larger interests of their family and their country." (Respondents were asked whether statement describes the way they feel.)

	March 1974	Sept. 1974	Jan. 1975	May 1975	June–Sept. 1976
Fully describes	47	59	55	55	43
Partially describes	35	24	27	27	38
Doesn't describe	19	18	18	19	18

From "The Polls: The Question of Confidence," by E. C. Ladd, Jr. In *Public Opinion Quarterly*, 1976–77, 40(4), 548. Copyright 1973 by The Trustees of Columbia University. Reprinted by permission.

inite dangers for the attitudinal bases of democracy. I can only assume that our capacity to bounce back from serious scandals and to revive those essential values must have its limits.

A "regressive" form of influence. Perhaps the most serious cost of corruption is that it tends to benefit society's "haves" at the expense of the "have-nots." My rough winners-and-losers assessments for machine politics, police corruption, and Watergate reflect that tendency: although some small, tangible, divisible benefits flow to have-nots (petty favors from the machine, for example), the larger and more lasting benefits of corruption go to the haves. This is not to deny my earlier assertion that some cases of corruption are broadly beneficial; it is instead to illustrate a general characteristic of corruption as a form of political influence.

This regressive tendency grows out of the fact that corrupt influence frequently requires the use of special access and connections, special knowledge, and money. These resources exist in limited supply and are unequally distributed through the social structure. The vast majority of citizens do not depend on these unusual resources to seek influence and to protect their interests. Instead, most citizens depend on our system's formal safeguards, guarantees, and established procedures. It is precisely those legally sanctioned parts of the political system that corruption circumvents. Those citizens may also depend on government services for their survival and livelihood, and such services can also be regressively redistributed by corruption. So although have-nots may receive occasional small benefits from corruption, in most cases they suffer the biggest costs. Some costs are immediate and tangible—lost services, misappropriated taxes—and others are intangible, widely shared, and long-term, such as lost political opportunities under the machine or threats to civil liberties and democratic values (Watergate). These intangible costs are no less real or serious simply because they are less easily recognized; in fact, as I have suggested already, they may be the most significant damages of all.

An overall assessment

Some corruption can be broadly beneficial. A much greater share of cases are simply insignificant, worthy of the attention of agency bookkeepers but not of the sensational public treatment they often get. Some cases of corruption are serious, however, and in these cases tangible and intangible costs far outweigh any benefits that flow to a few individuals.

In my admittedly subjective assessment, the costs of those serious cases—especially the regressive redistribution of benefits and the intangible damage to political trust—are so grave that they justify strong efforts against corruption. But these efforts must be carefully thought out, not hysterical; they must take into account the difficulties of reform discussed in Chapter 6, and above all they must begin with a careful judgment of which cases are damaging, which are beneficial, and which are simply not worth worrying about.

Is there a tolerable level of corruption? If we wish to live in the perfect republic, or if we believe that all laws and programs are well conceived and just, then the answer quite clearly is no. If we are willing to take our chances in the real world, however, the answer just as clearly must be yes. Specifying a tolerable level of corruption would be difficult, for that question takes us back to our most basic values and expectations about politics, and it also brings into play differences among political systems. Still, on a case-by-case basis, I would argue that instances of corruption become *less* tolerable the *more* they reinforce or increase social inequalities in the distribution of public policy benefits and in access to decision-makers, and the *more* they seriously threaten our trust in leaders, in institutions, and in each other. By the first standard, then, a hypothetical mayor's use of city employees to landscape his yard is more tolerable than fraud in a public works program that takes jobs away from the poor, even though the first kind of corruption is more egregious and much more likely to become a *cause celebre*. By the second standard, Watergate far outweighs graft in the General Services Administration, even though the latter case involved much more money. With these standards, however, comes the reminder that we cannot expect even successful efforts against the worst cases of corruption to usher in an era of total equality and justice. For just as corruption grows ultimately out of government's relationship to the society around it, the inequalities of corruption grow out of inequalities in society.

LEARNING TO LIVE WITH THE BEAST

What, then, can we and should we do about corruption? This is the question I encounter most frequently when I mention that I study the problem; it is also the question for which I have the fewest—and perhaps the least satisfying—answers. I have in Chapter 6 already extensively spelled out the difficulties of anti-corruption reforms. What I have left to say here amounts to observations about citizenship in a republic that celebrates democracy and in which corruption is still a fact of life.

Perhaps the most sweeping recommendation that some might infer from this analysis of corruption would be to cut back on the scale and pervasiveness of government's activities. If laws and regulations stand between what people want and what they get, creating pressures to break those laws, and if government policy processes create a bottleneck encouraging corrupt relationships and influence, why not get government out of the middle? This sort of recommendation is consistent with the notion that a large and active public sector is correlated with relatively large amounts of corruption.

This proposal undoubtedly would reduce corruption—if only by definition—since fewer roles and activities would be public ones. But it is not a strategy I could endorse, for corruption is but one problem our society faces, and it is far from the most serious one. Each program, law, and regulation—like each aspect of the policy process that makes it time-consuming, expensive, and uncertain—has a purpose and is directed at a specific objective. They should be judged on the basis of whether or not they accomplish worthwhile purposes and not primarily on whether or not they cause corruption. Judged on their merits, some laws, regulations, and governmental activities might indeed prove outdated, ineffective, or downright harmful, and would thus be candidates for repeal. But to discard programs and laws simply because they are associated with corruption would be to discard many policy initiatives that accomplish worthwhile purposes and whose loss would cause significant problems. There has been corruption, for example, in the inspection of meat-packing industries. Doing away with USDA inspections would solve that corruption problem very quickly. But would we know what we were buying the next time we went to the supermarket? Many complaints about the alleged corruption-inducing properties of governmental regulations are, in reality, arguments of economic self-interest from those affected by the regulations.

Some whose economic interests lie at the heart of their opposition to a law may raise the corruption issue as a smokescreen to make their stand more palatable. There is nothing wrong with advancing a self-interested viewpoint, but an obsession with corruption may keep us from recognizing one when we see it.

We must learn how to live with some corruption; the question is, how? Here is where the citizenship lecture comes in. Living with corruption entails, first, *sorting out the important cases from the inconsequential*. Many people and political observers in Pennsylvania, at least, seem to have trouble distinguishing between petty corruption and truly serious cases. A city councilmember's fiddling with his expense account on a trip occasions almost as much uproar as a serious scandal in a road-building program. One newspaper even voiced loud and righteous rage when it was revealed that the *National Geographic* magazines in a prominent state representative's office were paid for by the state. This sort of diffuse outrage serves no purpose; the last instance is probably not even corruption, by any definition. Such treatment of official misconduct merely produces the kind of superficial, diffuse, and episodic public concern that hampers reform, as noted in Chapter 6.

We should also try to *maintain realistic expectations* about honesty, efficiency, and levels of services in government. Public officials are human beings, often overworked, no more god-like than the rest of us; yet we sometimes demand superhuman virtues of them. We have a right to expect honesty and hard work out of public employees, but we cannot expect every one to perform perfectly in every situation. We should not conclude that when one person is caught in a corrupt transaction that he or she is typical of all. Perhaps we should compare the standards we impose upon public employees to those we impose on ourselves and ask which are more realistic.

Much the same can be said about the degree of efficiency and the level of services we expect to receive. Efficiency is a concept with no meaning in many areas of government activity. Many other governmental functions, such as urban policing, are more or less inherently inefficient. If these services *could* be provided efficiently and profitably, chances are they *would* be, but it would be by some private entrepreneur who would resist vigorously any public move into his or her business. Many services are left to government because they *cannot* be profitably and efficiently provided, a fact that often makes blanket comparisons of public and private enterprises inappropriate. We should not reflexively blame the cost or quality of government services on corruption (or indolence). Nor should we imagine that reform will suddenly enable governments to provide vastly better services at a sharply reduced cost. The problems of service delivery are real and diverse, and they only partly overlap with the problem of corruption.

We also must maintain our *political trust and a sense of forbearance*. This may sound like a proposal to put blindfolds on the cattle as they are led to slaughter, but it is not. Rather, if we desert political trust and engage in a politics that knows no forbearance, the result can only be *more* corruption (among many other problems). As I argued in Chapter 5, we forgot about the "politics of patience" for a time in the 1960s and in doing so helped produce Watergate. Political trust cannot be blind; where serious wrongdoing exists, it must be ended. Yet trust must be strong enough that we do not desert our system because of petty, unimportant cases of corruption. We must take advantage of the system's strengths in combatting severe cases rather than indulging in ill-advised institutional tinkering or launching into crusades in quest of some "quick fix." Forbearance must be strong enough for us to avoid "me-first" politics, even in response to serious revelations of wrongdoing—for down that road lie many dangers for democracy. I do not suggest that there is no place in politics for self-interest. We simply must remember that *how* decisions are made—and how well we protect the rights of all parties to political disputes—can be just as important as *what* decisions are made.

Finally, we should try to maintain a continuous *vigilance* instead of lapsing into the apathy-scandal-apathy cycle. This is difficult, for no one can spend an entire lifetime following political developments, and most of us would not if we could. Still, continuing interest in and knowledge of politics would serve several important purposes. It would have at least some supervision value, making it perhaps marginally more difficult to conceal wrongdoing. More important, though, is the possibility that this continuing political awareness would in time enable us to distinguish the serious from the insignificant types of official conduct and misconduct about which I have already written. It might also help us appreciate the central roles played by political trust and forbearance and understand the dangers to our society if those values are ever irretrievably lost.

This continuing interest in politics might even help us view government in a systemic perspective—as an uneasy aggregation of high-pressure roles within a central "bottleneck" setting in society that must somehow be managed by human beings much like ourselves. Its actions are at times clumsy, its services often unreliable. Its compromises are questionable, and the people who run it are at times dishonest. Yet it is the way we have chosen to conduct our public business—and for better or worse, most of the time it gives us the service we deserve.

CONCLUSIONS

There is little about the suggestions I have mentioned that could reduce corruption. Rather, they offer a strategy of accommodation, a way perhaps to allow us to worry (and to get angry) a bit less. This may be taken as a pessimistic response to corruption, but it is not intended that way. Struggles against official misconduct are not doomed. We do not have to sit passively by, mulling over the glories of democratic values while venal politicians pick our pockets. Most public servants are honest, and many reforms have proven successful. And if my observations on the beneficial or inconsequential nature of much corruption are correct, we may not have as much to worry about as we may at times think. When we *do* take the field to do battle with serious corruption, it will help to take along a map of the terrain, and I hope this book has provided that.

Can the citizenry be expected to make the sorts of delicate judgments I have proposed? This is a difficult question, involving not only the public's abilities and shortcomings but also the conduct of those whose task it is to examine and report on the political world. Scholars, critics, teachers, and journalists all have a hand in shaping the public's attitudes toward corruption and their standards of political judgment. At times, episodic and superficial public concern is more the fault of these political observers than of the public itself. John Dewey, writing more than 50 years ago, pointed out that until open inquiry offers the public the information and perspectives necessary for judgment, we will never know how good a judge the public can be. "The essential need," Dewey concluded, "is the improvement of the methods and conditions of debate, discussion and persuasion. That is *the* problem of the public. . . . [This] improvement depends essentially upon freeing and perfecting the processes of inquiry and of dissemination of their conclusions."[20]

It is difficult to say how much or what kinds of corruption we will encounter in years to come. I have already suggested that the danger of future Watergates is great, and a systemic view of corruption leads me to believe that other serious scandals will occur as well. Within that general observation, however, lie several variables. Some aspects of corruption's future depend upon what we do, as already suggested. Other aspects depend upon systemic trends—growth (or shrinkage) in the scale of the public sector, trends in mass attachments to government, even changes in political culture—conditions that can only be guessed at now. I am particularly concerned about the consequences of an age of scarcity or at least of a prolonged period of slow or no economic growth. It seems reasonable to guess that competition over the benefits of public policy would intensify sharply in an environment of scarcity and perhaps that the supply of such benefits would remain stagnant or decline. That sort of situation seems likely to lead to increased corruption, to declining political trust and civility, and to an intensification of corruption's regressive incidence. I hope these predictions never become more than mere speculation, but it is too early to say for sure.

In this book I have attempted to offer not only an understanding of corruption but also an appreciation of how *well* so many of our institutions work in the face of difficult systemic pressures. Politics is indeed the "art of the possible." That we have at times been had by dishonest practitioners of that art is indeed a fact. But in the long run, the strengths and weaknesses of our politics and institutions grow out of the strengths and weaknesses in ourselves. If we keep that in mind, our system will survive almost any challenge that corruption can present.

Notes

1. Colin Leys, "What is the Problem About Corruption," *Journal of Modern African Studies*, 3:2 (August 1965), p. 222.
2. *Ibid.*, p. 220.
3. James C. Scott, *Comparative Political Corruption* (Englewood Cliffs, N.J.: Prentice-Hall, 1972), Chapter 3.
4. Stanislav Andreski, "Kleptocracy: or, Corruption as a System of Government," pp. 346–357 in Arnold J. Heidenheimer (Ed.), *Political Corruption: Readings in Comparative Analysis* (New York: Holt, Rinehart and Winston, 1970). Andreski's perspective is also set forth in "Kleptocracy as a System of Government in Africa," pp. 275–290 in Monday U. Ekpo (Ed.), *Bureaucratic Corruption in Sub-Saharan Africa: Toward a Search for Causes and Consequences* (Washington, D.C.: University Press of America, 1979).
5. One long-term intangible cost, of course, is that the standards or penalties of justice become lighter *de facto* for those who can pay the bribe than for those who cannot or will not. This is a significant cost, exacted in the form of injustice. My discussion of it is deferred until later in this chapter because it is one of the intangible, long-term costs that emerge as a pattern from repeated instances of corruption rather than a direct material cost arising from any one case.
6. New York City, Knapp Commission, *The Knapp Commission Report on Police Corruption* (New York: George Braziller, 1972), pp. 65–66.
7. An early study of patronage and political activities in the ranks of Pennsylvania road-crew workers is Frank J. Sorauf, "State Patronage in a Rural County," *American Political Science Review*, 50:4 (December 1956), pp. 1046–1056.
8. William Watts and Lloyd A. Free, *State of the Nation III* (Lexington, Mass.: Lexington Books, D. C. Heath, 1978), Table 1-3, p. 10.
9. Data for the 1958–1972 responses are reported in Hazel Erskine, "The Polls: Corruption in Government," *Public Opinion Quarterly*, 37:4 (Winter 1973–1974), pp. 630–631; for 1974 and 1976, responses are reported in Everett Carll Ladd, Jr., "The Polls: The Question of Confidence," *Public Opinion Quarterly*, 40:4 (Winter 1976–1977), pp. 550 and 549 respectively.
10. Michael Margolis and Khondaker E. Haque, "Applied Tolerance or Fear of Government? An Alternative Interpretation of Jackman's Findings," *American Journal of Political Science* (forthcoming, 1981). Also on this point, see James Kuklinski and T. Wayne Parent, "Race and Big Government: Contamination in Measuring Racial Attitudes," *Political Methodology* (forthcoming).
11. On this issue, consider the following poll results (Gallup, March 26–31, 1951): "Do you think there is any tie-up between gamblers and persons in government in Washington? Do you think there is any such tie-up in this state/city?"

	Yes	No	No Opinion
Government in Washington	76%	8	16
State government	66	13	21
City government	53	24	23

188 Chapter 7

Consider this poll as well (Harris, April 18–23, 1973): "How serious a problem do you think corruption is on the federal/state/local level—very serious, somewhat serious, or not really serious?"

	Very serious	Somewhat serious	Not really serious	Not sure
Federal	52%	29	11	8
State	37	36	18	9
Local	31	29	32	8

Polls from Erskine, "The Polls: Corruption in Government," pp. 635 and 640.
12. Ladd, "The Polls: The Question of Confidence," p. 547. Data for 1959 and 1964 were gathered by the Institute for International Social Research; and for 1971–1976 by Potomac Associates. The 1976 data were collected by the Gallup Organization.
13. Ladd, "The Polls: The Question of Confidence," p. 548.
14. F. Christopher Arterton, "The Impact of Watergate on Children's Attitudes Toward Political Authority," *Political Science Quarterly*, 89:2 (June 1974), pp. 269–288; quoted material is from pp. 272 and 287.
15. See, for example, the following studies, all of which appear in *American Politics Quarterly*, 3:4 (October 1975): Harrell R. Rodgers, Jr., and Edward B. Lewis, "Student Attitudes Toward Mr. Nixon: The Consequences of Negative Attitudes Toward a President for System Support," pp. 423–436; Steven H. Chaffee and Lee B. Becker, "Young Voters' Reactions to Early Watergate Issues," pp. 360–385; Jack Dennis and Carol Webster, "Children's Images of the President and of Government in 1962 and 1974," pp. 386–405; and Robert Parker Hawkins, Suzanne Pingree, and Donald E. Roberts, "Watergate and Political Socialization: The Inescapable Event," pp. 406–422.
16. Roger G. Dunham and Armand L. Mauss, "Waves from Watergate: Evidence Concerning the Impact of the Watergate Scandal upon Political Legitimacy and Social Control," *Pacific Sociological Review*, 19:4 (October 1976), p. 478, and Table 1.
17. *Ibid.*, p. 483.
18. Watts and Free, *State of the Nation III*, Table 2-1, p. 30; see also discussion on p. 40.
19. Ladd, "The Polls: The Question of Confidence," p. 548.
20. John Dewey, *The Public and Its Problems* (New York: Henry Holt and Co., 1927), pp. 208 and 209.

Selected Bibliography

The following list of works is by no means comprehensive. Rather, it lists the sources likely to prove most helpful to readers who would like to look further into the topics of this book.

General works
Benson, George C. S.; Maaranen, Steven A.; and Heslop, Alan. *Political Corruption in America*. Lexington, Mass.: Lexington Books, D. C. Heath, 1978.
Berg, Larry L.; Hahn, Harlan; and Schmidhauser, John R. *Corruption in the American Political System*. Morristown, N.J.: General Learning Press, 1976.
Chambliss, William J. *On the Take: From Petty Crooks to Presidents*. Bloomington: Indiana University Press, 1978.
Eisenstadt, Abraham S.; Hoogenboom, Ari; and Trefousse, Hans L. (Eds.). *Before Watergate: Problems of Corruption in American Society*. New York: Brooklyn College Press, 1978.
Ekpo, Monday U. (Ed.). *Bureaucratic Corruption in Sub-Saharan Africa*. Washington, D.C.: University Press of America, 1979.
Friedrich, Carl Joachim. *The Pathology of Politics: Violence, Betrayal, Corruption, Secrecy, and Propaganda*. New York: Harper & Row, 1972.
Gardiner, John A., and Lyman, Theodore R. *Decisions for Sale: Corruption in Local Land-Use Regulation*. New York: Praeger, 1978.
Gardiner, John A., and Olson, David J. (Eds.). *Theft of the City: Readings on Corruption in Urban America*. Bloomington: Indiana University Press, 1974.
Heidenheimer, Arnold J. *Political Corruption: Readings in Comparative Analysis*. New York: Holt, Rinehart and Winston, 1970.
McCloskey, Paul N. *Truth and Untruth: Political Deceit in America*. New York: Simon and Schuster, 1972.
Rogow, Arnold A., and Lasswell, Harold D. *Power, Corruption and Rectitude*. Englewood Cliffs, N.J.: Prentice-Hall, 1963.
Rose-Ackerman, Susan. *Corruption: A Study in Political Economy*. New York: Academic Press, 1978.

Scott, James C. *Comparative Political Corruption*. Englewood Cliffs, N.J.: Prentice-Hall, 1972.
Wise, David. *The Politics of Lying: Government Deception, Secrecy and Power*. New York: Vintage Books, 1973.

Political machines

Bean, Walton. *Boss Ruef's San Francisco: The Story of the Union Labor Party, Big Business, and the Graft Prosecution*. Berkeley: University of California Press, 1952.
Callow, Alexander B. (Ed.). *The City Boss in America: An Interpretive Reader*. New York: Oxford University Press, 1976.
Callow, Alexander B. *The Tweed Ring*. New York: Oxford University Press, 1966.
Gosnell, Harold Foote. *Machine Politics: Chicago Model*. (2nd ed., with a foreword by Theodore J. Lowi and a postscript by Harold F. Gosnell). Chicago: University of Chicago Press, 1968.
Miller, Zane L. *Boss Cox's Cincinnati: Urban Politics in the Progressive Era*. New York: Oxford University Press, 1968.
O'Connor, Len. *Requiem: The Decline and Demise of Mayor Daley and His Era*. Chicago: Contemporary Books, 1977.
Rakove, Milton L. *Don't Make No Waves—Don't Back No Losers: An Insider's Analysis of the Daley Machine*. Bloomington: Indiana University Press, 1975.
Riordon, William L. *Plunkitt of Tammany Hall* (introduction by Arthur Mann). New York: Dutton, 1963.
Royko, Mike. *Boss: Richard J. Daley of Chicago*. New York: Dutton, 1971.
Stave, Bruce M. *The New Deal and The Last Hurrah: Pittsburgh Machine Politics*. Pittsburgh: University of Pittsburgh Press, 1970.
Stave, Bruce M. (Comp.). *Urban Bosses, Machines and Progressive Reformers* (introduction by Bruce M. Stave). Lexington, Mass.: Heath, 1972.
Steffens, J. Lincoln. *The Shame of the Cities* (introduction by Louis Joughin). New York: Hill and Wang, 1969.
Wendt, Lloyd, and Kogan, Herman. *Bosses in Lusty Chicago: The Story of Bathhouse John and Hinky Dink* (introduction by Paul H. Douglas). Bloomington: Indiana University Press, 1967, 1943.

Police corruption

Brown, W. P. *A Police Administration Approach to the Corruption Problem*. New York: State University of New York, 1971.
Daley, Robert. *Prince of the City: The True Story of a Cop Who Knew Too Much*. Boston: Houghton Mifflin, 1978.
Gardiner, John. *The Politics of Corruption: Organized Crime in an American City*. New York: Russell Sage Foundation, 1970.
Maas, Peter. *Serpico*. New York: Viking Press, 1973.
New York City, Knapp Commission. *The Knapp Commission Report on Police Corruption*. New York: G. Braziller, 1973.
Pennsylvania Crime Commission. *Report on Police Corruption and the Quality of Law Enforcement in Philadelphia*. St. Davids, Pa.: Pennsylvania Crime Commission, 1974.
Reiss, Albert J. *The Police and the Public*. New Haven, Conn.: Yale University Press, 1971.
Rubinstein, Jonathan. *City Police*. New York: Farrar, Strauss, and Giroux, 1973.
Sherman, Lawrence W. *Police Corruption: A Sociological Perspective*. New York: Doubleday, 1974.
Sherman, Lawrence W. *Scandal and Reform: Controlling Police Corruption*. Berkeley: University of California Press, 1978.

Simpson, Anthony E. *The Literature of Police Corruption* (foreword by Albert J. Reiss, Jr.). New York: John Jay Press, 1977.
Snibbe, J. R., and Snibbe, H. M. (Eds). *The Urban Policeman in Transition*. Springfield, Ill.: Charles C Thomas, 1973.

Watergate

Barber, James David. *The Presidential Character: Predicting Performance in the White House* (2nd ed.). Englewood Cliffs, N.J.: Prentice-Hall, 1977.
Ben-Veniste, Richard, and Frampton, George. *Stonewall: The Real Story of the Watergate Prosecution*. New York: Simon and Schuster, 1977.
Dean, John Wesley. *Blind Ambition: The White House Years*. New York: Simon and Schuster, 1976.
Drew, Elizabeth. *Washington Journal: The Events of 1973–1974*. New York: Random House, 1975.
Halpern, Paul J. *Why Watergate?* Pacific Palisades, Calif.: Palisades Publishers, 1975.
Jaworski, Leon. *The Right and the Power: The Prosecution of Watergate*. New York: Reader's Digest Press, 1976.
Lukas, J. Anthony. *Nightmare: The Underside of the Nixon Years*. New York: Bantam, 1977.
Magruder, Jeb Stuart. *An American Life: One Man's Road to Watergate*. New York: Atheneum, 1974.
Mazlish, Bruce. *In Search of Nixon: A Psychohistorical Inquiry*. New York: Basic Books, 1972.
Nixon, Richard Milhous. *The Presidential Transcripts* (with commentary by the staff of the *Washington Post*, including Bob Woodward and others). New York: Dell, 1974.
Schlesinger, Arthur M. *The Imperial Presidency*. Boston: Houghton Mifflin, 1973.
Wills, Garry. *Nixon Agonistes: The Crisis of the Self-Made Man*. Boston: Houghton Mifflin, 1971.

Campaign finance

Adamany, David W., and Agree, George E. *Political Money: A Strategy for Campaign Financing in America*. Baltimore: Johns Hopkins University Press, 1975.
Alexander, Herbert E. (Ed.). *Campaign Money: Reform and Reality in the States*. New York: Free Press; London: Collier MacMillan, 1976.
Alexander, Herbert E. *Financing Politics: Money, Elections, and Political Reform*. Washington, D.C.: Congressional Quarterly Press, 1976.
Alexander, Herbert E. (Ed.). *Sage Electoral Yearbook*. Beverly Hills, Calif.: Sage, 1979.
American Enterprise Institute. *Regulation of Political Campaigns: How Successful?* Washington, D.C.: American Enterprise Institute for Public Policy Research, 1977.
Belmont, Perry. *Return to Secret Party Funds*. New York: Arno Press, 1972.
Heard, Alexander. *The Costs of Democracy*. Chapel Hill: University of North Carolina Press, 1960.
Pollock, James Kerr. *Party Campaign Funds*. New York and London: A. A. Knopf, 1926.
Thayer, George. *Who Shakes the Money Tree? American Campaign Financing Practices from 1789 to the Present*. New York: Simon and Schuster, 1973.
Winter, Ralph K., in association with Bolton, John R. *Campaign Financing and Political Freedom*. Washington, D.C.: American Enterprise Institute for Public Policy Research, 1973.

Index

Adamany, D. W., 157, 162
Administrative procedures, chaotic, and emergence of machine politics, 45, 46–47
Agnew, S. T., 109, 129
Agree, G. E., 157, 162
Anderson, J., 161
Andreski, S., 174
Anti-corruption laws, 28–30 (*see also* Reform)
Apathy-scandal-apathy cycle, 150–151, 185
Arterton, F. C., 179–180

Banfield, E. C., 47, 48, 49
Barber, J. D., 114, 116–117, 133
Barbieri, A., 71*fn*
Bayh, B., 132
Black leadership, and machine politics, 64–65, 71*fn*
Bosses, *see* Political machines
Boston, 91–92
Bottleneck effects:
 and decision-making, reform, 142
 of government, 22–24, 133
 of police discretion, 76
 and political machines, 37–38, 53, 66
 and size of public sector, 32
 systemic factor in, 152

Brayton, "Blind Boss," 49
Bribery, 2, 11, 26, 29, 35*fn*, 43
 amount of money in, 142
 in patron/client interactions, 30–31, 145
 by police, 77–78, 85
 in policy process, 147
 by vice entrepreneurs, 94
Buckley v. *Valeo,* 155, 156
Burden, C., 170*fn*
Bureaucratization, in police work, 88–89
Business-political machine connection, 43–44

Campaign finance:
 as case study of reform, 153–158
 evaluation of finance reforms, 156–168
 post-Watergate reforms, 134–135, 145, 153
Caro, R. A., 60
Carter, J., 109, 132, 156, 166, 167–168
Chicago, 60, 65, 74 (*see also* Daley, Richard J.)
Chotiner, M., 120
Cities, *see* Urban areas
Clark, R., 139*fn*
Colson, C., 121

193

Command corruption, within police
    departments, 91–92, 102–103
Comprehensive Employment and
    Training Act (CETA), and
    patronage, 57–58, 66
Constraints on behavior, weakness of,
    in Nixon administration, 123–24
Corruption:
    amount of, 149–150
    complexities of, 151–152
    cost-benefit approach to, 172–175
    damage caused by, 175–183
    data problems in study of, 16–17,
        149–150, 161–162
    definitions of, 3–11
    and democracy, 172–188
    explanations for, 12–16
    history of, 1–3
    insignificant, 175
    learning to live with, 183–186
    overall assessment of, 182–183
    police, 72–107
    in political systems, 18–35 (*see also*
        Political machines; Watergate)
    as regressive form of influence, 182
    systemic roots of, 152–153
    tolerable level (?) of, 183
    tough cases in defining, 3–4, 9–11
    types of, 11–12
Corrupt Practices Act (1925), 154
Cost-benefit approach:
    to corruption, 172–175
    of deterrence and positive incentives,
        142–143
"Cover-ups," 11
Criminality, active police, 76–77
Criminal justice system, police in,
    87–88, 89–91, 103
Crisis of confidence, and corruption,
    trust, 177–181
Crisis rituals, Nixon's, 114–116
Croker, R., 56
Cynicism:
    about honesty of public officials,
        178–179
    of police, 81, 82
    political (since Watergate), 132–133

Dahl, R. A., 44
Daley, Richard J., 5, 42, 50, 59, 64, 68

Daley, Robert, 100–101
Data problems, 10–11, 16–17, 149–150,
    161–162
Dawson, W. L., 64, 65
Dean, J. W., 120, 121, 123
Decision-making:
    in government, 21–22, 27–30
    patron/client relations, and reforms
        in, 145–148
Demand-side reforms, 145–146
Democracy:
    and corruption, 172–188
    and political machines, 62–65
Democratic Party, 164–165, 167
Des Moines, 76–77
Deterrence strategies, 142
Dewey, J., 186
Discretion, wideness of police officer's,
    84–85
Dissent levels, in presidential
    administrations, 123–124
Diversion of resources and services,
    personal, 11
Dunham, R. G., 180

Economic arrangements, political
    corruption and, 25, 30–33
Economic development, level of, and
    corruption, 30–31
Ehrlichman, J., 112, 121
Elazar, D., 7, 25, 48, 49
Electoral procedures:
    chaos in, and emergence of machine
        politics, 45, 46–47
    and vote fraud, vote buying, 11
Ellsberg, D., 121
Enemies, Nixon administration's, 113,
    122
Enforcement:
    of anti-corruption laws, 28–30
    of campaign-finance reforms, 162
Equal Rights Amendment, 5
Erikson, E. H., 113
Ethnicity:
    in patronage acts, 57–58
    and police recruitment, 81
    and political machines, elections, 51
Exclusion, patterns of, 24
Executive Branch, U.S., 118–119, 123
    (*see also* Presidency, U.S.)

Extortion, 11, 35*fn*, 43, 142
  by police, 77–78

"Fair break" survey, 179–180
Falsification of data, records, 10–11
Fat cat myth, 156–157, 168
Federal Election Campaign Act (1971), and Amendments (1974), 154–155
Financial schemes, fraudulent, 11
Fines, amount of maximum, compared with bribery/extortion stakes, 142
Ford, G., 109
Fowler, E. P., 60
Franklin, B., 133
Free, L., 178
Frustration levels, Nixon administration's, 121–122

Gallup Poll, 6
Gambling, "honest outlets" for, 169*fn*
Giuliani, R., 101
Goldwater, B., 165
Government (*see also* Political systems):
  benefits conferred by, 20–21
  as "bottleneck," 22–24, 133
  corruption as propping up, 174–175
  decision-making in, 21–22, 24, 27–30
  loss of trust in, 177–181, 185
  popular attachment to, 24, 26
  as "the source," 21
  systemic perspective on, 185–186
Graft, "honest and dishonest," 44

Haldeman, H. R., 112, 119, 120, 121, 123, 124, 153
Halpern, P. J., 111, 113
Heinz, H. J., III, 164
Helms, J., 164
Hershkowitz, L., 50
Hofstadter, R., 47–48, 49, 140
Honest behavior:
  incentives for, 142–143
  in police officers, 95–96
Howe, L., 119
Hylan, M., 60

Immigration, and machine politics, 45–46, 47–50, 53–54
Incumbent bias, and campaign finance reforms, 165–166

Individualistic political culture, 25, 48
Industrial growth, rapidity of, and machine politics, 45, 46, 53–54
Influence:
  corruption viewed as, 173–174
  patterns of, 28
  in political system, 20
Information, lack of (data problems), 10–11, 16–17, 149–150, 161–162
Institutional-personal distinction, Nixon and blurring of, 120
Institutional perspective:
  on corruption, 14
  on police corruption, 73, 84–92, 101–103
  on political machine's emergence, 51–53
  on Watergate scandal, 110, 117–124
Institutional reforms:
  effectiveness of, 143–144
  post-Watergate, 135–136
Institutions, corruption as propping up, 174–175
Internal (police) corruption, 75–76

Jacobson, G. C., 159, 160, 165, 166
Johnson, L. B., 165
Jones, C., 148
Justice, police conceptions of, 89–91
  (*see also* Criminal justice system)

Kelly, J., 56
Kennedy administration, 3, 9–10
Kennedy, J. F., 119
Kickbacks, 11
King, Martin Luther, Jr., 4
Kleptocracy, 174
Knapp Commission, 74, 78, 87, 175
Krogh, E., 121

Labor movement, and political machines, 65
Ladd, E. C., 167, 178
Lasswell, H., 18
Law, the, and police work, 76, 90–91, 93–95, 103
Lawrence, D., 24, 59
Leadership, in political machine, 39, 40
Lee, R., 59, 71*fn*
Lefkowitz, J., 83

Index

Legal norms, corruption defined by, 8–9
Leuci, R., 86
Lexow Commission, 74
Leys, Colin, 172–174
Lincoln, A., 4, 118
Lineberry, Robert L., 60
Lipset, S. M., 124, 128
Local government, chaos in, and emergence of machine politics, 45, 46–47, 53
Louis VII (France), 1–2
Lowi, T., 61

Machine politics, *see* Political machines
Managerial visibility, police officers' low, 85
Market-oriented reform, 144–145
Mass resentment, politics of, 127–129
Material benefits, types of corruption leading to, 11–12
Mauss, A. L., 180
Mayhew, D. R., 166
Mazlish, B., 113
McCarthy, E., 164, 165, 168
McGovern, G., 108–109
Me-first politics, 181–182
Mellon, R. K., 24
Merton, R. K., 41–42, 54
Metzenbaum, H. M., 164
Middle-class political values, and machine politics, 67
Money (*see also* Bribery; Campaign finance; Extortion; Fines):
 and business-machine partnership, 44
 in patterns of influence and exclusion, 28
 as political resource, 33–34, 159–160
Moralistic political culture, 25, 48
Morals, and vice, 93–95
Moses, R., 60
Mott, S., 164

Nast, T., 36
Natcher, W. H., 170*fn*
Neiderhoffer, A., 81–82
Nepotism, 3, 11
Neustadt, R., 119, 120
New Deal, and political machine, 42, 66–67

New York City:
 police corruption in, 74, 81–82, 90, 101
 and Tammany Hall, 55–56, 60
Nixon, R. M.:
 abuses of power by, 111
 as active-negative character, 116–117
 administration of, and defining corruption, 3–10 *passim*
 crisis rituals of, 114–116
 fund-raising by, 134, 155
 internal competition in administration of, 121
 as "paranoid," 113–114
 pattern of recruitment by, 119–120
 psychological concepts about, 112–117
 and Watergate, *see* Watergate
Nkrumah, K., 174
Nye, J. S., 8

One-and-a-half party system, 165, 166
One-party bias, alleged, 164-165
"Original sin" conception of corruption, 175

PACs, *see* Political Action Committees
Partisanship, *see* Political parties
Patience, case for a politics of, 131–132, 185
Patronage practices, 1–2, 11, 176
 of political machines, 52, 57–59, 66
Peer-group pressures, on police, 86–87, 95–97
Penrose, B., 50
Perdue, L., 165
Personal-institutional distinction, Nixon and blurring of, 120, 122
Personalistic perspective:
 on corruption, 12–13
 on police corruption, 73, 79–84
 on political machine's emergence, 47–50
 on Watergate scandal, 110, 112–117
Personalistic reforms, 136, 141–143
Peters, J. G., 150–151
Phillips, K., 122
Platt, T., 49
Plunkitt, G. W., 44
Police corruption, 72–107
 consequences of, 97–101

Police corruption *(continued)*
  institutional approaches to, 73, 84–92, 101–103
  and peer-group socialization, 86–87, 95–97
  personalistic views on, 73, 79–84
  remedies for, 101–105
  systemic perspectives on, 73, 93–97, 103–105
  types and techniques of, 74–79
Police personality issue, 82–84
Police subculture, 86–87
Policing:
  organizational difficulties of, 84–87
  professionalism versus bureaucratization in, 88–91
Policy process, 24, 27–30
  in Nixon administration, 111, 113–114
  reforms in, 146–148
Political Action Committees (PACs), 160, 162, 163
Political contributions, *see* Campaign finance
Political cultures, 25–26, 48
Political discord (of late 1960s), 125–127
Political expression through campaign contributions, and finance laws, 163–164
Political machines, 36–71
  actual operation of, 56–65
  cost-benefit analysis of, 173
  death (?) of, 66–68
  and democracy, 62–65
  history of, 190
  leadership in, 39, 40
  myths about, 37
  nostalgia about role of, 59–62
  organizational analysis of "ideal," 38–41
  pacification effect of, 64–65
  performance and rewards measured by, 40–41
  political dynamics of, 41–44, 54–55
  theories of social context of, 44–56
  winners and losers in, 63
Political parties:
  and campaign finance laws, 164–165, 167–168
  and machine politics, 51–52
  and Watergate, 111

Political resource, money as, 33–34
Political systems:
  characteristics of, 24–33
  corruption in,, 18–35
  defined, 18–24
Politics:
  complexity of, 151–152
  of patience, case for, 131–132
Pomper, G., 156
Poor, the, and political machines, 41–43, 64–65, 67
Popular customs, 24, 26
Power, 11
Powers, J., 65
Presidency, U.S.:
  children's attitudes toward, 179–180
  the modern, 118–119, 123–124
Professionalism, in police work, 88
Prohibition, repeal of, 144–145
Public, the, 7
  apathy-scandal-apathy cycle in, 150–151, 185
  corruption's effect on trust by, 177–181
  police activity in sight of, 85–86
  and standards of conduct, 5–8
Public sector, relative size of, 31–32

Queensborough (N.Y.) Bridge, 60

Raab, E., 124, 128
Rakove, M., 64
Recruitment theory of police corruption, 80–82
Reform:
  and anti-corruption laws, 28–30
  of campaign finance, 153–168
  general approaches to, 141–148
  hope for, 148–149
  movements (1880s), 51–52
  options for post-Watergate, 134–136
  problems/difficulties of, 60–62, 140–141, 149–153, 160–162
  systemic, 134–135, 144–149
Regressiveness, of corruption, 182
Reiss, A. J., 79, 88–89
Republican Party, 164–165, 167
Resentment, politics of mass, 127–129
Revenge, politics of, Nixon's as, 131
Rigidification, Nixon's, 116–117

Index

Ripple effects of reforms, 152, 162–166
Roosevelt, F. D, 119, 120, 123
Roosevelt, J., 6
Rosenbaum, A., 65
Rotten-apple theory, 12–14
  of police corruption, 73, 79–80
Ruef, A., 50
Ryan, M., 49

Scammon, R.M., 122
Scott, J. C., 4, 28, 30, 145
Secrecy, in police subculture, 86–87
Selfishness, survey of, 181–182
Serpico, F., 86, 92
Settlement house movement, 65
Shapp, Milton, 1
Sheehy, G., 94
Shefter, M., 44, 55–56
Sherman, L. W., 74, 77–78, 84, 85, 87, 102
Social attachments and customs, 24, 25–26
Social distance, see Status gap
Social services, and political machines, 41–43, 66
Social unrest (late 1960s), 125–127
Society, and corruption, police, 99–101
Spoils system, and machine politics, 52, 57–59, 66 (see also Patronage practices)
Standards of conduct, 4–9
  legal norms, as, 8–9
  public interest as, 5–6
  public opinion as, 6–8
Status gap, between clients and decision-makers, 30–31, 145
Stave, B., 67
Subcultures, police, 86–87
Sufficiency issue, in campaign finance, 159
Supply-side reforms, 148
Systemic perspective:
  on bottleneck effect, 152
  on campaign finance reforms, 167–168
  on corruption, 15–16, 152–153
  on government, 185–186
  on police corruption, 73, 93–97, 103–105

Systemic perspective (continued)
  on political machine's emergence, 53–56
  on Watergate scandal, 110, 124–133
Systemic reforms:
  post-Watergate, 134–135
  types of, 144–149

Tammany Hall, 55–56, 60
Thayer, G., 153, 154
Theft, 11
  by police, 76–77
Thornburgh, R., 151
Traditionalistic political culture, 25, 26
Transactional types of corruption, 11–12
Truman, H. S., 119, 123
Trust, political, and corruption, 177–181, 185
Tweed, W. M., 36, 50
Two-party bias, and campaign finance laws, 164, 167–168

Unilateral types of corruption, 11
Urban areas:
  policing, 73–74, 84–87
  and political machines, 45, 46, 53–54, 59–62

Vice laws, and police responsibility, 90, 93–95, 103
"Victimless crimes," 103–104
Vietnam War, 125, 127
Vigilance, need for continuous, 185
Vollmer, A., 73
Voting irregularities, see Electoral procedures

Walker, J., 60
Wallace, G., 127–128
War, waging undeclared, 3–4, 10
Wards, and political machine, 51
Washington, G., 153
Watergate:
  analysis of, 108–133
  impact of, 133–137, 179–180
  and study of corruption, 2–8 passim, 12, 30, 136–137
  systemic roots of, 16
Wattenberg, B. J., 122

Watts, W., 178
Webman, J., 64
Welch, S., 150–151
Welch, W. P., 157
Wertheimer, F., 156
White, A. D., 47
Whyte, W. F., 91

Wills, F., 108
Wills, G., 114–115, 128
Wilson, J. Q., 57, 64
Wilson, J. W., 47, 48, 49

Yankelovich surveys, 179–181